A-Level Year 2
Psychology
Exam Board: AQA

Revising for Psychology exams is stressful, that's for sure — even just getting your notes sorted out can leave you needing a lie down. But help is at hand...

This brilliant CGP book explains **everything you'll need to learn** (and nothing you won't), with plenty of **in-depth psychological studies** to back up the theory. And of course, it's all written in a straightforward style that's easy to get your head around.

We've also included **exam-style questions** for every topic, along with a section of advice on how to pick up as many marks as possible in the final tests!

A-Level revision? It has to be CGP!

Contents

We deliberately haven't put any answers in this book, because they'd just be saying what's already in the book. So instead, here's how to write answers and do well.

Published by CGP

Editors:
Katherine Faudemer, Ceara Hayden, Kirstie McHale, Camilla Simson

Contributors:
Lauren Burns, Richard Carciofo, Elisa Grey, Nigel Holt, Christine Johnson, Tracey Jones, Kate Robson, Denise Say, Stuart Wilson

ISBN: 978 1 78294 331 0

With thanks to Mark Billingham, Lauren Burns and Glenn Rogers for the proofreading.
With thanks to Jan Greenway and Laura Jakubowski for the copyright research.

Cover image © Andrey Prokhorov/iStockphoto.com

With thanks to Science Photo Library for permission to reproduce the image on page 14.

Critical values tables on page 29 and page 30 abridged from Significance Testing of the Spearman Rank Correlation Coefficient by Jerrold H Zar from the Journal of the American Statistical Association © 1972 Taylor & Francis, reprinted by the publisher Taylor & Francis Ltd, http://www.tandfonline.com

Critical values tables on page 31 and page 33 abridged from FC Powell, Cambridge Mathematical and Statistical Tables, Cambridge University Press (1979).

Critical values table on page 32 abridged from Extended Tables of the Wilcoxon Matched Pair Signed Rank Statistic by Robert L McCornack from the Journal of the American Statistical Association © 1965 Taylor & Francis, reprinted by the publisher Taylor & Francis Ltd, http://www.tandfonline.com

Critical values table on page 35 abridged from Fundamentals of Behavioural Statistics (3rd Edn.) by R. Runyon and A. Haber © 1976 McGraw-Hill Education.
McGraw-Hill Education makes no representations or warranties as to the accuracy of any information contained in the McGraw-Hill Education Material, including any warranties of merchantability or fitness for a particular purpose. In no event shall McGraw-Hill Education have any liability to any party for special, incidental, tort, or consequential damages arising out of or in connection with the McGraw-Hill Education Material, even if McGraw-Hill Education has been advised of the possibility of such damages.

Clipart from Corel®
Printed by Elanders Ltd, Newcastle upon Tyne.

Based on the classic CGP style created by Richard Parsons.

The Psychodynamic Approach

In Year 1 you met some of the approaches in psychology. Here are a couple more for you to learn, starting with the psychodynamic approach. Psychodynamic theories explain behaviour with the unconscious — it all gets a bit weird here...

Freud Developed The **Psychodynamic** Approach

'**Psycho**' refers to the mind and '**dynamic**' refers to change or activity.
So, this approach emphasises the **active nature** of mental processes and their role in **shaping personality** and **behaviour**. This approach was developed by **Sigmund Freud** (1856-1939), in the 18th/early 19th centuries. It assumes that:

1) Human behaviour has **unconscious causes** that we're not aware of.

2) From birth, humans have a need to fulfil basic biological **motivations** — for food, sleep, warmth etc.

3) **Childhood experiences** are a really important influence on the development of adult personality and psychological disorders.

Bert's main motivation in life was to sleep. Lots.

Freud Said There Are Three **Levels of Consciousness**

Freud was interested in '**hysteria**', a disorder involving physical symptoms such as headaches, paralysis and blindness, but with no apparent physical cause. As his patients couldn't give any **conscious** reasons, Freud concluded they had an **unconscious** mind and that's where the cause of the hysteria was. He identified three levels of consciousness:

1) **Conscious**. This is what we are **aware** of at any given time, e.g. what we are seeing, hearing, smelling or thinking.

2) **Preconscious**. This is made up of **memories** that we can recall when we want to, e.g. we can recall our address, phone number, childhood memories or what we did at the weekend.

3) **Unconscious**. This is made up of memories, desires and fears which cause us extreme anxiety and have therefore been '**repressed**' or forced out of conscious awareness. However, the unconscious still influences behaviour. For example, it causes 'Freudian slips' and influences the content of our dreams. This part of our mind can be accessed with the help of a **psychoanalyst**, using the methods that Freud developed.

> Freudian slips are slips of the tongue believed to reveal a person's secret thoughts — e.g. calling your boyfriend/girlfriend by your ex's name.

Freud Said There Are **Three Parts** of the **Personality**

Freud claimed that the three main parts of the personality are the **id**, the **ego** and the **superego**, and these represent different levels of consciousness.

1) The **id** is the basic animal part of the personality that contains our innate, aggressive and sexual instincts. It wants to be satisfied by whatever means possible, and obeys the '**pleasure principle**'. It accounts for **unreasonable behaviour** and appears at **birth**.

2) The **ego** exists in both the conscious and unconscious parts of the mind and acts as a **rational** part known as the '**reality principle**'. It develops within the first three years after birth and balances the id and the superego to keep our behaviour in line.

3) The **superego** is in both the conscious and unconscious parts of the mind. This is the part of the mind that takes our **morals** into consideration and is involved in making us feel **guilty**. It develops around four to five years of age. It includes ideas about how to behave that we adopt from our parents.

The ego and the superego develop as the child goes through **five stages** of **psychosexual development** — the **oral**, **anal**, **phallic**, **latent**, and **genital** stages (more on this on page 4). Is anyone starting to think Freud was a bit nuts...?

The Psychodynamic Approach

Conflicts *Can Develop Between the* Parts of the Personality

1) So, as you know, the id, ego and superego represent different levels of **consciousness** and govern the way we **think** and **act**.

2) A way to see the relationships between these three aspects of the personality is by thinking of an **iceberg**. The **tip** of the iceberg is the **conscious** part of the mind made up of part of the ego and part of the superego. But the majority of personality comes from the **unconscious** mind, below the surface. It's made up of the id, a little of the ego and the rest of the superego.

3) Freud believed that these three different parts of consciousness can be in **conflict**. For example, there can be a conflict between the id and the superego because the id wants **instant satisfaction**, whilst the superego tries to impose **morals**.

4) These conflicts can lead to **anxiety**. It's then the ego's job to mediate between the id and the superego to **reduce** this anxiety.

5) It does this using one of several **unconscious** defence mechanisms:

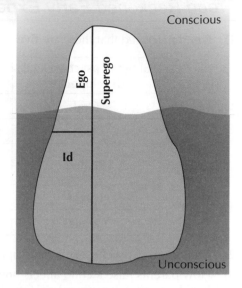

Repression

Repression involves the ego stopping **unwanted** and possibly **painful thoughts** from becoming **conscious**. For example, someone who experienced a **traumatic incident**, such as being mugged, may not recall it later. This is because they have **repressed** the memory.

Denial

Denial is where a threatening event or an unwanted reality is simply **ignored** and **blocked** from conscious awareness. For example, a drug addict might deny that they have a problem, or someone suffering from a bereavement might deny that their loved one has died.

Displacement

Displacement happens when a **negative impulse** is **redirected** onto something else. This could be another person or an object. For example, if your boss has made you angry at work, you might redirect your anger towards something else by kicking a door at home.

Practice Questions

Q1 Who developed the psychodynamic approach?

Q2 What are the three parts of the personality?

Q3 Give the three levels of consciousness outlined by Freud.

Q4 Which part of the personality obeys the pleasure principle?

Q5 What is displacement?

Exam Questions

Q1 Which one of these is **not** a defence mechanism?
   A denial   **B** repression   **C** conflict   **D** displacement   [1 mark]

Q2 Outline the structure of personality as explained by the psychodynamic approach.   [6 marks]

I won't really have to go and get a filling at the dentist...

I'm in denial, you say...? Oh well. Must be a conflict of the different parts of my personality. Or something. Anyway, enough about me. As you can see from these two pages, Freud had some funny old ideas, and as you'll see over the page, his methodology wasn't the most reliable... When you're ready, take a deep breath, and plough on.

The Psychodynamic Approach

If the id, the ego and superego weren't baffling enough, just wait until you read about Freud's psychosexual stages.

Freud Reckoned **Early Experiences** Influence Development

1) Freud proposed that there are **five** stages of development:

Stage of psychosexual development	Age	Characteristics
Oral	0 – 18 months	sucking behaviour
Anal	18 months – 3.5 years	keeping or discarding faeces
Phallic	3.5 – 6 years	genital fixation — Oedipus and Electra complex (see page 66)
Latent	6 years – puberty	repressed sexual urges
Genital	puberty – adult	awakened sexual urges

2) Each stage of psychosexual development focuses on **obtaining pleasure** through a certain part of the body.

3) How parents raise a child affects **how much** pleasure is obtained through that stage (e.g. how strict they are when potty training, and what type of role models they are).

4) If a child doesn't receive enough **pleasure**, or they receive too much, during a stage of development, they will become '**fixated**' at that stage.

> For example, during the oral stage, a conflict could occur when being weaned off breast feeding. This could lead to a fixation in later life, characterised by traits such as **nail biting**, **smoking** or abnormal **eating behaviours**.

5) This experience is all **repressed into the unconscious**, but influences adult personality. Severe fixation could lead to a psychological **disorder**.

Freud Carried Out **Case Studies**

As part of **psychoanalysis**, Freud did **case studies** on his patients using several **methods** to reveal the **conflicts**, **fears** and **desires** buried in their unconscious mind. These problems could then be faced, allowing the patient to understand and resolve them.

Freud (1909) — The case study of Little Hans

Method:	Freud carried out a **case study** of a child called Hans who had a phobia of horses. Hans was observed by his father, who made notes of Hans's dreams and stuff he said, and passed them on to Freud for analysis.
Results:	Hans was afraid of horses because he thought they might bite him or fall on him. During the study he developed an interest in his 'widdler' (penis). His mum had told him not to play with it or she'd cut it off. Hans told his dad about a dream where he was married to his mum and his dad was now his grandfather.
Conclusion:	Freud's interpretation was that Hans had reached the **phallic stage** of development and showed evidence of the 'Oedipus complex' — he wanted to have an exclusive relationship with his mother and was jealous of his father. Hans had sexual feelings for his mother, shown partly by his dream of marrying her. The horse symbolised Hans's father because, to him, they both had big penises. His fear of horses is an example of **displacement** (page 3) — a **defence mechanism** that protected him from his real fear of his father. Hans suffered from **castration anxiety**. He was afraid that he would be castrated by his father if he found out about his feelings for his mother. This was symbolised by Hans's fear that a horse would bite him.
Evaluation:	This was a **case study**, meaning that it provided lots of **detailed data** about one subject, but it does mean the results can't be **generalised**. The findings provided evidence to support Freud's theories. However, the results were based entirely on observation and interpretation. This means a cause and effect relationship **can't** be established. There could be **other explanations** — for example, Hans's anxiety may have come from his mother threatening to cut his penis off. Also, before the study Hans had been frightened by a horse falling down in the street, which could explain his fear of them. Freud analysed information from Hans's father, so the results could be **biased**.

The Psychodynamic Approach

The **Psychodynamic Approach** Has **Strengths** and **Weaknesses**

Like every approach in psychology, the psychodynamic approach has some strengths and weaknesses.
A lot of its **weaknesses** are related to the **research methods** used by Freud.

Strengths

1) The psychodynamic approach was the first theory to focus on **psychological causes** of disorders. Before this, the focus had been on **physical causes** or things like possession by **evil spirits**.

2) It was also one of the first approaches to suggest that mental health disorders may be linked to **unresolved conflicts** related to **biological needs**.

3) It offers methods of **therapy** (such as psychoanalysis) which may also uncover unconscious conflicts. Patients can then **understand** the causes of their problems and so **resolve** them and release their anxieties.

4) Freud's theory places emphasis on how experiences in early childhood can affect **later development**. This has formed the basis for lots of other important theories.

So... hearing voices. Ever get pushed out of the sand pit at school...?

Weaknesses

1) Freud's claims are based on his subjective interpretations of his patients' dreams, etc. Therefore they're often **unreliable** and **open to bias**.

2) Freud's theories are related to the unconscious mind, which can't be accessed. As such, his theories are **unfalsifiable** (i.e. they can't be proved wrong).

3) **Psychoanalysis** may take a long time and so be very expensive. The childhood conflicts that are 'uncovered' may be emotionally distressing and possibly inaccurate, depending on the reliability of the patient's memory, the techniques used to uncover them and the analyst's interpretations.

4) The focus is on the patient's **past**, rather than on the problems that they are **currently suffering**.

5) The approach is based on case studies of people in 'distress', so the findings can't be **generalised** to everyone else.

6) The unscientific research methods mean it's not possible to establish **cause and effect**.

Practice Questions

Q1 Identify the five stages of psychosexual development.

Q2 Give an example of behaviour seen in the first psychosexual stage.

Q3 Outline the method and results of Freud's case study of Little Hans.

Exam Questions

Q1 Read the item below and then answer the question that follows.

> As an adult, Frank bites his fingernails and smokes. He has put on lots of weight because he overeats.

Explain how Frank's personality could be explained using the psychodynamic approach to psychology. [4 marks]

Q2 Describe and evaluate the psychodynamic approach to psychology. [16 marks]

I've always wondered if Little Hans had little hands...

Right, so you should now have a good idea of what the psychodynamic approach is all about. Make sure you remember to learn the strengths and weaknesses of the approach — examiners love asking you to evaluate things, and they might even be sneaky enough to get you to contrast the psychodynamic approach with another approach.

Humanistic Psychology

Now for the humanistic approach to psychology. This approach was developed mainly by Carl Rogers and Abraham Maslow during the 1950s. It's an interesting one, and has influenced counselling today.

Humanistic Psychology Focuses on the Individual

1) Humanistic psychology focuses on the person as a **whole**.

2) Humanistic psychologists believe that all people are **inherently good** and that they're **driven** to achieve their **full potential**.

3) Unlike other types of psychology, it takes into account the **feelings** of the individual rather than just their observable behaviour. It treats every person as being **unique**.

4) Because of this, it has an **idiographic** approach rather than a **nomothetic** approach (see page 48) — it focuses on studying the **individual** rather than producing general rules which come from summarising a group of people.

5) Humanistic psychology assumes that a person's behaviour is caused by their **subjective feelings** and their thoughts about **themselves** (their **self-concept**), especially about how they can become **better people** and **learn** new things.

6) It disagrees with the strictly deterministic ideas of other approaches, which assume that human behaviour occurs in cause and effect relationships. Instead, it believes that human behaviour is determined by **free will**. People can **choose** how to behave — and their behaviour isn't caused by external or biological factors, or even the past.

Maslow Developed a Hierarchy of Needs

1) Humanistic psychology suggests that people are **motivated** to use their own free will to allow them to reach their **fullest potential**.

2) People can be motivated by lots of things — some needs are shared, and others are individual. For example, we're **all** motivated to find food and water, but we **differ** in whether we're motivated to do things like learn a new language or become a football star.

3) **Maslow (1943)** came up with a 'need theory' of motivation — he devised a **hierarchy** to show how human needs can be **categorised** and **prioritised**. This is known as **Maslow's hierarchy of needs**:

5) At this level you realise your **fullest potential** — you've become the best you're capable of being.

4) At this level you're focused on **achievement** and **gaining respect** from others.

3) At this level you consider **affection**, **acceptance** and **belonging** to be most important.

2) At this level you strive to feel **safe** physically, psychologically and economically.

1) At this level you source the food, water, shelter and sleep you need to **stay alive** (as well as sex to reproduce).

4) In a nice change from psychologists trying to explain what has happened when something has gone wrong with someone, Maslow was more interested in explaining how people try to make themselves the best that they can be. He believed that we spend our lives trying to reach the **top** of the hierarchy, but that **hardly anyone** ever gets there. Sad. He also stated that until **lower level needs** are met, you **can't** attempt to satisfy higher level needs.

5) This seems to make sense in some cases of **real life** — e.g. who'd be interested in reading a psychology book if they were extremely hungry or in immediate physical danger...

6) However, humanistic psychology is quite a **westernised concept**, i.e. western culture encourages individual growth, rather than prioritising the needs of the social group.

7) Also, humanistic psychology assumes that everyone has the ability to self-actualise. But this could be **incorrect**, as self-actualisation may be limited to the most intelligent, well-educated people.

Humanistic Psychology

Self-Actualised People Have Certain Characteristics

According to Maslow, once people have **achieved** all their **previous needs** in the hierarchy, they are ready for **self-actualisation**. He came up with a list of **characteristics** that a self-actualised person might show.
These include:

1) A strong sense of **self-awareness**.
2) A **fully accepting** view of themselves and others for who they are.
3) The ability to deal with **uncertainty** and the **unknown**.
4) A strong sense of **creativity**.

Maslow believed that self-actualisation could be measured using what he called '**peak experiences**'.
These are times where the person feels **wonder** and **euphoria** towards the world around them.
After these experiences, people often feel **inspired**, with a renewed sense of **self-awareness**.

There is Limited Evidence for Maslow's Hierarchy of Needs

There is **little evidence** or research to support the hierarchical nature of Maslow's hierarchy of needs.
Maslow supported his hierarchy with biographical evidence of famous 'self-actualisers'. However, the hierarchy doesn't explain why some people with the characteristics of a self-actualised person **deprive** themselves of basic needs such as food and shelter (e.g. Mother Teresa).

Despite the limited evidence, a study by **Aronoff (1967)** tested whether the higher levels of the hierarchy are only satisfied once the lower levels have been satisfied and found support for this idea:

	Aronoff (1967) — Job demands and the hierarchy of needs
Method:	Aronoff compared people in two jobs in the British West Indies — **fishermen** and **cane cutters**. Cane cutters got paid according to how much cane was cut by the whole group, even when they were off sick. So they had high **job security**, although wages were low. In contrast, fisherman worked alone, doing more challenging work. So they were **less secure** in their job, although they earned more overall. Both groups of people were assessed to see which level they were at on Maslow's hierarchy of needs.
Results:	More **cane cutters** were at the **lower levels** of the hierarchy, still trying to achieve safety and security than **fishermen**, many of whom had satisfied the lower levels of the hierarchy.
Conclusion:	Only those men who had satisfied lower levels of the pyramid would chose to become fishermen, allowing them to develop high self esteem. This suggests that people **cannot reach** the **higher levels** of Maslow's hierarchy until they have **satisfied** the **lower levels**.
Evaluation:	The study supports Maslow's hierarchy of needs theory, and it has **ecological validity** as it studied people in their natural environment. However, it only studied people from one **culture**, so the results can't be **generalised** to the wider population.

Practice Questions

Q1 What does humanistic psychology assume that people are driven to do?

Q2 What is the lowest level in Maslow's hierarchy of needs?

Q3 What is self-actualisation?

Q4 What is meant by a 'peak experience'?

Exam Questions

Q1 Which is these is **not** associated with humanistic psychology?
    A free will   **B** psychosexual stages   **C** determinism   **D** self-actualisation   [1 mark]

Q2 Briefly outline and evaluate Maslow's hierarchy of needs.   [8 marks]

I need my duvet, a cup of tea, a book to read — and that'll do for now...

Humanistic psychologists believe that it's no good studying a load of people and then coming up with a 'one size fits all' rule. They acknowledge that everyone is unique, and that behaviour is more likely to be a result of individual feelings and thoughts. Maslow was one humanistic psychologist, and you'll find out all about Rogers over the page...

Humanistic Psychology

Rogers *Also Talked About* Self-Actualisation

1) Like Maslow, Rogers believed that all people try to achieve **self-actualisation**. He also claimed that all people are **inherently good** and that they're **motivated** to achieve their **fullest potential**.

2) However, Rogers didn't believe the route to self-actualisation was as **strict** as Maslow had described. Instead of working their way up a hierarchy of needs, Rogers thought that people move towards self-actualisation depending on their own **thoughts** about themselves and the way that they're **treated** by others.

3) From this, he believed that you'll develop in a **psychologically healthy way** if your path to self-actualisation is not blocked. Blockages (e.g. being raised in a difficult environment) can lead to **psychological problems**.

4) Rogers believed that everyone has a **need** to be regarded by others in a good light, and to be shown love, affection and respect. This is particularly important for children, who want to **seek approval** from their parents. They'll be more psychologically **happy** if they get this approval, or **unhappy** if they feel that their parents are **disappointed** or **displeased** with them.

Rogers *Described* Two Parts *of the* Self

1) Rogers outlined the differences between how someone **sees themselves** (their **self-concept**) and how they would **like to be** (their **ideal self**).

2) He suggested their self-concept is created and develops in a way which depends on whether they receive **unconditional positive regard** or whether **conditions of worth** are set for them.

Unconditional Positive Regard

- This is where the person gets affection and support **no matter what** their behaviour is like.
- We need unconditional positive regard to have a **positive self-concept**.

Conditions of Worth

- This is where approval and affection is given as a result of **behaving** in a certain way.
- Although this treatment can help someone learn to fit in with the rules of social life, Rogers believed that it could **stop** them from reaching **self-actualisation**. This is because the person may focus on keeping **other people happy** rather than developing their own personality.

3) If they have unconditional positive regard and then receive **love** and **acceptance** for their behaviour, they will experience **congruence** — and become a **fully-functioning person**.

4) However, if they are set conditions of worth then their **ideal self** becomes something different to the **self-concept**, and the person will experience **incongruence** (see below).

Rogers *Developed His Ideas Into a Form of* Therapy

1) Rogers believed that many people's psychological problems were caused by **incongruence**.

2) This is where there is a **mismatch** between someone's **self-concept** and their **ideal self**. His therapy aimed to remove this incongruence by making it possible for the person to become their ideal self.

3) His therapy was known as **client-centred therapy**, also known as **person-centred therapy**.

4) As the name suggests, the therapy focuses on the **client** — they're **in charge** of what is talked about, and it's their responsibility to eventually **solve** their own problems.

5) The therapist's job is to try and make the client **aware** of their thoughts, actions and behaviours. They can do this by carefully **rephrasing** the client's sentences and **repeating** them back.

> For example, a conversation might go like this:
>
> **Client:** I find my parents really annoying. They're always going on at me and won't let me do what I want.
>
> **Therapist:** So, you're feeling quite frustrated. Your parents treat you like you're still a child and not an adult.

6) **Unconditional positive regard** (i.e. not judging), **genuineness** and **empathy** are really important in person-centred therapy. The therapist is **supportive** of the client no matter what they do or say, with the aim that the client will come to **value** themselves.

Humanistic Psychology

Rogers's Therapy Seems to **Work**

There's quite a bit of **evidence** that Rogers's person-centred therapy is effective.

For example...
Gibbard and Hanley (2008) studied the impact of person-centred therapy on a group of patients suffering from common mental health disorders such as anxiety and depression. They studied almost **700 people** over **five years**. A **questionnaire** was used to measure the extent of their condition **before and after** therapy. It was found that nearly **70%** of the participants showed a **significant improvement** in their mental health after taking part in person-centred therapy.

Humanistic Psychology has **Strengths** and **Weaknesses**

Strengths

1) Humanistic psychology is a very **positive** approach, which states that people are striving to be better.
2) **Free will** is a major part of humanistic psychology, which is less restrictive than more deterministic approaches (see page 44). Humanistic psychologists believe that a deterministic approach is no good for understanding the **complex nature** of human behaviour.
3) The approach treats people as **individuals** and takes the **whole person** into account, rather than reducing individual behaviours to cause and effect responses.
4) Research in this approach gathers **qualitative data** (see page 22) which is **rich in detail**. Rogers **recorded** many of his therapy sessions so they could be **analysed**, making it possible to observe the **successes** as a result of the therapy.
5) The **counselling techniques** which have come from the approach have been shown to be **effective**.

Weaknesses

1) The approach places **less emphasis** on factors such as the role of **genes**, etc. than the **biological** approach.
2) The humanistic approach **lacks objectivity** — it's largely based on feelings and **subjective** reports, and so it's hard to test in a scientific way. It also features things that are hard to **measure**, such as self-actualisation.
3) The approach is **idiographic**, which means it doesn't create generalised laws which can be applied to everyone, making it a **less scientific** approach.

Practice Questions

Q1 What is meant by congruence?
Q2 What was Rogers' therapy called?
Q3 How has humanistic psychology influenced counselling?
Q4 Give one strength and one weakness of the humanistic approach.

Exam Questions

Q1	Outline the role that conditions of worth may play in achieving self-actualisation.	[2 marks]
Q2	Discuss how humanistic psychology contributes to understanding and explaining psychological problems in people.	[16 marks]

So, you're feeling unhappy about having to do this revision...

Has that helped? Has it made you more aware of yourself? Hmm, I'll try again. "So, you're feeling unhappy about having to do this revision, and you just can't believe the teachers are being this mean to you. What rotters."
Any better? Well it's tough — you're just going to have to get on with it. I'm not sure I'd make a very good therapist...

Localisation of Function

You were introduced to biopsychology in Year 1 — this section covers the extra things you need to learn. First up, it's a page about brains. Ever really thought about what's going on up there...? Nah, me neither. Luckily for you, biopsychologists have and it's pretty interesting stuff. Lots of tricky names coming up though, so brace yourself...

Localisation of Function — Certain Bits of the Brain Do Certain Things

Certain areas of the brain are thought to be responsible for particular functions, e.g. vision, language, coordination... This is known as **localisation of function**:

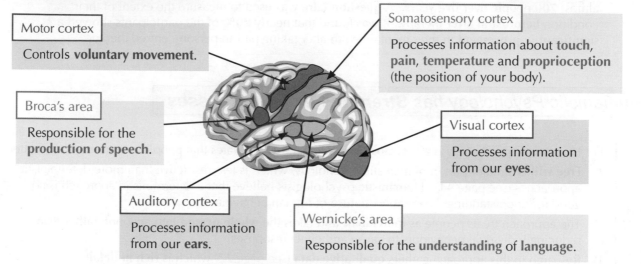

Motor cortex
Controls **voluntary movement**.

Somatosensory cortex
Processes information about **touch**, **pain**, **temperature** and **proprioception** (the position of your body).

Broca's area
Responsible for the **production of speech**.

Visual cortex
Processes information from our **eyes**.

Auditory cortex
Processes information from our **ears**.

Wernicke's area
Responsible for the **understanding** of language.

The **Brain** is Divided into **Two Hemispheres**

1) The brain is split into **two hemispheres** (halves) — the **right hemisphere** and the **left hemisphere**.

2) The two hemispheres are **connected** by the **corpus callosum**.

3) Different **functions** are **dominant** in each hemisphere.

4) In most people, **Broca's** and **Wernicke's** areas are only found in the **left hemisphere** — so it handles the bulk of **language** functions. The left hemisphere is also generally responsible for **logic**, **analysis** and **problem solving**.

5) The **right** hemisphere is more concerned with things like **spatial** comprehension, **emotions** and **face recognition**.

6) This is known as **hemispheric lateralisation of function**.

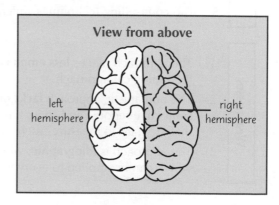

View from above

left hemisphere

right hemisphere

The **Two Hemispheres** Can **Communicate** via the **Corpus Callosum**

In general, each **hemisphere** deals with **information** from the **opposite side** of the body.

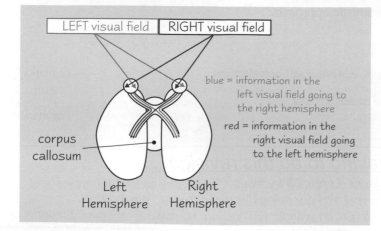

LEFT visual field   RIGHT visual field

blue = information in the left visual field going to the right hemisphere

red = information in the right visual field going to the left hemisphere

corpus callosum

Left Hemisphere

Right Hemisphere

For example...

1) Information from the **right visual field** (that's the right half of what you see) goes to the **visual cortex** in the **left hemisphere**.

2) Information from the **left visual field** goes to the **visual cortex** in the **right hemisphere**.

3) Information passes through the **corpus callosum** to whichever side of the brain needs to deal with it.

Localisation of Function

Split Brain Surgery Gives an Opportunity for Research

1) In very severe cases of **epilepsy**, the only treatment available is to **sever** the **corpus callosum**. This stops seizures spreading across the brain.

2) But a **side effect** of splitting the hemispheres is that **information** can no longer move between them.

3) Scientists have used **split brain surgery patients** to study the different roles of the two hemispheres — take a look at Sperry's study...

Sperry (1968) — Effects of split brain surgery

Method:	The study involved a combination of **case studies** and **experiments**. The 11 participants had undergone split brain surgery as a result of epilepsy that couldn't be controlled by medication. A control group was used who had no hemisphere disconnection. In one of the experiments, participants covered one eye and looked at a fixed point on a projection screen. Pictures were projected onto the **right** or **left** of the screen at high speeds so that there was no time for eye movement.
Results:	If the picture was shown in the **right visual field**, all of the participants could say or write what it was without a problem. But if the image was flashed onto the **left** the split brain participants couldn't say or write what they'd seen. They could however select a corresponding object with their left hand, which represented what had been shown to their left eye (right hemisphere), even though they didn't know why they had selected this object.
Conclusion:	This shows that **different areas** of the brain specialise in **different functions**. The **left** hemisphere (which receives visual information from the right visual field) can **convert** sight into spoken and written language. Usually information entering the right hemisphere can cross over to be processed in the left. As the results show, this **can't** happen in **split brains**, so the information going to the right hemisphere can't be converted into language at all. However, the right hemisphere can still produce a non-verbal response.
Evaluation:	Using case studies as well as experiments meant that Sperry obtained both **qualitative** and **quantitative** data. Also, using both research methods meant that the **reliability** and the **validity** of the study were increased. However, the study only used 11 participants, which is a very **small sample** size for being able to generalise the results to others. But, it would have been difficult to find a large number of split brain patients to study. Epilepsy is usually caused by **brain damage** and the patients had also been on **medication** which may have affected their brains. Therefore, it is hard to conclude that the ways they processed information would be the same as for people **without** epilepsy or split brain treatment. The study has also been criticised in terms of **ecological validity** — the experimental situation was artificial, so it's difficult to **generalise** the results to real-life situations.

Practice Questions

Q1 What is the function of the somatosensory cortex?

Q2 Which hemisphere does information from the right visual field go to?

Q3 What is split brain surgery?

What are you looking at?

Exam Questions

Q1 Look at the diagram of the left hemisphere below.

Area X

    a) Name the area labelled X in the diagram. [1 mark]

    b) Complete the following sentence. The area labelled X is responsible for
    A voluntary movement.   **B** vision.
    C speech production.   **D** proprioception. [1 mark]

Q2 a) Outline one study which provides evidence for hemispheric lateralisation of function. [4 marks]

    b) Evaluate the study described in part a). [4 marks]

Brings a whole new perspective to being in two minds about things...

It's all a bit confusing this split brain stuff, so don't panic if you don't get it straight away. Just take your time and draw out some diagrams to help you — it'll click eventually. Nightmare stuff, this, if you get your left and right muddled up...

Plasticity

Brain engaged — it's about to get deep...

The Brain is **Constantly Reorganising** Itself

1) The brain has the ability to **alter** its **structure** and **function** in response to changes in the environment.

2) This is known as **plasticity**. Here's how it works:

   - Information takes a **pathway** through the brain, travelling from one **neuron** to the next via **synapses**.
   - When we're presented with new **information**, new **neural pathways** begin to form.
   - **Using** a neural pathway **strengthens** it — the more a pathway is used, the stronger the connections between the neurons become.
   - If a neural pathway is **not used** it becomes **weaker**.

Harold was fully aware that 'practice would make perfect'.

3) This constant **rewiring** and **reorganisation** of the brain is the basis of how we **learn** and **adapt to changes** in our **environment**. For example, when we first carry out a new action, we are not very good at it. If we **repeat** the action over and over again (i.e. **practise** it), the pathways **strengthen** and we **get better** at the action.

4) Plasticity was previously thought to only occur in **babies** and **children**. Although plasticity is **greatest** in the **developing brain**, it is now widely accepted that plasticity occurs **throughout adult life** too.

There's Lots of **Evidence** for Plasticity

Different areas in the **somatosensory cortex** and the **motor cortex** of the brain represent different **parts of the body**. This is known as **cortical representation**. For example, one area of the somatosensory cortex processes sensory information from your lips and another area processes sensory information from your toes.

Lots of studies providing support for plasticity have focused on changes in cortical representation — this is known as **cortical reorganisation**.

	Elbert et al (1995) — Plasticity in musicians
Method:	**Nine musicians** who played either the violin, cello or guitar were compared to **six non-musicians**. A technique called **magnetic source imaging** was used to measure the area of the **somatosensory cortex** representing the **digits of the left hand** of each participant.
Results:	The area of the somatosensory cortex representing the digits of the left hand was **larger** in the stringed instrument players than in the controls.
Conclusion:	These findings suggest that the **increased** amount of **sensory processing** required from the left hands of stringed instrument players results in **structural changes** in the brain, providing support for plasticity.
Evaluation:	Other researchers argue that the increased representation of the left hand digits in the musicians may have been **genetic** rather than as a result of playing an instrument. In other words, they may have been good musicians because of a natural trait. The study used a fairly **small sample size** so may not be representative.

The left hand carries out lots of fast, fine movements when playing a stringed instrument. A large amount of sensory information is also processed, for example, to detect the amount of pressure being applied to the strings.

Studies have also provided **evidence** of plasticity in the **motor cortex**.

- **Karni et al (1995)** used fMRI (see p.14) to show that learning and practising a sequence of finger movements over a period of four weeks led to activation of a larger area of the motor cortex when carrying out the sequence. This suggests that some **reorganisation** had occurred.

- **Nudo et al (1996)** mapped the motor cortex of adult monkeys before and after training in a task which mainly required use of the digits. They found that the representation of the digits in the motor cortex increased. They then carried out training in a task that mainly used the forearm. They found that the forearm representation increased and the digit representation decreased. This suggests that plastic changes are **continuous** and **reversible** (at least in monkeys).

Plasticity

Plasticity Can Allow Functional Recovery After Brain Damage

1) **Brain damage** can be caused by serious head injuries, strokes, tumours, infections, etc.

2) This **brain damage** can result in **loss of function**. For example, damage to Broca's area can result in the loss of speech, damage to the auditory cortex can cause loss of hearing, etc.

3) The brain has the potential to **recover** some of this lost function.

4) This is thought to be due to **plasticity** — the brain begins to **rewire** itself.

5) There is evidence that **healthy areas** of the brain located **near** the damaged area begin to **take over** the function of the damaged area.

Using the Affected Area Can Encourage Functional Recovery

After a stroke which has caused loss of function on one side of the body (e.g. the right arm), some patients are prevented from using their non-affected side (e.g. their left arm). This forces them to 're-learn' how to use their affected arm. This method is known as **constraint-induced movement therapy** (**CIMT**).

Advantages

- Numerous studies have shown that CIMT produces **cortical reorganisation** which results in **regained** or **improved function**.

- The principles of CIMT can also be applied to patients who suffer from **aphasia** as a result of stroke damage. Instead of communicating in other ways, e.g. drawing pictures, using sign language, etc. they play a game which requires them to try and **speak** a word presented on a card. Studies have shown that this therapy caused dysfunctional areas near the damaged area to become **functional** again.

People with aphasia struggle to speak correctly, for example, they may use the wrong word or use the wrong sounds in the word.

Disadvantages

- CIMT can be very **frustrating** for the patient.

- CIMT needs to be very **intensive** to be effective. Patients are often required to train the affected limb for several hours a day, for consecutive weeks and have their unaffected limb restrained for 90% of the time that they are awake.

- It is most effective in treating patients who have suffered **mild** to **moderate** strokes. If there's lots of damage to the brain, it can be much harder to regain function.

Practice Questions

Q1 What is meant by cortical representation?

Q2 Outline the findings of Elbert et al's (1995) study.

Q3 What brain scanning method did Karni et al (1995) use in their study?

Q4 What does CIMT stand for?

Q5 Give one disadvantage of CIMT.

Exam Questions

Q1 Doris has recently had a stroke which has caused loss of function in her left arm. Describe how the brain's plasticity could allow her to regain function in her left arm. [2 marks]

Q2 Outline and evaluate evidence for plasticity within the brain. [8 marks]

I think I'm going to need an electrician...

Crikey. Isn't the brain amazing? It's constantly reorganising to learn, adapt and even fix itself. I know it's tricky to get your head round all of this, but read these pages through a couple more times and you'll soon get those neural pathways strengthened up — use it or lose it, my friend.

Studying the Brain

As you've probably gathered by now, biopsychologists really like the brain, and they've got a few tricks up their lab coat sleeves for studying it. First up, functional magnetic resonance imaging. Also known as fMRI, luckily...

fMRI Scans Show Brain Activity

Functional magnetic resonance imaging (fMRI) scans are **3D** scans providing **structural** and **functional** information. They show **changes** in **brain activity** as they actually happen, by using a really strong magnetic field and radio waves:

1) **More oxygenated blood** flows to **active areas** of the brain (to supply the neurons with oxygen and glucose).

2) Molecules in **oxygenated blood respond differently** to a **magnetic field** than those in deoxygenated blood.

3) So the **more active areas** of the brain can be **identified** on an fMRI scan.

Uses of fMRI

1) fMRI scans are used to research the **function** of the brain as well as its structure. If a participant **carries out** a task whilst **in the scanner**, the **part** of the brain that's involved with that function will be **more active**. (It's often coloured by the computer so that it shows up more easily.)

2) For example, a participant might be asked to **move** their **left hand** when in the fMRI scanner. The areas of the brain involved in moving the hand will **show up** on the fMRI scan.

3) fMRI scans can be used to **diagnose medical problems** because they can also show **damaged** or **diseased areas** of the brain.

4) They are also used to study **abnormal activity** in the brain. For example, Shegrill et al (2001) used fMRI to show which areas of the brain were **active** during **hallucinations** in a patient with **schizophrenia**.

This fMRI scan looks down on the brain from above. The red area is active when the person moves their left hand.

fMRI scans are a really useful tool for biopsychologists, as they provide a **non-invasive** way of studying the brain. However the machines are very **expensive** to buy and run. They also require people to lie very still in an enclosed space for a period of time, which can be a problem for people who suffer from **claustrophobia** (fear of confined spaces). They have **poor temporal resolution** — this means they don't show changes over **time** accurately.

EEGs Show Electrical Activity

1) An **electroencephalogram (EEG)** shows the **overall electrical activity** of the brain. It picks up the signal of many neurons firing together — not individual neurons.

2) Multiple **electrodes** are placed on the **scalp** and the electrical activity in the brain is recorded for a period of time.

3) This produces a **pattern of waves**. These patterns represent different levels of **arousal** or **consciousness**. For example, the different stages of sleep each have their own typical wave patterns.

Uses of EEGs

1) EEGs are commonly used in **sleep studies**.

2) They have also been used in the study of conditions such as **depression** and **schizophrenia**. E.g. a meta-analysis by Boutros et al (2008) showed that patients suffering from schizophrenia displayed **abnormal EEG wave patterns** compared to controls.

3) **Abnormal EEGs** have also been identified in patients suffering from eating disorders such as **anorexia nervosa**.

4) This means EEGs have the potential to be used as a **diagnostic tool**.

Stage 1	~~~~~~~
Stage 2	~~~~~~~
Stage 3	~~~~~~~
Stage 4	~~~~~~~
REM Sleep (active sleep)	~~~~~~~

These EEG wave patterns show brain activity during the different stages of sleep.

EEGs and ERPs (see next page) are also **non-invasive**, and they are **cheaper** to carry out than fMRI scans. Although they have a **good temporal resolution**, they have **poor spatial resolution** — this means it's hard to work out which area of the brain the waves originate from.

Studying the Brain

ERPs Show Electrical Activity in the Brain in Response to a Stimulus

1) Biopsychologists can also look at how an EEG wave pattern **changes** in **response** to a **stimulus**.
2) This change is known as an **event-related potential (ERP)**.
3) If a **specific stimulus** is presented, it produces a **specific change** in the wave pattern:

normal wave pattern

stimulus

It's important to remember that the EEG represents the activity of the whole brain — not individual neurons.

4) Biopsychologists have identified **different ERPs** which are produced in response to **different stimuli**.

Uses of ERPs

1) ERPs have been used a lot in **memory** research, as they give biopsychologists lots of clues about **information processing** in the brain.
2) Research has shown **differences** in the ERPs of people suffering from certain **psychiatric disorders** compared to healthy individuals. For example, Miltner et al (2000) found that people with **phobias** had an ERP of a **greater amplitude** in response to images of the objects they feared, compared to non-phobic individuals.

Post-mortem Examinations Show the Structure of the Brain

1) **Post-mortem examinations** involve **dissecting** (cutting up) the brain of a person who has **died**.
2) This allows researchers to physically look at the **internal structure** of the brain.

Uses of Post-mortem Examinations

Before modern techniques such as brain scanning were invented, post-mortems were one of the only ways of studying the brain.

1) If a person had a **medical condition** when they were alive, a post-mortem could show up any **structural abnormalities** that could **explain their condition**.
For example, a study by Brown et al (1986), which used post-mortem examinations, showed that patients who had suffered from **schizophrenia** had **enlarged ventricles** in their brains.
2) Post-mortems have provided **evidence** for **localisation of function** in the brain.
For example, **Paul Broca** carried out post-mortem examinations on two patients who developed **speech problems** as a result of **brain damage**. Both patients had damage to the **same area** of the brain, so Broca concluded this area (which we now know as **Broca's area**) was involved in **speech production**.

An obvious **disadvantage** of post-mortem examinations is that the person has to have **died** before the examination can be carried out, so they will **not benefit** from any of the findings.
A **disadvantage** of **all** of these methods of studying the brain, is that although they do give us information about what's going on in the brain, they **don't** allow **cause and effect** to be established. For example, the enlarged ventricles in people with schizophrenia **haven't** necessarily been **caused** by schizophrenia.

Practice Questions

Q1 Give one problem with functional magnetic resonance imaging (fMRI).
Q2 What does an electroencephalogram (EEG) show?

Exam Questions

Q1 Briefly outline how functional magnetic resonance imaging (fMRI) works. [4 marks]

Q2 Briefly explain one advantage and one disadvantage of using electroencephalography to study the brain. [4 marks]

I wonder what level of arousal your EEG would show right now...

I don't know about you but I think all this stuff is pretty neat. In fact, there are whole areas of research in psychology that just wouldn't have been possible without these techniques, so hats off to the scientists who came up with them.

Biological Rhythms

The Beatles. Whitney Houston. Elvis. They all had rhythm, and so do you. You don't have to write a song on it (unless you really want to) but you do need to know about it. And these lovely pages are here to help.

Biological Rhythm Cycles *Vary* in *Length*

Biological rhythms can be classified according to how long their cycle lasts.

1) **Circadian rhythms** — have cycles that generally occur **once every 24 hours**.
   For example, we will usually go through the **sleep-wake cycle** once every day.

2) **Infradian rhythms** — have cycles that occur **less than once every day**.
   For example, the menstrual cycle. **Sabbagh and Barnard (1984)** found that when women
   live together their menstrual cycles may **synchronise**. It isn't clear why, but it may be
   linked to **pheromones** (chemicals that can affect the behaviour or physiology of others).

3) **Ultradian rhythms** — have cycles that occur **more than once every 24 hours**.
   For example, the sleep cycle has several repeating stages of light and deep sleep. Research
   using **EEGs** to monitor brain activity during sleep has shown that a **regular** sleep pattern is
   really important. Disrupting these cycles can have very serious **consequences** (see next page).

Living together had led to more than just Kim and Mia's menstrual cycles synchronising.

Biological Rhythms are *Regulated* by *Internal* and *External Influences*

The timing of biological rhythms is determined by factors both **inside** and **outside** our bodies.

Endogenous pacemakers

1) Some aspects of our biological rhythms are set by **genetically determined** biological structures
   and mechanisms **within the body**.

2) The **suprachiasmatic nucleus** (SCN), part of the **hypothalamus**, seems to act as an
   internal clock to keep the body on an approximate 24-hour sleep-waking cycle.

3) It is sensitive to light and regulates the **pineal gland**, which secretes **melatonin** — a hormone
   which seems to induce sleep. When there is **less** light, more melatonin is produced.
   When there is **more** light, secretion is reduced and waking occurs.

4) **Menaker et al (1978)** lesioned this structure in hamsters — their sleep-waking cycle was **disrupted**.

Exogenous zeitgebers

1) These are influences outside of the body that act like a **prompt**, which may trigger a **biological rhythm**.

2) **Light** is the most important zeitgeber. **Siffre (1975)** spent six months in a cave. He had **no clocks** and
   no natural light as zeitgebers. His sleep-waking cycle **extended** from a 24-hour to a 25-30 hour cycle.
   It therefore seems that natural light is needed to fine-tune our normal 24-hour cycle.

Endogenous and Exogenous Factors *Interact*

Endogenous and exogenous factors **interact** to regulate the timing of our biological rhythms.

1) In some cases, endogenous factors may **completely determine** a cycle. **Pengelly and Fisher (1957)** found that
   squirrels will hibernate even when kept in laboratory conditions very different from their natural environment.

2) However, many animals can **react more flexibly**, especially humans who are able to adapt to their surroundings.
   We can make ourselves stay awake and **change the environment** to suit our needs, e.g. by using artificial light.

3) **Cultural factors** are also important. For example, Eskimos often live in permanent daylight or permanent
   night-time but can maintain **regular daily sleep cycles** — so the cycle can't just be determined by levels of
   light acting on the pineal gland.

4) **Individual differences** can also affect the rhythms. **Aschoff and Wever (1976)** found that in a group of people
   isolated from daylight, some maintained their **regular** sleep-wake cycles. Other members of the group displayed
   their own very **extreme** idiosyncrasies, e.g. 29 hours awake followed by 21 hours asleep. This also shows that
   factors must interact to control or influence biological rhythms.

Biological Rhythms

Disrupting Biological Rhythms can have Negative Consequences

When endogenous pacemakers become out of line with exogenous zeitgebers, it can **disrupt** the sleep-wake cycle.

1) In the natural environment, zeitgebers normally **change slowly**, e.g. light levels during the year change gradually.
2) However, in modern society, zeitgebers can change quickly. This can have **negative effects** on our ability to function — slowing **reaction times**, impairing **problem-solving skills**, and limiting our **ability to concentrate**.

Jet lag

1) Jet planes allow fast travel to **different time zones**. Leaving the UK at 9am means that you'd get to New York at about 4pm UK time. New York is 5 hours behind the UK, so the local time would be about 11am.
2) Consequently you'll feel sleepy at an **earlier (local) time**. If you then went to sleep you would wake-up earlier and be **out of sync** with local timing. It appears easiest to **adapt** by forcing yourself to stay awake.
3) It can take **about a week** to fully synchronise to a new time zone. **Wegman et al (1986)** found that travelling east to west (**phase delay**) seems easier to adapt to than travelling west to east (**phase advance**).
4) **Schwartz et al (1995)** found that baseball teams from the east coast of the USA got **better results** travelling to play in the west than teams based in the west did when travelling to play in the east.

Shift work

Modern work patterns mean some people work shifts throughout the 24-hour period, disrupting their sleep cycle.

Czeisler et al (1982) studied workers at a factory whose shift patterns appeared to cause sleep and health problems. The researchers recommended **21-day shifts** (allowing more time for workers to adapt), and changing shifts **forward in time** (phase delay). After implementing the changes **productivity** and **job satisfaction** increased.

As described on p.19, psychological research such as this can have a positive impact on the economy.

Research on Biological Rhythms has Limitations

1) Findings from animal studies can't accurately be **generalised** to humans — humans have greater **adaptability**.
2) Studies that have deprived humans of natural light have still allowed **artificial light**, which may give many of the **benefits** of natural light — this reduces the **validity** of these studies.
3) Things like **individual differences** need further study. Some people are more alert early in the day, and others later on, and the speed with which we **adapt to disruptions** can vary. It's difficult to determine whether a person's lifestyle is a **cause or effect** of their biological rhythms.
4) If we fully understand what causes the problems linked to jet lag and shift work, we can **minimise** or **avoid them**, reducing accidents in work environments. There are different ways to deal with these problems, e.g. taking time to **naturally adjust**, or using **drugs** to reduce the effects of sleep deprivation.

Practice Questions

Q1 What is an infradian rhythm?

Q2 Give an example of an exogenous zeitgeber.

Exam Questions

Q1	Distinguish between circadian and ultradian rhythms.	[2 marks]
Q2	Outline the effect of endogenous pacemakers and exogenous zeitgebers on the sleep-wake cycle.	[8 marks]
Q3	Discuss research studies that have examined the role of endogenous pacemakers and exogenous zeitgebers in human biological rhythms.	[16 marks]

"I didn't mean to fall asleep Miss — the melatonin made me do it..."

It's scientific fact that if you're a rock star, your biological rhythm immediately changes to 'We Will Rock You' by Queen. Actually, that's not scientific at all. Nor is it fact. When you've had a decent crack at all the questions on this page, think about what your rock rhythm would be... Are you ready? It's 'We Will Rock You', by Queen. Fact.

The Scientific Process

You met research methods in Year 1, but there's more you need to know I'm afraid. This section covers all the extra stuff you need, and recaps on a few things you'll have seen already. You'll probably remember the scientific process from Year 1 — it's all about how we develop and test scientific ideas. Best get on with it then...

Science is about **Establishing Truths**

1) Scientific research should be **objective** — independent of **beliefs** or **opinions**.

2) So, the methods used should be **empirical** — based on **data**, not just theory. The best way to make sure of this is to carry out an **experiment** that collects **quantitative data** and has strictly **controlled variables**.

3) This means that you should be able to **replicate** the research, and also to establish **cause** and **effect**.

Science Answers Real-life **Questions** and **Tests Hypotheses**

Science tries to explain **how** and **why** things happen — it **tests hypotheses** and **constructs theories** by asking questions. This is the **scientific process**:

> 1) **Ask** a question — make an **observation** and ask **why or how** it happens.
>
> 2) **Suggest** an answer, or part of an answer, by forming a **theory** (a possible explanation of the observations).
>
> 3) Make a **prediction** or **hypothesis** — a **specific testable statement**, based on the theory, about what will happen in a test situation.
>
> 4) Carry out a **test** — to provide **evidence** that will support the hypothesis (or help to disprove it).

Suggesting explanations is all very well and good, but if there's **no way to test** them then it just ain't science. A theory is **only scientific** if it can be tested.

Science is All About **Testing Theories**

It starts off with one experiment backing up a prediction and theory. It can then end up with all the scientists in the world **agreeing** with it and you **learning** it. Stirring stuff. This is how the magical process takes place:

1) The results are **published** — scientists need to let others know about their work, so they try to get their results published in **scientific journals**. These are just like normal magazines, only they contain **scientific reports** (called papers) instead of celebrity gossip. All work must undergo **peer review** before it's published.

> • **Peer review** is a process used to **ensure the integrity** of published scientific work. Before publication, scientific work is sent to **experts** in that field (**peers**) so they can assess the **quality** of the work.
>
> • This process helps to keep scientists **honest** — e.g. you can't '**sex-up**' your conclusions if the data doesn't support it, because it **won't pass** peer review.
>
> • Peer review helps to **validate conclusions** — it means published theories, data and conclusions are more trustworthy. But it **can't guarantee** that the conclusions are 100% right. More **rounds** of predicting and testing are needed before they can be taken as '**fact**'.
>
> • Sometimes **mistakes** are made and bad science is published. Peer review **isn't perfect**, but it's probably the best way for scientists to **self-regulate** their work, and to ensure **reliable** scientific work is **published**.

2) Other scientists read the published theories and results, and try to **repeat them** — this involves repeating the **exact experiments**, and using the theory to make **new predictions** that are tested by **new experiments**.

3) If all the experiments in all the world provide evidence to back it up, the theory is thought of as scientific 'fact'.

4) If **new evidence** comes to light that **conflicts** with the current evidence, the theory is questioned all over again. More rounds of **testing** will be carried out to see which evidence, and so which theory, **prevails**.

Popper (1969) Argued that **Theories** Should be **Falsifiable**

1) **Popper (1969)** argued that theories are **abstract**, so it's impossible to **prove them right** through **empirical research**.

2) Instead, he claimed that a theory is **scientific** if it's **falsifiable** — if it can be proved **wrong**. So, every **test** of a theory should be an attempt to **falsify** it.

3) This sounds a bit weird, but if you think about a **non-scientific** psychological theory then you can see how it fits. For example, Freud's psychodynamic explanation of gender development (page 66) is **non-falsifiable** — you can't prove it wrong because it's based on the unconscious mind.

The Scientific Process

Theories Get **Tested** Over and Over and Over and Over and...

Our currently accepted theories have survived this '**trial by evidence**'. They've been tested **over and over and over** and each time the results have backed them up. **BUT**, and this is a big but (teehee), they never become totally undisputable fact. Scientific **breakthroughs or advances** could provide new ways to question and test a theory, which could lead to **changes and challenges** to it. Then the testing starts all over again...

Science Uses **Paradigms**

1) A **paradigm** is a set of principles, methods and techniques which define a scientific discipline.

2) **Kuhn (1970)** believed that for something to be a science, it needs to have a paradigm. This has resulted in **two different opinions** as to whether psychology is truly a science.

3) Some believe that psychology **has a paradigm**. It was initially **behaviourism**, but then it underwent a change to cognitive psychology. This change in principles and practices is known as a **paradigm shift**.

4) Others argue that psychology might be made up of **mini-paradigms**, and so psychology is in a state of **pre-science** (it hasn't quite become a widely recognised science yet).

Psychological Research Can Impact the *Economy*

Despite the ongoing debate as to whether psychology is a true science, psychology has a big impact on the world. Psychologists conduct research into a wide range of areas. Their findings can have implications for the **economy**.

E.g. People with untreated mental health disorders may need more time off work

- People suffering from conditions like **depression** or **obsessive-compulsive disorder** which aren't being treated may need to take more days off work than those who are receiving treatment.

- **Treatments** for mental health disorders come about as a result of **psychological research** (e.g. cognitive-behaviour therapy, antidepressants, etc.), and can **help** people continue a normal lifestyle, such as going to **work**. Less time off work is **better** for the economy.

E.g. Research into sleep behaviour can help shift workers

- Modern work patterns mean some people work shifts throughout the 24-hour period, disrupting their **sleep cycle**.

- **Czeisler et al (1982)** studied workers at a factory whose shift patterns appeared to cause sleep and health problems. The researchers recommended **rotating shifts** every **21 days** (allowing more time for workers to adapt), and changing shifts forward in time (phase delay).

- The employees had previously worked a backwards rotation — working during the nights for the first week, late afternoons in the second week and only mornings during the third week (phase advance). They would then restart the pattern again in the fourth week.

- After implementing the changes, **productivity** and **job satisfaction** increased.

- **More productive** workers lead to a **better** economy.

Practice Questions

Q1 What is empirical research?

Q2 Describe the meaning of a 'paradigm' and 'paradigm shift' in reference to psychology.

Exam Questions

Q1 Which of the following is **not** a feature of science?

    A objectivity   **B** subjectivity   **C** falsifiability   **D** replicability   [1 mark]

Q2 Briefly discuss the implications of psychological research for the economy.   [6 marks]

The features of psychology — tall, muscular, good sense of humour...

You need to know about the features of science — objectivity, the empirical method, replicability, falsifiability, theory construction, hypothesis testing, paradigms and paradigm shifts. Think how good you'll be at Scrabble® then.

Reliability and Validity

All research studies involve testing or measuring participants. If you want the results to be meaningful, the tests need to be reliable and valid. And if you want to pass your exam you need to know what reliability and validity mean.

Reliable Tests Give Consistent Results

Reliability refers to how **consistent** or **dependable** a test is. A reliable test carried out in the **same circumstances**, on the **same participants** should always give the **same results**. There are different types of reliability:

1) Internal Reliability

- **Different parts** of the test should give **consistent results**.
- For example, if an IQ test contains sections of supposedly equal difficulty, participants should achieve similar scores on all sections.

> The internal reliability of a test can be assessed using the **split-half method**. This splits the test into two halves, e.g. odd and even numbered questions, and the results from each half should produce a **high positive correlation**.

2) External Reliability

- **External reliability** — the test should produce **consistent results** regardless of **when** it's used.
- For example, if you took the same IQ test on two different days you should achieve the same score.

> The external reliability of a test can be assessed using the **test-retest method**. This involves **repeating** the test using the **same participants**. A reliable test should produce a **high positive correlation** between the two scores. A problem with this is that the participants may have changed in some way since the first test, e.g. they may have learnt more. To avoid this, external reliability can be checked using the **equivalent forms test**. This compares participants' scores on two different, but equivalent (equally hard), versions of the test.

3) Inter-observer Reliability

- The test should give **consistent results** regardless of **who** administers it.
- For example, if two researchers observe behaviour and categorise infants as showing signs of a strong attachment or a weak attachment, they should both record the same score.

> This can be assessed by **correlating** the scores that **each researcher** produces for **each participant**. A **high positive correlation** should be found.

Valid Tests Give Accurate Results

Validity refers to how well a test measures what it **claims to**. For example, an IQ test with only **maths questions** would not be a valid measure of **general intelligence**. There are different types of validity:

1) **Face validity** — the extent to which the test looks, to the participants, like it will measure what it is supposed to be measuring.
2) **Concurrent validity** — the extent to which the test produces the same results as another established measure, e.g. two different IQ tests should produce the same measure of IQ. Inferential tests can be used to determine whether both measures are highly correlated, and therefore valid (see page 27).
3) **Ecological validity** — the extent to which the results of the test reflect real-life.
4) **Temporal validity** — the extent to which the test provides results that can be generalised across time.

Reliability and Validity

Validity Can Be Assessed in Different Ways

- A quick (but not very thorough) way of assessing validity is to simply **look** at the test and make a judgement on whether it **appears** to measure what it claims to. For example, an IQ test that just consisted of maths questions could be identified as having low validity by this method.
- **Comparing** the results of the test with the results of an **existing measure** (that's already accepted as valid) can help to determine the validity of the test.
- The results of the test can be used to **predict** results of **future tests**. If the **initial** results **correlate** with the **later** results it suggests that the test has some validity and can continue to be used.

Reliability and Validity Can Both be Improved

There are several ways that the **reliability** and **validity** of tests can be **improved**:

Standardising research

Standardising research involves creating **specific procedures** which are followed every time the test is carried out. This ensures that all the researchers will test all the participants in **exactly the same way**, e.g. in the same sequence, at the same time of day, in the same environment, and with all participants receiving exactly the same instructions. This reduces the possibility of extraneous variables affecting the research. Therefore it will help to improve **external reliability** and **inter-observer reliability**.

Mark had spent all morning standardising the procedure and was feeling pretty smug about the end result.

Operationalising variables

1) **Operationalising variables** involves **clearly defining** all of the research **variables**.
2) For example, in a study of whether watching aggressive TV influences aggressive behaviour, the terms '**aggressive TV**' and '**aggressive behaviour**' need to be defined.
3) 'Aggressive TV' could include cartoons or human actors. One of these might influence human behaviour and the other might not — this needs to be taken into account when planning, carrying out and drawing conclusions from the investigation.
4) Similarly, 'aggressive behaviour' could refer to physical and verbal aggression, or just physical aggression.
5) Clarifying this from the start improves the **reliability** and **validity** of the test.

> Pilot studies allow the reliability and validity of a test to be assessed in advance, which then gives the opportunity for improvements to be made.

Practice Questions

Q1 Explain the difference between internal reliability and external reliability.
Q2 How does the split-half method test for internal reliability?
Q3 Why does standardisation help to improve the reliability and validity of research?

Exam Questions

Q1 Briefly explain how validity could be assessed in psychological research. [4 marks]

Q2 Briefly outline how reliability could be improved in psychological research. [4 marks]

Reliable tests? Who cares. Reliable results are what you need right now.

So, it turns out that 'reliable' and 'valid' are more than just terms to bandy around and throw into answers with some sort of vague idea that they're good things for studies to be. They've got specific meanings you need to know. These examiners are so demanding — it's like they've got nothing better to do than sit around thinking up stuff for you to learn.

Data Analysis

Content analysis is a research method used to analyse secondary data (see next page) and data you've already collected (e.g. through unstructured interviews). It involves splitting the data into assigned categories. It's usually an easy and inexpensive research method to use, but it can be time consuming, and may be subjective.

Qualitative Data Can Be Tricky to Analyse

1) Once **quantitative data** (i.e. numbers) is collected, it can be **easily** and **objectively** analysed.

2) However, **qualitative data** (such as an interview transcript) is sometimes seen as 'of **limited use**' because it's difficult to analyse **objectively**.

Thematic analysis is a form of qualitative analysis — it involves subjective decisions

Thematic analysis is one of the most frequently used forms of qualitative analysis. It involves making **summaries** of data and identifying **key themes** and **categories**.

- Firstly, the researcher becomes **familiar with the data**. Then they start to **look** for different themes, **review** the themes, **define** and **name** the themes and then **write** a report.

- However, different researchers may read different things into the themes — it can be **subjective**.

- Such analysis may give the basis for **hypotheses**, e.g. about what may be found in other sources / other things the participant may say — the hypothesis formation is therefore **grounded in the data** (but could still be subjective).

Strengths

1) Qualitative analysis preserves the **detail** in the data.

2) Creating hypotheses during the analysis allows for new **insights** to be developed.

3) Some **objectivity** can be established by using **triangulation** — other sources of data are used to check conclusions (e.g. previous interviews). With more sources researchers can cross-check their interpretations.

Criticisms

1) How do you decide **which categories to use** and whether a statement fits a particular category?

2) How do you decide what to **leave out** of the summary, or which quotations to use?

These are **subjective** decisions and researchers may be **biased**, possibly showing statements or events **out of context**.

Content Analysis is a Way to Quantify Qualitative Data

1) Because of the **detail** (and hence the **insight**) that **qualitative** data can give, some researchers prefer to **avoid** 'reducing' it to **numbers**.

2) Instead they analyse the data into **categories** or '**typologies**' (e.g. sarcastic remarks, statements about feelings, etc.), **quotations**, **summaries**, and so on.

3) This is called **content analysis** and the method is outlined below.

4) **Hypotheses** may be developed during this analysis so that they are 'grounded in the data'.

Using content analysis can reduce ethical issues, as participants aren't directly involved in the research.

- A **representative sample** of qualitative data is first **collected** — e.g. from an interview, printed material (newspapers, etc.) or other media (such as TV programmes).

- **Coding units** are identified to analyse the data. A coding unit could be, for example, an **act of violence**, or the use of **gender stereotypes** (though both of these must be given valid **operationalised definitions** first — e.g. a definition of an 'act of violence').

- The qualitative data is then **analysed** to see **how often** each coding unit occurs (or **how much** is said about it, etc.).

- **Statistical analysis** can then be carried out.

Strengths
- A **clear summary** of the patterns in the data may be established.
- Once a coding system has been set up, **replication** is easy, improving reliability.

Limitations
- Often an individual's judgement is used to define coding units, so they can be **subjective**.
- Reducing the data to particular coding units **removes detail**, and the true meaning of things may be lost when taken out of context.

Data Analysis

There are **Advantages** and **Disadvantages** of **Quantifying Data**

Advantages of Quantifying Data

1) It becomes **easier** to see **patterns** in the data, and easier to **summarise** and **present** it (see pages 24-26).
2) **Statistical analysis** can be carried out.

Disadvantages of Quantifying Data

1) Care is needed to avoid **bias** in defining **coding units**, or deciding which behaviours fit particular units.
2) Qualitative data has **more detail** (**context**, etc.), which is **lost** when it's converted into **numbers**.

Psychologists Gather **Primary** and **Secondary Data**

Researchers gather **primary** and **secondary data** when they collect results.

- **Primary data** — information collected during a researcher's direct observations of participants, e.g. test results, answers to questionnaires, observation notes.

- **Secondary data** — information collected from other studies. This data can be used to check the validity of studies, or used to provide evidence to support or discredit a new theory.

Summarising Lots of Studies is Called a **Meta-Analysis**

Both **quantitative** data and **qualitative** data can be analysed using a **meta-analysis**. This is where you analyse the results from loads of different studies and come up with some **general conclusions**.

They're a good way of **bringing together data** (which is a general aim of the scientific process), and by doing this they reduce the problem of **sample size**. However, one problem is that there are often loads of **conflicting results** out there, which obviously makes doing a meta-analysis a bit tricky...

Practice Questions

Q1 What is quantitative data?
Q2 Give one limitation of analysing qualitative data.
Q3 What is content analysis?
Q4 Give one advantage of quantifying qualitative data.
Q5 What is the difference between primary and secondary data?
Q6 What is a meta-analysis?

Exam Questions

Q1 Briefly outline how thematic analysis is used to analyse qualitative data. [2 marks]

Q2 Outline and evaluate how content analysis can be used to analyse qualitative data. [4 marks]

Why not do a content analysis of this book?

You could count the hilarious jokes for example... On second thoughts, maybe you should just make sure you're clear on all the stuff on these pages instead. That's probably a much better use of your time. And content analysis has its problems anyway, as I'm sure you know... If you don't, have another read through of its strengths and limitations.

Summarising the Data

Here's a quick recap of some of the different ways to present data. You'll probably remember most of this from Year 1 — happy days. But you need to know about histograms too, so don't just merrily skip these pages.

Data *Can be Presented in* Various Ways

1) **Qualitative** data from observations, interviews, surveys, etc. can be presented in a **report** as a '**verbal summary**'.

2) The report would contain **summaries** of what was seen or said, possibly using **categories** to group data together. Also **quotations** from participants can be used, and any **research hypotheses** that developed during the study or data analysis may be discussed.

3) When **quantitative** data is **collected** (or **produced** from **qualitative** data) it can be **summarised** and presented in various ways. Read on...

Tables are a Good Way to Summarise Quantitative Data

- **Tables** can be used to clearly present the data and show any **patterns** in the scores.

- Tables of '**raw data**' show the scores **before** any **analysis** has been done on them.

- Other tables may show **descriptive statistics** such as the mean, range and standard deviation.

Ice cream flavour	Quality (score out of 10)		
	Tastiness	Thickness	Throwability
Chocolate	5	7	6
Toffee	8	6	7
Strawberry	6	5	4
Earwax	6	9	8

Table to Show the Qualities of Different Flavour Ice Cream

Harold and Madge could spot a good table a mile off.

Examiners sometimes like to make you do some **maths** with the numbers in **tables** and **graphs**.

EXAMPLE:

What **percentage** of the participants who obeyed were boys?

	Boys	Girls
Number of participants who obeyed	36	24
Number of participants who didn't obey	52	64

To find the percentage, divide the number of boys who obeyed by the total number of participants who obeyed, then multiply by 100.

Find the total number of participants who obeyed: 36 + 24 = 60

Percentage of boys among those who obeyed: (36 ÷ 60) × 100 = **60%**

Don't panic if you're asked to do some maths, just read the question carefully and take it step by step — don't rush it.

Summarising the Data

Nearly done — just a little bit more...

Line Graphs are Good for Showing More Than One Set of Data

Line graphs are for use with **continuous data**. The **independent variable** is plotted along the **x-axis** and the **dependent variable** is plotted up the **y-axis**.

They show the plotted data points, which are then **joined up** with **straight lines**.

It can be useful to combine **two or more** line graphs on the same set of axes — then it's easy to **make comparisons** between groups.

If you need to plot a line graph, you'll get marks for labelling the axes (including the units), accurate plotting, and including a title.

Bar Charts Can be Used for Non-continuous Data

Bar chart showing the mean number of words recalled by two groups in a memory experiment.

Bar charts are usually used to present '**non-continuous data**' (like when a variable falls into **categories** rather than being measured on a numbered scale).

This bar chart shows the mean number of words recalled by different groups in a memory experiment.

Note that the columns in bar charts **don't touch** each other. Also, it's preferable to always show the **full vertical scale**, or **clearly indicate** when it isn't all shown (otherwise it can be **misleading**).

Scattergrams Can Tell You if Two Variables are Related

Scattergrams are used when you've got **two different variables** — you plot one variable along the bottom of the graph, and the second one up the side. Scattergrams are good for showing whether there's a **correlation**.

EXAMPLE:

Gill is investigating the relationship between height and scores on a depression index.

Height (cm)	Depression Score
150	20
164	32
100	10
130	18
140	30

- Choose a suitable scale for each axis.

- Carefully plot the data points — but don't join them up.

- Instead, you can draw a line of best fit to show a trend — draw a line which passes through or as near to as many of the points as possible.

Summarising the Data

... okay — I lied... one more and then you're done.

Histograms are for When You Have Continuous Data

Histograms show data measured on a 'continuous' scale of measurement.

This histogram shows the time different participants took to complete a task.

Each column shows a **class interval** (here, each class interval is 10 seconds), and the columns **touch** each other.

It's the **height** of the column that shows the number of values in that interval. (**All** intervals are shown, even if there are **no scores** within them.)

Histograms are for when you have continuous data. This includes things like height, temperature and time — things that fall on a continuous scale. Non-continuous data includes things like exam grades, types of ice cream and names of football teams — things that fall into distinct categories.

Practice Questions

Q1 What kind of information is typically shown in tables?

Q2 What kind of data is shown on bar charts?

Q3 What does each column in a histogram represent?

Exam Questions

Q1 A sample of children were observed in an observational study. Their attachment styles were recorded below.

	Secure	Insecure-avoidant	Insecure-resistant
Number of children	56	17	7

Calculate the percentage of the children from the sample who had a secure attachment. [2 marks]

Q2 Draw a bar chart showing the percentage obedience for boys and girls from the table on page 24. [6 marks]

Q3 Look at the table below, then answer the questions that follow.

Participant	1	2	3	4	5	6	7	8	9	10
Percentage Mark on Psychology Exam	70	50	20	85	90	60	30	24	10	75
Average Number of Minutes Exercise per Day	30	20	5	50	75	60	10	15	5	40

a) Draw a scattergram to display the data shown in the table above. [3 marks]

b) Draw a line of best fit through your data points. [1 mark]

Data? I can't, I lost her number...

There's nothing too tricky here, the only new bit is histograms — the rest of this stuff should be ringing bells from Year 1. Make sure you know all of it though. It'd be a shame to get your bar charts mixed up with your histograms. Believe me, I've seen it... it's really not pretty. More importantly, it'll lose you marks, and nobody wants that.

Inferential Statistics

You were introduced to inferential statistics in Year 1, but there's quite a bit more you need to know about them. Yay. This stuff can be tricky to get your head around at first, but don't panic, it's all explained here. Best get on with it then...

Inferential Statistics are about Ruling Out Chance

1) You can never be 100% certain that results aren't all down to chance. So instead of 'proving' a hypothesis, you have to be content with finding out whether it's **likely** to be true. This is called **statistical significance**.

2) If your results are statistically significant, it means that you can **read something into them** — they're unlikely to be just down to chance.

3) If your results are **not statistically significant**, it means they could have happened by chance rather than being the effect of changes in your independent variable, so you can't really read anything into them.

Use Statistical Tests to Find Out if Your Results Mean Anything

1 • The first thing you do is write out your **null hypothesis** — this is the prediction you want to **test**.
 • In a statistical test, you assume that your null hypothesis is **true** for the time being, and that any hint of a significant difference between your groups (or correlation between your variables) is actually just a **fluke**.

2 • Next you choose a **significance level** — this is a '**level of proof**' that you're looking for before you read anything into your results.
 • The smaller the significance level, the stronger the evidence you're looking for that your results aren't just down to chance.
 • A significance level is a **probability**, and so is a number between 0 and 1.
 • (Probabilities near 1 mean things are very **likely**, and probabilities near 0 mean things are very **unlikely**.)
 • Significance levels are always **very small** — usually 0.05 (5%) or less. (Because a significance level is very **small**, events with probabilities smaller than the significance level are very **unlikely** to happen.)

Doreen was convinced that her winning streak was statistically significant. Mary was less sure.

3 • You then turn all your experimental results into a single **test statistic**.
 • Then you can find out what the **probability** is that this test statistic, and therefore your results, were the result of a **fluke** (making your **null hypothesis true** after all).

4 • If the probability of your results being a fluke is **less than** the significance level (e.g. 5%), then it's pretty safe to say that your null hypothesis **wasn't actually true**. You can therefore assume that the **difference** you've noticed between your groups was down to the change you made in your **independent variable**.
 • This is what stats-folk mean when they talk about 'rejecting the null hypothesis'. (If you reject your null hypothesis, you assume your **alternative hypothesis** is true instead.)

5 • If you reject your null hypothesis, you can proudly shout out that your results are **statistically significant**.

6 • If you **don't reject** the null hypothesis, it means that your results could have occurred **by chance**, rather than because your null hypothesis was wrong.
 • If this happens, you've proved **nothing** — not rejecting the null hypothesis doesn't mean it **must be true**.

7 • Using a significance level of **0.05** (5%) is okay for most tests.
 • If the probability of your results being down to chance is **less than** or **equal to** this ($p \leq 0.05$), then it's **pretty good evidence** that the null hypothesis **wasn't true** after all. So the researchers can be at least **95% confident** in their conclusion.
 • If you use a significance level of **0.01** (1%), then you're looking for **really strong evidence** that the null hypothesis is untrue before you're going to reject it. The researchers can be at least **99% confident**.

Inferential Statistics

There are Two Types of **Potential Error**

It's possible to make errors when you're deciding whether or not to reject the null hypothesis.

A **Type I error** is when you **reject** the null hypothesis when it was **actually true**.

The significance level gives you the **probability** of this happening. E.g. a $p = 0.05$ level means the probability that the null hypothesis is actually true is **5%**.

This is why significance levels are **small**.

A very small significance level (e.g. 0.01 or 1%) is used when you need to be very confident in your results, like when testing new theories.

A **Type II error** is when you **don't reject** the null hypothesis when it was **actually false**.

This can happen if your significance level is **too small** (e.g. if you want very strong evidence of the need to reject a null hypothesis and so use a 0.01 significance level).

So if you don't reject your null hypothesis, even if your alternative hypothesis was significant at $p = 0.05$, then there's a **95% chance** you'll have made a **Type II** error.

Choosing significance levels is a **compromise** — if the level you choose is **too big** you risk making a Type I error. If the significance level you choose is **too small**, you could make a Type II error.

There are **Various Ways** to **Test Significance**

1) Remember that you can never be 100% sure that a hypothesis is correct — it's always possible that results are just due to **chance**.

2) Significance levels are assigned to establish the **probability** of the result being due to chance, and if this is acceptably low (e.g. 5%), then you can reject the **null hypothesis**.

3) **Inferential statistical tests** help to decide whether or not to reject the null hypothesis. However, there are many **different tests** and it is crucial that you use the **correct one** for your data. We'll get to the specific tests over the next few pages.

4) You use inferential tests to calculate what's called an **observed value** (the value you get when you carry out the test on your results). The observed value is then **compared** against a **critical value**, which is provided for each test in a **critical value table**. This indicates whether or not the results are significant.

5) In some tests, if the observed value is **more than or equal to** the critical value, the results are considered to **be significant**. In others, the observed value must be **equal to or less than** the critical value to **show significance**.

You Need to Know How to Use **Critical Values Tables**

Example: A psychologist investigating eating behaviour uses **Spearman's rho correlation coefficient** to analyse his data set. His null hypothesis is that there will be **no correlation** between mood and calorie consumption. His alternative hypothesis is that there **will be a correlation** between mood and calorie consumption. He tested **20 participants** and produced an **observed value of 0.518**.

To test the significance of his results, the psychologist must **compare** his observed value against the critical values for Spearman's rho correlation coefficient.

1) Firstly he must decide if it's a one-tailed or a two-tailed test.

A **one-tailed test** is used when the researcher has predicted an association and has also stated which way the results will go (i.e. a directional hypothesis, such as 'the lower the mood, the higher the calorie consumption').

A **two-tailed test** is used when the researcher has predicted an association, but hasn't stated which way the results will go (i.e. a non-directional hypothesis). The hypothesis in this correlation is non-directional, so it's a two-tailed test.

Inferential Statistics

2)   The observed value is then looked up in a critical value table.

Some of the critical values for a Spearman's rho correlation coefficient are shown here. As the test is **two-tailed**, the researcher needs to look at the row of significance levels for two-tailed tests.

3)   Read off the table.

If the psychologist wants to see if his results are significant at the $p = 0.05$ level, he should use the column highlighted in purple.

N = the number of values in the data set. As there were **20** participants in this study, the **critical value** at the $p = 0.05$ level = **0.447**.

4)   Make a conclusion about significance.

For the data to be significant, the **observed value** from the Spearman's rho calculation must be **greater than or equal to** the relevant **critical value**.

The observed value in this experiment is **0.518**, which is **greater than 0.447**. This means that the psychologist's results **are significant** at the $p = 0.05$ level. Consequently, the researcher can **reject** his null hypothesis, and **accept** his alternative hypothesis.

Level of significance for two-tailed test			
0.10	**0.05**	**0.02**	**0.01**
Level of significance for one-tailed test			
N	**0.05**	**0.025**	**0.01**	**0.005**
15	0.443	0.521	0.604	0.654
16	0.429	0.503	0.582	0.635
17	0.414	0.485	0.566	0.615
18	0.401	0.472	0.550	0.600
19	0.391	0.460	0.535	0.584
20	0.380	0.447	0.520	0.570
21	0.370	0.435	0.508	0.556
22	0.361	0.425	0.496	0.544

Critical values of Spearman's rho correlation coefficient.

Several Things Determine Which Inferential Test Should be Used

Inferential statistics allow you to make an educated guess about whether or not a hypothesis is correct. Deciding which inferential test you use for your data is determined by the following factors:

Experimental Design

Research may have either **related measures** (if a repeated measures or matched participants design was used), or **unrelated measures** (if an independent measures design was used).

Research Aims

Some inferential statistics test whether there is a **significant difference** between two (or more) groups of scores:

*   For example, 'did the participants in group A have significantly higher average scores than those in group B?'.
*   This is what happens in an **experiment**. The IV is manipulated to see if it produces **changes** in the DV that are significantly different from the **control condition** (or other experimental conditions).

Some inferential statistics test to see if there is a **significant association** between two (or more) variables:

*   For example, whether they occur together more than would be expected by chance.
*   This is what we look for in **correlation studies** — to see if two variables are positively or negatively associated, more than would be expected by chance factors alone. If they are, a **significant** correlation has been shown.

Level of Measurement / Type of Data

Studies can collect different types of data, which affects how it can be analysed.

*   **Nominal data** — This is the most basic level of measurement — a **frequency count** for completely **distinct categories**. For example, in a study where a confederate pretends to need help, you could assign each passer-by to either an 'altruistic' category (if they helped) or a 'non-altruistic' category (if they did nothing).
*   **Ordinal data** — All of the measurements relate to the **same variable**, and measurements can be placed in ascending or descending **rank order**, e.g. on a **rating scale** for aggression where 1 = 'not aggressive' and 10 = 'extremely aggressive'. But you can't say a person with a score of 10 is twice as aggressive as a person with a score of 5, just which one was **more** or **less** aggressive.
*   **Interval data** — Measurements are taken on a scale where **each unit is the same size**, e.g. length in centimetres. Interval data places participants along an objective, scientific scale. You then know exactly how far apart the scores are. E.g. in a race, participant 'F' was quickest, in 15.8 seconds and participant 'B' was second, in 16.5 seconds. Technically, an **absolute zero point** is needed to make judgements about whether one score is twice that of another. When we have this (e.g. 0 seconds, 0 centimetres, etc.) then we call it a **ratio scale**.

Spearman's Rho and Pearson's *r*

If the thought of maths in general, and statistics in particular, makes you want to run for the hills, then take a ticket and get in line. But don't worry — you only need to know when each test is used and how to interpret the results — you don't have to calculate the observed values (except for the sign test (see page 33)... there's always one).

Spearman's Rho is a **Correlation Coefficient**

Spearman's rho can also be used on interval or ratio data if they're not normally distributed.

1) Spearman's rho correlation coefficient is an observed value used to see if there's a significant association between two variables that have at least **ordinal** data.

2) To work out (and then test the significance of) **Spearman's rho** correlation coefficient, you need values for two different variables (e.g. hours of sleep and test scores for 10 students).

Example: A psychologist is investigating the relationship between sleep and cognitive function. His hypothesis is that students who get **more** hours of sleep the night before a test will score **higher** in the test. Students' hours of sleep the night before a test and their test scores are shown below.

Spearman's rho can be used to establish concurrent validity (page 20).

Student	Hours sleep	Test score (%)
A	3	12
B	6	71
C	9	83
D	4	46
E	5	38
F	13	94
G	10	100
H	1	15
I	8	32
J	12	87

Spearman was no ordinary rower...

3) Using the Spearman's rho calculation, the psychologist calculates an observed value of **0.867** (3 s.f.).

4) The observed value is very close to +1, showing that there is a **strong positive correlation** between hours of sleep and test score.

5) The result of the calculation is then compared with a critical value.

6) For the data to be significant, the observed value must be **greater than or equal to** the relevant critical value in the table.

Positive correlation means the variables rise and fall together. A negative correlation would mean that as one variable increases, the other decreases.

7) As the hypothesis is directional, a one-tailed test is used.

	Level of significance for two-tailed test			
	0.10	*0.05*	*0.02*	*0.01*
	Level of significance for one-tailed test			
N	*0.05*	*0.025*	*0.01*	*0.005*
7	0.714	0.786	0.893	0.929
8	0.643	0.738	0.833	0.881
9	0.600	0.700	0.783	0.833
10	0.564	0.648	0.745	0.794
11	0.536	0.618	0.709	0.755
12	0.503	0.587	0.671	0.727

In this example, you read the values off the N = 10 row, as there are 10 participants.

8) From the table it can be seen that the critical value for $p = 0.05$ is **0.564**. The observed value (0.867) is **greater than** this, therefore the results are **significant** at the $p = 0.05$ level.

9) The psychologist **can reject** the null hypothesis.

Spearman's Rho and Pearson's *r*

Pearson's *r* is also a **Correlation Coefficient**

Pearson's *r* can also be used to establish concurrent validity (page 20).

1) A Pearson's *r* test investigates the association between two variables. Both variables must have **interval** or **ratio** data and be **normally distributed**.

2) The correlation between the two variables will fall between –1 and +1. This value is called *r*.

3) The closer *r* is to –1 or +1, the stronger the relationship.

4) If *r* is **positive**, the relationship between the two variables is positive (one **goes up** as the other **goes up**). If *r* is **negative**, the relationship between the two variables is negative (one **goes down** as the other **goes up**). Makes sense if you think about it...

Example: A psychologist was investigating the hypothesis that there is a **relationship** between weight and serotonin levels. **Five** participants had their weight recorded and had a blood test to determine their serotonin level, measured in nanograms per millilitre. Their results are shown in the table.

Student	Weight (kg)	Serotonin Level (ng/mL)
A	61	160
B	58	245
C	55	282
D	64	172
E	60	161

5) Using the Pearson's *r* test, the observed value is **–0.854** (3 s.f.). You can ignore the minus sign though (it just shows it's a negative correlation), so it's **0.854**.

6) For Pearson's *r*, the observed value must be **greater than or equal to** the critical value to be significant.

7) Before you look up the critical value, you'll need to calculate the **degrees of freedom (*df*)**. For Pearson's *r*, this is $N - 2$. So in this case, it is 3 (since $5 - 2 = 3$).

8) The hypothesis is **non-directional**, which means it's a two-tailed test. So the critical value for $p = 0.05$ is **0.878**.

9) The observed value (0.854) is **less than** this, so the results are **not significant** at the $p = 0.05$ level.

10) The psychologist **cannot reject** the null hypothesis.

	Level of significance for two-tailed test			
	0.10	**0.05**	**0.01**	**0.001**
	Level of significance for one-tailed test			
df = N – 2	**0.05**	**0.025**	**0.005**	**0.0005**
2	0.900	0.950	0.990	0.999
3	0.805	0.878	0.959	0.991
4	0.729	0.811	0.917	0.974
5	0.669	0.754	0.875	0.951

Practice Questions

Q1 A psychologist conducts a Spearman's rho test and calculates an observed value of 0.4. She used 12 participants and had a two-tailed hypothesis. Use the table on page 30 to determine if her data is significant at the $p = 0.05$ level.

Q2 What type of data can a Pearson's *r* test be used for?

Exam Question

Q1 A psychologist investigated the relationship between TV watching and weight. These are the results.

Participant	1	2	3	4	5	6
TV watching per day (mins)	180	124	80	52	12	16
Weight (kg)	64	70	68	62	55	54

a) Name an appropriate statistical test that could be used to analyse the results in the table. [1 mark]

b) Given that the correlation coefficient is 0.716 (3 s.f.), determine if the results are significant at the $p = 0.05$ level. [2 marks]

You'll be given the critical values tables in the exam, so you don't need to learn them. Phew.

Rho, rho, rho your boat, gently down the stream...

Don't get freaked out by these pages of tables of critical values. You don't have to memorise them — just make sure you feel comfortable being able to use them to work out whether your data is significant or not...

Wilcoxon and The Sign Test

*Drum roll please... I now proudly introduce the Wilcoxon Test. *Rapturous applause, whoops and cheers*.*

The **Wilcoxon** Test is a Test of Difference for **Related** Data

The Wilcoxon test is a test of difference for related data. It is used when:

- A **hypothesis** states that there'll be a **difference** between two sets of data.

- The data is **ordinal**.

- The experiment is a **repeated measures** or **matched pairs** design.

> *See page 29 if you don't know what ordinal data is.*

> **Example:** A psychologist is investigating **two methods** of memorising words. Her hypothesis is that Method 1 will be **more effective** than Method 2. Her **null hypothesis** is that there will be **no difference** between the two methods.
>
> Each participant will do two memory tests — one for each method, in a **repeated measures** design. The results are shown below.

	Participant no.	1	2	3	4	5	6	7	8
No. words recalled	Method 1	6	5	10	6	8	5	9	8
	Method 2	7	7	8	8	7	6	9	9

1) The Wilcoxon test involves working out the **difference** between participants' scores across **both conditions**. If one condition gives considerably different results to the other, the data will be **significant**.

2) The Wilcoxon test is used to calculate an observed value of **8.5** for the results above.

3) Compare this observed value with the critical value from the critical values table for this test.

4) The observed value must be **less than or equal to** the **critical value** to be significant.

5) In this case *N* is **7**. For a Wilcoxon test, *N* is calculated by only including participants who **did show** a difference between the two conditions.

> *Participant 7 scored 9 using both methods. This is why their score isn't included when calculating N.*

	Level of significance for two-tailed test			
	0.10	*0.05*	*0.02*	*0.01*
	Level of significance for one-tailed test			
N	*0.05*	*0.025*	*0.01*	*0.005*
5	0			
6	2	0		
7	3	2	0	
8	5	3	1	0
9	8	5	3	1
10	10	8	5	3
11	13	10	7	5
12	17	13	9	7
13	21	17	12	9

6) As the psychologist's hypothesis is directional, a **one-tailed test** is used.

7) From the table you can see that the critical value for *p* = 0.05 is **3**.

8) The observed value (8.5) is **more than** this, therefore the results are **not significant** at the *p* = 0.05 level.

9) The psychologist **cannot reject** her null hypothesis.

Toby laughed in the face of rejection. He quite liked bins.

Wilcoxon and The Sign Test

You Can Use the **Sign Test** When You've Got **Nominal** Data

One of the easiest statistical tests to use is the **sign test**. It compares scores in data from **repeated measures** or **matched pairs** designs by turning the **change** in scores into **nominal** data. You could be asked to **calculate** the observed value here — so make sure you learn the method.

Example hypothesis:	Participants' scores on a depression index before drug treatment will be significantly different to their scores after treatment.

Depression Index (1-20)	Participant no.	1	2	3	4	5	6	7	8
	Before Treatment	12	5	6	8	10	12	15	9
	After Treatment	5	6	4	2	3	2	16	9

1) The **difference** between each participant's two scores is calculated:

Participant no.	1	2	3	4	5	6	7	8
Difference	7	1	2	6	7	10	1	0
Sign (+/−)	−	+	−	−	−	−	+	

Always subtract in the same direction, noting if the result is a positive or negative value. Any differences of zero are removed from the results.

2) Add up the number of positive signs and negative signs. The **smallest** one is the **observed value**.

3) There are **5 negative** signs and **2 positive** signs. So the observed value is **2**.

4) The observed value must be **less than or equal to** the **critical value** to be significant.

5) Since the hypothesis is non-directional, a **two-tailed test** is used. Here, N is the number of participants not including zeros (7).

6) In this case, the **critical value** is 0. Since the observed value is **greater than** 0, the results are **not significant**.

	Level of significance for two-tailed test			
	0.10	**0.05**	**0.02**	**0.01**
	Level of significance for one-tailed test			
N	**0.05**	**0.025**	**0.01**	**0.005**
5	0	—	—	—
6	0	0	—	—
7	0	0	0	—
8	1	0	0	0
9	1	1	0	0
10	1	1	0	0
11	2	1	1	0

Practice Questions

Q1 What type of data can a Wilcoxon test be used on?

Q2 What types of research design can a sign test be used on?

Q3 Describe the steps of the sign test.

Exam Question

Q1 Read the item below, then answer the question that follows.

> Bella investigated students' stress levels on a scale of 1-10 before and after their Psychology exam (1 = low stress, 10 = high stress). She hypothesised that they would be significantly more stressed before the exam than after the exam. Her results are shown in the table:
>
> | Participant | 1 | 2 | 3 | 4 | 5 | 6 | 7 | 8 | 9 | 10 |
> | --- | --- | --- | --- | --- | --- | --- | --- | --- | --- | --- |
> | Stress level before exam | 8 | 7 | 9 | 10 | 5 | 6 | 8 | 9 | 9 | 10 |
> | Stress level after exam | 4 | 3 | 5 | 8 | 8 | 7 | 9 | 8 | 5 | 4 |

Use the sign test to determine if Bella's results support her hypothesis. [4 marks]

No U-turns permitted ahead...

Oh wait — wrong sort of sign test. Although they won't tell you how to drive, the Wilcoxon and sign tests are mighty useful. Just remember — the Wilcoxon is for ordinal data and the sign test uses nominal data.

t-Tests and the Mann-Whitney Test

Spearman's, Pearson's, Wilcoxon... not only are the stats confusing, but the names aren't that easy to remember either. They certainly like their fancy names. Here we have the t-tests and the Mann-Whitney test. Hoorah.

> It's also called a dependent t-test.

The **Related *t*-Test** is Used in **Repeated Measures** Designs

The **related *t*-test** is a test of difference (or similarity) for **repeated measures** or **matched pairs** designs.
It's used when you have **interval** or **ratio** data which is normally distributed. A trusty example will make it clearer:

Example: A psychologist investigated the hypothesis that the weight of participants will be significantly **lower** after following a new diet plan, than their weight before. In a **repeated measures design**, participants' weight was recorded before and after the trial diet.

Participant	Weight before diet (kg)	Weight after diet (kg)
A	94	71
B	82	63
C	96	68
D	85	76

1) Running a related *t*-test on this data gives an observed value of **4.903** (3 d.p.).

2) The **degrees of freedom (*df*)** are calculated by doing $N - 1$. So here, $df = 4 - 1 = \mathbf{3}$.

3) The observed value in a related *t*-test must be **greater than or equal to** the **critical value** to be significant.

4) As the psychologist's hypothesis is directional, a **one-tailed test** is used.

5) From the table you can see that the critical value for $p = 0.05$ is **2.353**.

6) The observed value for *t* (4.903) is **greater than** this, therefore the results **are significant** at the $p = 0.05$ level. The psychologist **can reject** the null hypothesis.

	Level of significance for two-tailed test			
	0.10	*0.05*	*0.02*	*0.01*
	Level of significance for one-tailed test			
df = N − 1	*0.05*	*0.025*	*0.01*	*0.005*
1	6.314	12.706	31.821	63.657
2	2.920	4.303	6.965	9.925
3	2.353	3.182	4.541	5.841
4	2.132	2.776	3.747	4.604
5	2.015	2.571	3.365	4.032

Abridged from Statistical Tables for Biological Agricultural and Medical Research (6th ed.) © 1963 R.A Fisher and F. Yates. Reprinted with permission of Pearson Education Limited.

The **Unrelated *t*-Test** is Used in **Independent Measures** Designs

It shouldn't come as a great surprise that the unrelated *t*-test is similar to the related *t*-test.
The main difference is that in the **unrelated *t*-test**, there should be **two separate groups** of participants (i.e. unpaired).

Example hypothesis: There will be a significant **difference** between male and female Psychology test scores.

> It's also called an independent t-test.

1) An unrelated *t*-test on this data gives an observed value of **0.719** (3 d.p.).

2) To calculate the degrees of freedom, add up the number of participants in both groups and subtract 2. So here, it'll be $4 + 4 - 2 = \mathbf{6}$.

3) Look up your value of *t* in a **critical values table**.

4) The observed value must be **greater than or equal to** the critical value for the results to be significant.

5) The hypothesis is non-directional, so it is a **two-tailed** test.

6) The table shows the critical value is 2.447 for $p = 0.05$.

7) The observed value of *t* (0.719) is **less than** this, so the results are **not significant**.

8) This means the null hypothesis **cannot** be rejected.

Female Test Score (%)	Male Test Score (%)
84	78
70	90
80	65
92	73

	Level of significance for two-tailed test			
	0.10	*0.05*	*0.02*	*0.01*
	Level of significance for one-tailed test			
df	*0.05*	*0.025*	*0.01*	*0.005*
4	2.132	2.776	3.747	4.604
5	2.015	2.571	3.365	4.032
6	1.943	2.447	3.143	3.707

Abridged from Statistical Tables for Biological Agricultural and Medical Research (6th ed.) © 1963 R.A Fisher and F. Yates. Reprinted with permission of Pearson Education Limited.

t-Tests and the Mann-Whitney Test

The **Mann-Whitney Test** is Used with **Ordinal Data**

The **Mann-Whitney Test** is a test of difference (or of similarity) for data from an **independent measures** design. It focuses on **ranks** and is used when you have **ordinal** data. Take a look at the following example:

> **Example:** Two groups took part in a study investigating whether drinking one **vitamin drink** daily for 4 weeks improved **verbal memory** test performance compared to a group who had no vitamin drinks.

Number of words recalled	Vitamin group	19	13	9	12	21	15	14
	No vitamin group	7	5	10	8	6	11	18

1) Using the Mann-Whitney test, an observed value, U, is calculated. Here, $U = \textbf{7}$.

2) This table shows the critical values for U for a one-tailed test at $p = 0.01$.

3) In the Mann-Whitney test, the observed U value must be **less than or equal to** the critical value to be **significant**.

4) As N_1 and N_2 are both **7**, the critical value is 6.

5) As $U = 7$ here, it can be concluded that there's **no significant difference** between the two groups.

6) This means the **null** hypothesis **cannot** be rejected.

	N_1				
	5	**6**	**7**	**8**	**9**
5	1	2	3	4	5
6	2	3	4	6	7
N_2 **7**	3	4	6	7	9
8	4	6	7	9	11
9	5	7	9	11	14

Abridged from Fundamentals of behavioural statistics (3rd Edn.) by R. Runyon and A. Haber © 1976 McGraw-Hill Education.

Practice Questions

Q1 When can a related *t*-test be used?

Q2 What type of data is a Mann-Whitney test used on?

Exam Questions

Q1 Donel is investigating a new drug to lower blood cortisol level. He divides participants into two groups and both groups partake in the same stressful event. The first group have been taking a placebo drug for one month, whilst the second group have been taking the new drug for one month. Their cortisol levels are then recorded after the event.

Name an appropriate statistical test that Donel could use to analyse his findings. Explain your answer. [4 marks]

Q2 Read the item below, then answer the questions that follow.

> Two separate groups of participants took part in a study to investigate the influence of music on stress levels.
>
> The researcher's hypothesis stated that the addition of music would make an event more stressful.
>
> Both groups took a simulated driving test and were then asked to rate their stress levels.
>
> **Group A** completed the driving test whilst listening to loud music.
> **Group B** did not listen to music during the driving test.
>
> The results are given in the table:
>
> | Stress Level (1 = Low, 10 = High) | Group A | 8 | 7 | 8 | 8 | 9 | 10 | 2 | 4 | 6 |
> |---|---|---|---|---|---|---|---|---|---|---|
> | | Group B | 2 | 4 | 1 | 5 | 3 | 8 | 2 | 1 | 7 |

a) Write a hypothesis for the experiment described above. [2 marks]

b) Given that the observed $U = 14.5$, determine whether the results are significant at the $p = 0.05$ level. [2 marks]

Oh man... Whitney didn't see the sign on page 33...

I don't blame you for groaning at not only this massive amount of statistics, but also these increasingly bad jokes. But... keep your spirits up and your brain switched on, and you'll be flying through these pages in no time at all.

Chi-Squared and Choosing the Right Test

As the sun starts to set, the owls awaken and the bats begin to flutter, we come to the end of the tale of inferential statistics. It has been a momentous journey, full of ups and downs. But, to finish... here's one more good 'un.

The **Chi-Squared Test** is Used with **Nominal Data** and **Independent Samples**

There's no better way of explaining this than showing you an example. So, hey presto...

> **Example:** A student is interested in seeing whether finding reality TV programmes **entertaining** is related to being either **male** or **female**. His results are shown in the table below.

The **Chi-Squared test** tests the **null hypothesis**. In this example, the null hypothesis would be that there's **no association** between finding reality TV entertaining and being male or female — this is shown by the **expected frequencies**. Under the null hypothesis, the expected frequencies show that **equal amounts** of men and women find reality TV entertaining, and equal amounts do not.

	Men	Women	Totals
Finds reality TV entertaining (expected frequency)	19 (27)	35 (27)	54
Does not find reality TV entertaining (expected frequency)	41 (33)	25 (33)	66
Totals	60	60	120

John was stunned that the "chai test" involved more than just "add boiling water and brew for 4 minutes".

The expected frequencies are worked out using the following formula:

$$E = \frac{\text{row total} \times \text{column total}}{\text{overall total}}$$

The **Expected** and **Observed** Frequencies are **Compared**

> In a Chi-Squared test, the **expected frequencies** tell you what the outcome would be if the **null hypothesis** was **true**. They indicate that there would be **no difference** between groups. The **observed frequencies** are the **actual results**.
>
> So, if there is a **big difference** between the expected and the observed frequencies, it is more likely that the results **will be significant** — they won't match what would happen if the null hypothesis was true.

1) This example has an observed value, χ^2, of **8.62**.

2) You can use a critical value table to see if this is significant.

3) In a Chi-Squared test, **degrees of freedom (df)** = (No. of rows − 1) × (No. of columns − 1). In this example $df = (2 − 1) \times (2 − 1) = 1$.

df	Level of significance for two-tailed test				
df	0.20	0.10	0.05	0.02	0.01
1	1.64	2.71	3.84	5.41	6.64
2	3.22	4.60	5.99	7.82	9.21
3	4.64	6.25	7.82	9.84	11.34
4	5.99	7.78	9.49	11.67	13.28
5	7.29	9.24	11.07	13.39	15.09
6	8.56	10.64	12.59	15.03	16.81

Abridged from Statistical Tables for Biological Agricultural and Medical Research (6th ed.)
© 1963 R.A Fisher and F. Yates. Reprinted with permission of Pearson Education Limited.

The table was critical in the formation of Hank and Yasmine's holiday romance.

4) For the Chi-Squared result to be significant, χ^2 needs to be **greater than or equal to** the critical value.

5) In this example, the results are significant as the critical value at $p = 0.05$ is 3.84, which is **less than** 8.62.

6) This means that the **null** hypothesis is **rejected**.

Chi-Squared and Choosing the Right Test

It's Really Important to **Choose** the **Right Test** for the Job

When deciding which inferential statistics test to use, you need to think about several **factors**. These include things like the **research aims**, the **level of measurement** or **types of data**, and the **experimental design** that is being used in the study.

Repeated and **independent measures** designs test to see if there is a **significant difference** between two or more groups of scores. **Correlation studies** test to see if there is a **significant relationship** between two variables.

This table can help you to decide which test you need to use in different situations.

	Nominal	*Ordinal*	*Interval/Ratio*
Repeated Measures or Matched Pairs Design	sign test	Wilcoxon	related *t*-test
Independent Measures Design	Chi-Squared test	Mann-Whitney	unrelated *t*-test
Correlation	Chi-Squared test	Spearman's rho	Pearson's *r*

The tests which require interval or ratio data (the related and unrelated t-tests and Pearson's r) are called parametric tests. To use them, the data must be normally distributed.

Make Sure You **Check** if your **Hypothesis** Has a **Direction**

- When looking up critical values it's important to remember to look back to the hypothesis.

- You need to know whether it's **directional** or **non-directional**, so that you can tell whether your test is **one-tailed** or **two-tailed**.

Remember, a directional hypothesis states which way the results will go, whereas a non-directional hypothesis doesn't.

- It's also important to remember to check whether your **observed value** needs to be **greater than** or **less than** the critical value for the test you are doing — it differs for each statistical test.

Practice Questions

Q1 When would a researcher use a Chi-Squared test?

Q2 What do expected frequencies show?

Q3 Which inferential test would you use in a repeated measures design which gathered nominal data?

Q4 Name three different inferential tests which can be used with ordinal data.

Exam Questions

Q1 Read the item below, then answer the question that follows.

> Ian is interested in whether there is an association between being an only child and having a pet.

Name a suitable inferential test for this study and explain your answer. [4 marks]

Q2 Complete the sentence below.
Ashley is investigating the correlation between the time it takes someone to swim 100 m and their height.
To determine the significance of his results, he should use a:

A sign test   **B** Chi-Squared test   **C** Spearman's rho test   **D** Pearson's *r* test   [1 mark]

Just to throw another spanner in the works, you say "kai", not "chi"...

... but this isn't an inferential statistical test speaking exam (and thank goodness for that, by the way), so that's useless info. What will help, though, is knowing the factors which affect which statistical test you should choose. Luckily for you, there's a nifty little table above. Think of it as an early birthday present.

Reporting on Psychological Investigations

Once the research study has been done you'd think that'd be the end of it and the poor overworked psychologist could have a break. But no — the study has to be written up, and it has to be done in a certain way. Some people are so picky.

Reports on Psychological Studies Have a Specific Structure

Title The first thing a report needs is a **title**. It should say what the study's **about** and include the **independent variable (IV)** and the **dependent variable (DV)**. For example, 'An Investigation into the Effect of Hunger on Reaction Times'.

Abstract The abstract's a **concise summary** of the report (often no more than 120 words), telling the reader about the research and findings without them having to read the **whole report**. It should include brief descriptions of the **aims** and **hypotheses** of the study, the **method**, and a summary of the **results**. The abstract should also contain interpretations of the findings and any significant **flaws** in the study. A lot to fit into a small space...

Introduction The introduction is a general **overview** of the **area** being studied, including **existing theories**. It should also discuss a few **studies closely related** to the current study.

Aim and Hypotheses The aim is a sentence stating the **purpose** of the study. For example, 'To investigate whether reaction times are affected by hunger levels'. The hypothesis is what's actually going to be **tested**, and should include the **independent variable** and the **dependent variable**. For example, 'Hunger will have no significant effect on reaction times'.

Method The method describes **how** the research was **carried out**. Someone should be able to **replicate** the study by following the method, so it needs to be **detailed**. It should include information on:

The **design of the investigation**, for example:
- The **research method** used, e.g. field experiment, interview.
- The **research design**, e.g. repeated measures, and any potential problems with the design.
- How **extraneous variables** were **controlled**, e.g. counterbalancing, randomisation.
- How **materials**, e.g. **word-lists**, **questions**, etc. were chosen.
- How **ethical issues** were dealt with.

The **procedure used**:
- This should be a blow-by-blow account of **what happened** each time a participant took part.
- It should start with **how** the researcher and the investigation were **introduced** to the participant and how **informed consent** was obtained.
- It needs to include what was **said** to the participants (the standardised instructions), how the study was **carried out** and how the participants were **debriefed**.
- The method should also contain details of how the **data** was **recorded**.

The **use of participants**, for example:
- The **number** of participants used.
- The **demographics** of the participants, e.g. age, employment, gender, etc.
- The **sampling method** used.
- How participants were **allocated** to **conditions**.

The **resources used**, for example:
- The **materials** used, e.g. questionnaires, pictures, word lists, etc.
- Any **apparatus** used — it's often useful to include diagrams or photographs of these.

Reporting on Psychological Investigations

Results
The results of the study can be reported as **descriptive** or **inferential** statistics. Descriptive statistics include **tables**, **graphs** and **charts** (see p.24-26). Inferential statistics (see p.27-37) involve doing **statistical tests** on the data. The results section needs to include explanations of **why** certain tests were chosen, e.g. because the study was looking for a correlation. They should also include the **results** of the test — the observed value, the critical value and level of significance.

Discussion
The discussion covers a range of things including:

- **An explanation of the findings** — **summarising** the results and **relating** them to the **aim** and **hypothesis**. It should be stated whether or not the null hypothesis is rejected. Any **unexpected** findings should also be addressed and explained here.
- **The implications of the study** — for example, whether the study relates to **real-life situations**, e.g. interviews, exams, etc.
- **The limitations and modifications of the study** — any **problems** or **limitations** need to be explained, along with modifications that could **improve** the study.
- **The relationship to background research** — the results need to be related to the **background research** covered in the introduction. The data should be compared to other data and comments made on whether or not the findings of the study support the findings of other studies.
- **Suggestions for further research** — some ideas for further research should be included.

References
The references section contains a list of all the books, articles and websites that have been used for **information** during the study. It allows the reader to see where the information on the **research** and **theories** mentioned in the report (e.g. in the introduction) came from. References should be presented in **alphabetical order** of first author's surname.

Appendices
Any **materials** used, e.g. questionnaires or diagrams, can be put in the appendix. **Raw data** and **statistical test calculations** also go here.

When Ellie said she needed help with her appendix, a hospital trip wasn't what she had in mind.

General Tips
The report should be written in the **third person**, e.g. 'the participants were asked to recall numbers' rather than 'I asked the participants to recall numbers'. The language used should be **formal**, e.g. 'the participants in the study were an opportunity sample', rather than 'the participants were basically anyone we could get hold of.'

Practice Questions

Q1 What should be included in an abstract?

Q2 In which section of a report would you find an overview of the research area?

Q3 List six things that should be included in a method.

Q4 Name two types of statistics that could be included in the results section of a report.

Q5 In which section should materials such as questionnaires be included?

You've achieved your aim and reached the end of the section — result...

If you're the kind of person that has their own special celebratory dance for moments of crowning glory or achievement, I suggest you perform it now — because this is the end of the section. If you've made it this far and learned everything in between then you are now (unofficially) an unstoppable psychological research machine. And very smart, too.

Gender Bias

It's easy for psychologists to make statements that can disguise any differences between men and women. Or, they might say there are differences when there aren't any. So, watch out for sneaky gender bias.

There are **Different Types** of **Gender Bias**

Gender bias is a preference towards one gender. It can either **exaggerate** or **minimise** differences between males and females. There are different types of **gender bias** that may crop up in psychological theories and research.

Alpha Bias

1) Alpha bias is where differences between males and females are **exaggerated**.
2) This type of bias can be used to **undervalue** one of the sexes.
3) The differences are sometimes attributed to differences in **biology** — for example, differences in **genetics** or **hormones**.

My friend is always being mean about my little car, but he's just got Alpha Romeo bias.

Beta Bias

1) Beta bias is where differences between males and females are **ignored** or **minimised**.
2) This can happen when studies just include participants of **one gender** but then the conclusions are applied to the **whole population**.

Research can also be **androcentric** (male-centred) or **estrocentric** (female-centred).

Androcentrism

1) This is where **males** are viewed as being at the centre of culture.
2) In psychological terms, male behaviour is seen as the **norm**. This can mean that theories made in relation to males are also **applied to women**, or it can mean that **any differences** that women display are seen as **exceptions** to the rule.

Estrocentrism

1) This is where **female** behaviour is seen as the **norm**.
2) This is a much **rarer** phenomenon than androcentrism.

Some **Research Designs** Can Make Gender Bias **More Likely**

Research designs are really important, because the **research methods** that psychologists use can cause the results and conclusions to be **gender biased**. Different research designs can **unintentionally** cause either **alpha bias** or **beta bias**.

1) When a **research question** is first proposed and an **aim** is formed (see page 38), psychologists need to be careful that they're not unconsciously including any gender **stereotypes**. For example, studies on aggression often use male stereotypes to provide a measure of what it means to be aggressive.

2) **Participants** for research should be selected in a non-biased way. Many early studies in psychology only used **male university students**, and this could have had the effect of producing **beta biased** theories. They would have been based on results from males, but **generalised** to the **whole population**.

3) Researchers can sometimes unconsciously treat male and female participants **differently** during a study. To avoid this, they should make sure that male and female participants are spoken to in the **same manner**. If participants are treated differently, the researchers will be introducing **extraneous variables** that may produce a false **gender difference** in the results that **isn't actually there**.

4) Researchers should be aware that **gender stereotypes** can affect their **expectations** about the outcomes of research. These expectations can affect the **results** that they record, or the way that they **interpret** their results. For example, in an **observational study** comparing men and women, researchers should be careful not to just record behaviours that fit in with their ideas about how men and women **should** behave. They also shouldn't be led to **interpret** their results to show a gender difference that **isn't actually there**.

Gender Bias

Not All Studies are Published

1) Gender bias can be created as a result of **publication bias**.

2) It has been reported that studies that produced **positive findings** are more likely to be published than studies that don't find any differences. In terms of gender research, this would mean that studies showing a **difference** between males and females would be **more likely** to appear in **scientific journals** than ones with no gender differences.

3) This can **exaggerate differences** between males and females, and so produce an **alpha bias**.

Theories Can Show Gender Bias Too

There are plenty of **theories** out there that show gender bias...

Freud's theories

- **Freud's** theories usually described **male behaviour** as the **norm**, explaining female behaviour as anything which differed from the norm. For example, Freud proposed that when girls find out that they don't have a penis, they suffer from what he termed '**penis envy**' (page 66).

Asch's theory

- Asch's research into **conformity** was **androcentric** — he used a **male-only** sample, meaning that his results couldn't be generalised to women.

> You learnt about Asch's research in Year 1 — it's briefly described on the next page if you need to jog your memory.

Bem's theory

- **Bem's (1974)** theory of **psychological androgyny** (page 60) is a **beta biased** theory. Her theory centres on the idea that the most psychologically healthy men and women can **choose** which **personality traits** they want to have, regardless of whether they're typically masculine or feminine qualities.

- In other words, she classed the various masculine and feminine traits as all being on a **level playing field**. This is why the theory is **beta biased**. It ignores the fact that different traits are **valued** differently in **society** — for example, a lot of masculine traits are valued highly.

Practice Questions

Q1 What is alpha bias?

Q2 What is beta bias?

Q3 What is meant by androcentrism?

Q4 Explain one way that research design can create a gender biased experiment.

Q5 Why might Freud's theories be considered androcentric?

Exam Question

Q1 Read the item below, and then answer the questions that follow.

> A researcher is designing an experiment to study conformity amongst university students.
> He intends to use a sample of 50 male students from his university and record whether they are affected by minority influence in a shape-naming task.

Outline why the researcher's study could be considered to be androcentric. [2 marks]

You just can't win...

Studies that appear to be 'gender neutral' could actually be showing beta bias. There might simply be no difference between the two genders, or it might be the case that the difference is being ignored or minimised due to the design of the research. It's a right old mine field out there. Don't take everything as gospel — remember to question everything.

Cultural Bias

The list of stuff to think about when you're evaluating an experiment goes on and on... and on and on. There's yet another thing to add on now — cultural differences. And these can throw up all kinds of issues.

Psychologists *Have Often* Ignored Cultural Differences

Culture refers to the set of **customs**, **social roles**, **behavioural norms** and **moral values** that are **shared** by a group of people. As psychology developed in **western** countries, researchers would typically study people who were **available** — people from their own cultural background. Historically, there hasn't been much research to **compare** people of **different** cultures. There are various possible **reasons** for this:

1) Researchers **assumed** that people from **western** cultures are essentially the **same** as people in **other** cultures. So, whatever was found about people from one culture was **applied** to all other people.

2) It may have been assumed that **non-western** cultures were more '**primitive**' and less **worthy** of study.

3) Researchers who wanted to do **cross-cultural** research couldn't because they lacked **time** and **resources**.

Research Methods *Can Cause* Cultural Bias

Cultural bias can be the result of a researcher's **assumptions** and **research aims**.
Berry (1969) identified **two** main **approaches** to research which could lead to cultural bias:

'Universality' means using one set of rules or theories to explain everything.

Etic research

- **Etic research** is research from a specific culture which is then applied to other cultures to find **universal laws**, giving the studies **universality**.
- It's possible that there are lots of these. All humans have basically the **same physiology** and many behaviours are found in **all cultures**, e.g. language, attachment formation, aggression.
- However, because studies have to take **samples** of the population, it's **difficult** to **generalise** the findings to **all** cultures. If researchers do this, they could be guilty of **bias** in the form of an **imposed etic**.

Emic research

- **Emic research** is research based on a specific culture that's used to understand that culture from within. It isn't generalised to other cultures. Instead it studies **variations** in behaviour **between** groups of people. This avoids the problem of cultural bias through an imposed etic (i.e. making universal laws).
- However, bias may still occur by **exaggerating** differences **between** different cultural groups, and neglecting to look at the differences **within** the cultural groups.
- This is what happens in claims like 'people from country X are more generous than people from country Y'. Even if evidence showed that, on average, country X residents are more generous, it's still likely that many of them aren't, and that many people from country Y are. So it's important not to neglect the **variety** found **within** groups — individual differences.

The issue of **sub-culture bias** is also important — etic or emic bias for sub-groups **within** larger groups. For example, research on relationships might **focus** on studying **heterosexuals**, and so **neglect homosexual** relationships (**emic bias**). The findings might then be **generalised** to homosexual relationships, despite not having studied them (**etic bias**).

Ethnocentrism *is a Type of* Cultural Bias

Ethnocentrism is where our own culture is taken as the **norm** that we judge other cultures against. Ethnocentric research is **centred** around the one culture it's **based** in — so because most psychological studies have studied people from **western** cultures, a lot of them are **ethnocentric**. For example:

- Asch's (1951) research into **conformity** involved seeing whether people would **change** their answer to an **easy** question (judging the length of a line) to **conform** with the people around them. (You learnt about this study in Year 1.) This study was **ethnocentric** because it only studied **Americans**. It showed **etic bias** because Asch **generalised** the results to members of groups that hadn't actually been studied.
- **Further research** found **variations** in **levels** of conformity depending on the **culture** being studied.

- Milgram's (1963) study of **obedience** (you looked at this in Year 1 too) challenged the view that the German soldiers who had carried out the Holocaust must be inherently evil. Milgram found that people could commit evil acts because of the **situation** they were in, rather than because of their **character**. However, he used **American** participants in his study, and **didn't** take **cultural differences** between **Germany** and the **USA** into account, making this an **imposed etic**.

Cultural Bias

Cultural Bias Has Social Implications

Culturally biased **studies** will produce culturally biased **theories**. This has important **implications** for society because psychologists might be making claims that aren't actually true. It's especially problematic when biased views influence **psychological practice**, e.g. understanding and treating **abnormality**.

1) **Cochrane and Sashidharan (1995)** found that people of **African-Caribbean origin** in the UK were up to **seven** times more likely than white patients to be diagnosed with **schizophrenia**. The rate of schizophrenia in the Caribbean is **no higher** than in the UK, so it seems that African-Caribbeans **don't** have a **genetic predisposition** towards it.

2) **Littlewood and Lipsedge (1989)** found that African-Caribbean patients were often prescribed **stronger** doses of **medication** than white patients, even though their **symptoms** were the **same**. This suggests that their symptoms are **interpreted** as being more **severe** than they actually are.

3) These findings could be the result of **culture biased assumptions** influencing how people's behaviours are **interpreted**. It seems that all patients may be judged against **norms** for the **white population**, even if they're originally from a different culture.

There are Problems With Doing Cross-Cultural Research

Cross-cultural research can help to reduce cultural bias, but the results aren't always **valid**.

1) Even with a **translator** it can be **difficult** to **interpret** what participants say and do — some beliefs and customs may be difficult for people from other cultures to understand. This means that findings can be **misinterpreted** and research can be **ethnocentric** because the researchers judge behaviour against their own **cultural norms**.

2) **Cross-cultural replications** of studies are difficult to do. **Smith and Bond (1988)** argued that perfect cross-cultural replications are impossible because **procedures** will have different **meanings** to people in different **cultures**. This means that studies can lack **validity** — they might not be testing what they aim to test.

There Are Ways to Reduce Cultural Bias in Research

Cultural bias usually **isn't intentional**, so it can be difficult to prevent. However, there are ways to **reduce** it:

1) Research should recognise **cultural relativism**. This is accepting that there are no universal standards for behaviour, and that any research done must take into account the culture it takes place in.

2) Samples should be **representative** of the groups you want to generalise the results to — they should include all relevant sub-groups.

3) **Berry (1969)** recommended conducting research in **meaningful contexts** and using **local researchers** who are part of the culture being studied. This **avoids** the problems of an **imposed etic**.

Practice Questions

Q1 What is the difference between etic and emic research?
Q2 What is ethnocentrism?
Q3 How did Asch's (1951) research show etic bias?
Q4 Explain one of the difficulties encountered in cross-cultural research.
Q5 What is cultural relativism?
Q6 Outline one thing which could be done to reduce cultural bias in psychological research.

Exam Question

Q1 Outline the impact of cultural bias on psychological research. [6 marks]

Cultural bias — too much theatre and art, not enough revision...

So to do a super-duper psychological study you need to make sure that your research is neither etic nor emic, that it doesn't show sub-culture bias and it isn't ethnocentric. No problem. Assuming that you know what those words mean.

Free Will and Determinism

Hey, guess what — you don't actually have to look at these pages at all. But you can choose to look at them of your own free will... But it's probably best if you do look at them, even if you don't really want to. Flippin' exams.

There's **Debate** About **Whether** People have **Free Will**

Psychology aims to explain **why** people **behave** in certain ways. The **free will versus determinism** debate centres around whether people can **choose** how to behave, or whether what they do is **influenced** by **other forces**.

Free will

People are able to **choose** how to behave — their behaviour **isn't** a response to **external** or **biological** factors, and **isn't** influenced by **past behaviour**.

Comments on free will

- People can **explain** behaviours in terms of **decisions** and **intentions**.
- However, **free will** is **subjective** — someone might **think** they're **choosing** how to behave, but actually be **influenced** by **other forces**.
- Some people with **psychological** disorders **don't** appear to have **free will**, e.g. people with **OCD** feel that they **can't control** their thoughts and actions.

Determinism

All of the physical events in the universe (including human behaviour) occur in **cause and effect relationships**. So, our thoughts, beliefs and behaviours are determined by **past events** and **causes**. This is a **scientific** view that implies that complete knowledge of a cause and effect relationship will mean you can **predict** future behaviour in the same situation.

Comments on determinism

- The determinist approach is very **scientific**. Other scientific subjects (e.g. physics) have shown that events in the **physical universe** operate according to **cause and effect** relationships that follow certain laws.
- However, determinism is **unfalsifiable** — it can't be proved wrong, because it assumes that events **can** be the **result** of **forces** that **haven't** been **discovered** yet.

Yes, Colette had in fact chosen to wear her hair like this of her own free will.

Different **Psychological Approaches** Fall on **Different Sides** of the **Debate**

- Most psychological approaches are **determinist** to a certain extent, because they look for **patterns** and **causes** of behaviour. If the answer was always just that behaviour was down to free will, psychologists wouldn't have much to study. Many approaches do **acknowledge** the existence of **free will** though.

- As opposed to **hard determinism**, which completely rules out the idea of free will, **soft determinism** is the viewpoint that we choose our behaviour, but the choices that we make are a result of our own personality traits and intentions. Most **psychological approaches** hold this view, just to different **degrees**:

1) **Psychodynamic** — **Freud** argued that behaviour is **determined** by **unconscious forces**. This is known as **psychic determinism**. For example, if you forget to go to a dentist's appointment, you might consciously think it was an accident. But Freud would claim it was actually determined by **unconscious influences**, e.g. you didn't really want to go. However, he also acknowledged that behaviours have many causes, including **conscious intentions**, e.g. a person can **choose** to have psychoanalysis.

2) **Biological** — Behaviours are **determined** by biological influences, e.g. genetics and brain structure. For example, **schizophrenia** has been linked to genes and brain structure abnormalities. The idea that this is the **sole cause** of behaviour is known as **biological determinism**.

3) **Cognitive** — Behaviour is the result of both **free will** and **determinism**. The approach looks for **patterns** in how the brain **processes** external information, and what **behaviours** this leads to. However, it acknowledges that people use cognitive processes like **language** to **reason** and make **decisions**.

4) **Behaviourist** — **Skinner** claimed that behaviour is **determined** by the **environment** and is the result of **punishment** and **reinforcement**. This is known as **environmental determinism**. Everyone has a different **history of reinforcement**, so knowing this about someone would allow you to **predict** their behaviour. If the environmental **conditioning** changes then their **behaviour** will also change.

5) **Humanistic** — This approach falls on the **free will** side of the debate. Humanistic psychologists believe that individuals are **in control** of their behaviour and are trying to achieve **personal growth**.

Holism and Reductionism

Reductionism is About Explaining **Complex** Things in **Simple Terms**

Reductionism — **Reductionism** is the **scientific** view that it should be possible to explain **complex** things by **reducing** them to their most **simple** structures or processes. In psychology this means explaining **behaviour** by boiling theories down to some **basic principles** — e.g. **aggression** is caused by **conditioning**. Testing this in an experiment means that it's possible to establish **cause and effect**. However, experiments are often **unrealistically simplified** and **ignore** other **influences**, so they may not be testing real behaviour.

Holism — **Holism** is the argument that human behaviour is more **complex** than the processes that other sciences study, e.g. chemical reactions. This means it should be viewed as the **product** of **different influences**, which all **interact**. Trying to **separate** these influences by just studying one of them means that complex behaviour can be **misunderstood**, so a holistic approach avoids this problem. However, it's **difficult** to **test** integrated theories because you can't **isolate** the **variables** — this means it's **hard** to establish **cause and effect**.

Rose (1976) Talked About **Levels of Explanation** in Psychology

Rose (1976) put forward a range of explanations used in psychology, from the most **reductionist** (and therefore the **most scientific**), to the most **holistic** (and therefore the **least scientific**).

the molecular level (physics) → the cellular level (biochemistry) → parts of individuals (biology) → the behaviour of individuals (psychology) → the behaviour of groups (sociology)

These are known as **levels of explanation** — how reductionist or holistic an explanation of something is.

Different **Psychological Approaches** Fall on **Different Sides** of the **Debate**

1) **Psychodynamic** — by considering unconscious forces and childhood experiences, the psychodynamic approach is a relatively **holistic** approach. For instance, Freud emphasised that personality is the result of **interaction** between different **components**, such as the id and the ego, which is a more **holistic** view.

2) **Biological** — all behaviours can be explained as the product of biological influences like **genetics**, **brain structure** and **brain chemistry**. This is **biological reductionism**. It aims to establish **cause and effect**, but it **focuses less** on other influences on behaviour, e.g. behavioural or social.

3) **Cognitive** — the brain's cognitive processes are compared to the working of a computer — **machine reductionism**. There is input, various stages of processing, and then an output. This is reductionist because it doesn't explain why humans function **differently** to computers, e.g. they can forget.

4) **Behaviourist** — all human behaviour (except biological reflexes and instincts) is shaped by the environment through the processes of classical and operant conditioning. This is known as **environmental (stimulus-response) reductionism**. Other possible influences (e.g. genetic, social) are focused on less.

5) **Humanistic** — the approach is **holistic** as it studies the individual in context and tries to understand their subjective experiences. It uses **self-report** techniques, rather than breaking down behaviour into its component parts. Humanistic psychologists **disagree** with reducing behaviour to cause and effect reactions.

Practice Questions

Q1 Outline the argument for the existence of free will.

Q2 Explain the difference between reductionism and holism.

Q3 Is the behaviourist approach reductionist? Explain your answer.

Exam Questions

Q1 Outline the difference between hard determinism and soft determinism. [2 marks]

Q2 Outline **two** types of reductionism. [4 marks]

Keep things as simple as possible — yep, that's my idea of a good theory...

There's lots of new terminology on these pages, so don't go rushing past it — stick around until you know your free will from your holism. You can then impress the examiners by flashing your new-found vocabulary around.

The Nature-Nurture Debate

This has got to be one of the biggest debates of all time — are you the product of your genes or your environment? Well, unfortunately the conclusion is a bit less exciting than you might expect — it's probably just a bit of both.

The **Nature-Nurture Debate** Has a **Long History**

Firstly, let's just get the definitions of **nature** and **nurture** absolutely clear:

- **Nature (genotype)** — **innate** characteristics determined by **physiological** and **genetic** factors.
- **Nurture** — the influence of the **environment** and **learning** experiences.

1) Philosophers have debated for centuries about **how far** human behaviour is the product of **innate characteristics**, and how far it's the product of the **environment**.

2) For example, in the 18th century there was debate between **nativists** and **empiricists**. **Nativists** like **Jean Rousseau** argued that all human characteristics were in-born. **Empiricists** like **John Locke** claimed that everyone is a '**blank slate**' when they're born, so the **environment** 'writes' unique characteristics onto us.

3) Nowadays, almost all psychologists accept that **nature** and **nurture** must **interact**, because personality and behaviour seem to be influenced by **both**. This is known as the **interactionist** approach.

- Rats raised in **bare**, dark cages have been compared to rats that grew up in **stimulating** environments.
- It's found that the rats raised in the unstimulating environments do **less** well in problem-solving tasks and **learn** much more **slowly** than the other rats.
- This suggests that **environment** can affect **innate genetic potential**.

4) The debate now focuses on the **relative contribution** of **inherited traits** and the **role of the environment** in accounting for behaviour.

It's **Hard** to **Separate Nature** and **Nurture**

The **interactionist approach** states that nature and nurture **interact** to form a person's character.

1) **Gottesman (1963)** suggested that people have a **reaction range**. This means everyone has a certain **genetic potential** for things like intelligence and height — the **genotype**.

2) The **environment** determines **how much** this potential is fulfilled (how people turn out) — the **phenotype**.

3) For example, someone with a **high** genetic potential for intelligence, who didn't go to school, may have the same **IQ** as someone with **low** genetic potential for intelligence, who received a good education.

1) The **diathesis-stress model** suggests that people have **genetic predispositions** for disorders like schizophrenia.

2) A person with a **higher diathesis (vulnerability)** is **more likely** to develop the trait, but whether they do depends on the amount of **stress** they **experience** (i.e. the environment).

1) One influence can sometimes **override** another. For example, **phenylketonuria (PKU)**, is a **genetic** metabolic disorder that can cause brain damage.

2) But if the person **doesn't eat** particular **proteins**, then the disorder **won't** get **worse**. This shows how **environment** can **override** a **genetic disposition**.

Determining how far nature or nurture control characteristics can be complicated by **genotype-environment correlations** — correlations between a person's genes and their environment. **Plomin et al (1977)** identified **three types** of genotype-environment correlations:

1) **Passive** — people with similar **genes** (e.g. members of the same family) are likely to experience similar **environments**. For example, two siblings may be aggressive because they have both **inherited** aggressive tendencies from their parents, or because their parents' predisposition towards aggression means that they provide a hostile home **environment**.

2) **Reactive** — **genetically determined** characteristics may **shape** a person's **experiences**. For example, people **react** more **positively** towards **attractive** people, so the kind of environment a person experiences depends partly on their **inherited** characteristics.

3) **Active** — people with particular **inherited** tendencies might **seek out** certain **environments**, which will then **shape** their behaviour just as their genetic background does. **Bandura (1986)** called this **reciprocal determinism** — environment determines behaviour and behaviour determines environment.

The Nature-Nurture Debate

Nature-Nurture *Influences* Can be *Studied* Using *Different Methods*

Family studies

- If **family** members **share** a trait more **frequently** than unrelated people do, then this could imply a **genetic influence** for that behaviour. For example, **Solyom et al (1974)** showed that phobias can run in families.
- However, similarities between family members may actually be the result of their **shared environment** — relatives might **learn** the behaviour from each other through **observational learning**.

Adoption studies

- These compare an **adopted child** with its **biological** and **adoptive parents**. If the child has more **similarity** with its **adoptive** parents then this would imply that **nurture** is **important**, because they share the same **environment**.
- **Similarity** with the **biological parents** suggests that **nature** is more **important**. **Plomin et al (1988)** showed a **stronger** correlation of **IQ** within **biological** families than adopted families.

Twin studies

- **Identical (MZ) twins** share **100%** of their **genes**. **Non-identical (DZ)** twins share about **50%** of their **genes**. So if **MZ** twins are more likely to **share** a characteristic than **DZ** twins, it implies a **genetic influence**. This is shown by **concordance rates** — concordance means how likely it is that both people in a pair will have a certain characteristic, given that one of them does. For example, **Holland et al (1988)** found a **56% MZ concordance** for anorexia (i.e. in MZ twins, if one twin had anorexia, then 56% of the time both twins did), compared to **5% DZ concordance**. Which suggests that **genes** influence the development of anorexia.
- However, if a trait was **completely genetic** then MZ concordance would be **100%**, so their behaviour must also be **influenced** by **environment**. For example, people might treat MZ twins more **similarly** than DZ twins. As such, it's more **useful** (but also more **difficult**) to do research on twins who **haven't** been brought up **together**.

Different *Psychological Approaches* Fall on *Different Sides* of the *Debate*

1) **Psychodynamic** — Freud argued that personalities are the result of an **interaction** of nature and nurture. He emphasised the importance of **inborn instincts** and drives (represented in the id). However, he also said that **experiences** can result in **fixations** in the stages of **development**.

2) **Biological** — emphasises **genetically** determined brain structures and processes. **Evolutionary** psychology states that many behaviours, e.g. aggression, are genetically influenced because they have **survival value**. However, the **environment** influences brain **development**, so learning can **override** genetic predispositions.

3) **Cognitive** — studies **genetically** determined mental processes, but accepts that the **environment** influences their **development** and **functioning**. **Piaget's** theory of **cognitive development** argues that **environmental** stimulation is needed for the **genetically** determined process of development to **unfold**.

4) **Behaviourist** — all behaviours are **learnt** through **conditioning**, apart from inborn **reflexes** and **instincts** (e.g. blinking). This approach falls most heavily on the **nurture** side of the debate.

5) **Humanistic** — behaviour is part of a **natural** need to reach your **full potential** (to self-actualise — see p.6). However, whether you reach it depends on your experiences in the world, and so the humanistic approach falls more towards the **nurture** side of the debate.

Practice Questions

Q1 What is the interactionist approach to the nature-nurture debate?

Q2 Outline two ways of studying the relative influence of nature or nurture.

Q3 Outline two approaches to psychology that focus more on nurture than nature.

Exam Question

Q1 Briefly outline the nature-nurture debate in psychology. [2 marks]

I hope it's not nurture — this isn't a very stimulating environment...

Nature or nurture — this debate is as old as they get. Luckily, you only have to worry about it for your exams. So, I recommend you learn this stuff really well, walk into that exam room, add your thought to this endless debate in a knowledgeable and memorable way, then walk back out again and leave the experts to continue arguing about it.

Idiographic and Nomothetic Approaches

Some topics in psychology lend themselves to an idiographic approach, and others are more suited to a nomothetic approach. I can tell you're wondering what that's all about, so you're in luck — here's a page especially for you.

The **Idiographic** and **Nomothetic** Approaches Have Different **Aims**

The Nomothetic Approach

1) In psychology, the nomothetic approach applies **general laws** and **theories** to explain behaviour across a **whole population**.

2) Nomothetic research uses **research methods** such as **laboratory experiments** and **correlational research**, which involve **groups** of participants to draw **general conclusions**.

3) It usually uses **quantitative methods** to draw conclusions.

Nomothetic studies try to use large samples to get lots of data.

Sometimes a nomothetic approach uses idiographic methods, or vice versa.

The Idiographic Approach

1) The idiographic approach focuses on the **individual** in detail.

2) It looks at what makes each person different, and **avoids** making general laws and theories.

3) Idiographic research uses **research methods** such as **case studies**, **interviews** and **observations**, that focus on the individual.

4) It usually uses **qualitative methods** to analyse its findings.

Idiographic and Nomothetic Approaches Have **Strengths** and **Weaknesses**

Evaluation of the Nomothetic Approach

1) The **research methods** frequently used in the nomothetic approach mean that it's a pretty **controlled**, **objective** and **scientific** approach. The **theories** it produces can then be **scientifically tested**.

2) However, these research methods can lack **ecological validity**, and so can't **reliably** be **generalised** to real life.

3) In creating general laws, **individual differences** are ignored. So, it's less useful for explaining behaviour that **doesn't fit in** with the norms of the general laws.

Evaluation of the Idiographic Approach

1) The idiographic approach focuses on the **individual**, so it can give a more **complete** explanation of behaviour than the nomothetic explanation.

2) However, this often means that **fewer people** are studied (but in more detail), so it's tricky to **generalise** findings to larger populations. It can also be seen as a **less scientific** approach than the nomothetic approach.

3) On the other hand, **detailed studies** of individual cases can help to **develop nomothetic laws** by providing extra information. For example, theories of memory have often come about from laboratory studies **combined** with more detailed case studies of people who have suffered from brain damage.

Different **Psychological Approaches** Fall on **Different Sides**

1) **Psychodynamic** — can be seen as having **both** nomothetic and idiographic components. For example, Freud's theory of **psychosexual development** (see page 4) assumed that the same stages could explain everyone's development, showing a **nomothetic approach**. However, his approach was also partially **idiographic** because it involved investigating how an individual experiences the world through the use of case studies.

2) **Biological** — aims to find the cause of behaviour in **biological structures** and **processes**. It assumes these are the same across the population, so it's a **nomothetic approach**.

3) **Cognitive** — assumes the same **mental processes** apply across the population, and so falls more towards being a **nomothetic approach**.

4) **Behaviourist** — psychologists from the behaviourist approach apply **cause and effect laws** to explain behaviour in general, which is thought to be a result of classical and operant **conditioning**. So it is a **nomothetic approach**.

5) **Humanistic** — this approach is heavily focused on **individuals** and their drive for self-actualisation (see page 6). It's therefore completely on the **idiographic** side of the debate.

Socially Sensitive Research

Some Research Raises **Sensitive Social Issues**

1) As well as the ethical guidelines that psychologists have to stick to when they plan research (you should remember these from Year 1), there are also **ethical implications** when it comes to what the **research findings** might tell us.

2) Findings from psychological research may highlight **social issues** that create negative effects or reactions in society.

3) They might lead to certain groups of people being **stigmatised**, or even to **laws** being passed that put some people at a disadvantage.

4) This sort of research is known as **socially sensitive research**. It can be defined as research that may have **implications** for the **individuals** in the research, or for **groups in society**, such as the participants' families, or particular cultural groups.

Research into genetic influences raises many issues

1) Research into whether there are genetic influences on **criminal behaviour** could have important consequences. For example, genetics could be used as a **defence** against being convicted for a crime, or could be used to **stigmatise** people who have the relevant genes even if they haven't shown any antisocial behaviour.

2) Also, there's the possibility of **compulsory genetic testing** to identify people with a particular gene.

3) Such **screening** could also identify genes linked to psychological disorders such as **schizophrenia**.

4) Although this may potentially help people it could also lead to **anxiety** and **social stigma**, especially as people may have a **genetic vulnerability** for a disorder but not actually **develop it**.

Using a factor like race as an independent variable is a very sensitive issue

1) Some studies using **IQ tests** have shown possible **racial differences** in **intelligence**.

2) The issue is whether this is an **appropriate topic** for research because of **social tensions** that the results and conclusions may produce.

3) Such research is often **discredited** because of **methodological problems** with the IQ tests that were used. For instance, they may have been **biased** towards some social-cultural groups. An example of this is an IQ test developed by **Yerkes (1917)**. Many of the questions in the test required **cultural knowledge** of the US, therefore lower scores were due to a **lack of culturalisation**, rather than **low intelligence**.

5) There's an argument that socially sensitive research **shouldn't** be carried out for ethical reasons. However, other people argue that researchers have to carry out this type of research because it could help society **as a whole**. For example, research showing that the father can be the primary caregiver has had a positive effect on the economy. (You might remember this research from looking at attachment in Year 1.)

Practice Questions

Q1 What's the difference between idiographic and nomothetic approaches?

Q2 Which side of the idiographic/nomothetic debate does the biological approach to psychology sit on? Explain why.

Q3 How might research into genetic influences raise socially sensitive issues?

Exam Questions

Q1 Which approach aims to find general laws to explain behaviour?
   A idiographic   **B** holism   **C** nomothetic   **D** free will   [1 mark]

Q2 a) Briefly outline what is meant by an idiographic approach to psychology.   [2 marks]

   b) Explain one limitation of an idiographic approach to psychological investigation.   [2 marks]

Q3 Describe one example of research that could be considered socially sensitive.
   Give reasons for your answer.   [4 marks]

They're an argumentative bunch, those psychologists...

There are debates going on all over the place in psychological research — nature-nurture, holistic-reductionist, idiographic-nomothetic... you name it, it's being argued about. More importantly for you — make sure you're prepared for the exam, and can discuss these debates in the context of the various psychological topics you know all about.

Evolutionary Explanations for Partner Choice

If you've ever wondered why we find certain characteristics attractive in people, evolutionary psychology has some explanations. If you've never wondered this, evolutionary psychology still has some explanations.

Evolutionary Psychology Says Our Preferences are Evolved Adaptations

1) **Evolutionary psychologists** believe that the **psychological processes** that people use to choose a partner come from **evolution**.

These processes may not be conscious.

2) The idea is that these processes came about because, in the past, when humans lived as **hunter-gatherers**, having them made people well **adapted** to the environment. (There's more about the mechanics of this below.)

3) A key part of this explanation is the theory that **attractive traits** are **reliable indicators** that a partner is a good bet for passing on our genes. For example, **Singh** found that **waist to hip ratio** was related to **attractiveness** in women, and argued that this is because it's a reliable indicator of a woman's ability to **reproduce**:

> **Singh (1993)** got **male participants** aged 18-22 to rank **drawings of female figures** with a waist to hip ratio (WHR) of 0.7 to 1.0 (i.e. waist size 70% to 100% of hip size) in terms of attractiveness and ability to have children. The drawings with a waist to hip ratio **0.7** were rated the **most attractive** and the **most able to have children**.
>
> **Singh (2002)** argued that low WHR is a reliable indicator of **health** and ability to **reproduce** in women. He cited evidence that females have **higher WHR** before puberty and after menopause (i.e. low WHR correlates with fertility), and that high WHR in women has been shown to correlate with health issues like **diabetes**.

Attractive Characteristics Evolve Through Sexual Selection

1) **Natural selection** is the process where characteristics that make an individual more **likely to reproduce** and pass on their **genes** become more prevalent in a population.

2) Darwin's theory of natural selection, which is generally accepted, says that this is how **evolution** happens.

3) One of the processes of natural selection is **sexual selection**:

- Within a species there are certain **characteristics** that make an individual more able to **find a partner** (e.g. being physically attractive) and **reproduce** (i.e. fertility).

- These characteristics give an individual a **reproductive advantage**, therefore they become **more prevalent** because they're more likely to be **passed on** to future generations. This is known as **sexual selection**.

- There are **two types** of sexual selection:

> **Intra-sexual selection** takes place when males compete (often aggressively) and the winner is rewarded with the female. The female is **passive** in this process — she doesn't choose her own mate.

> **Inter-sexual selection** takes place when males compete for the **attention** of a female. The female plays an **active** role, choosing her mate.

In some species females compete for males, but this is quite rare.

There Can Be Conflict Between Natural Selection and Sexual Selection

1) As well as traits that give a reproductive advantage, natural selection also happens with traits that give a **survival advantage** — traits that make it more likely an individual will **survive** long enough to reproduce (e.g. health).

2) Sometimes the traits that are **attractive** to a mate make an individual **less likely** to survive, so sexual selection can **conflict** with natural selection more generally. For example, female peacocks find the **long, brightly coloured tails** of male peacocks attractive, but very brightly coloured tails are more noticeable to **predators**.

3) One theory from **evolutionary psychology** explaining why this happens is the **handicap principle**:

> **The Handicap Principle**
>
> **Zahavi (1975)** argued that displaying a noticeable **handicap to survival** (e.g. a large colourful tail) actually indicates survival strength. Zahavi called this the **handicap principle**.
>
> If an individual has managed to survive (and their ancestors survived long enough to reproduce) **despite** having the unhelpful characteristic, then they must have **superior genes**.

4) The handicap principle can be applied to humans too. For example, **masculine facial features** (e.g. a strong jaw) result from high levels of **testosterone**. Testosterone causes the immune system to be **less responsive**, so having these features indicates a **cost** to the individual. This cost means masculine facial features can be seen as an **honest indicator** of 'quality' genes — they're only displayed by individuals who can **afford** the handicap.

Evolutionary Explanations for Partner Choice

Evolution Could Explain Gender Differences in Partner Preferences

Buss (1989) did a cross-cultural study which looked for gender differences in partner preferences.

Buss (1989) — Gender differences in mate selection

Method: Questionnaires were used to collect data from over 10 000 men and women from 37 different cultural groups. The questionnaires covered demographic information such as age, gender and marital status. They also asked about preferences for variables such as marriage, age differences and characteristics in a mate (e.g. intelligence, sociability and financial prospects).

Results: Women valued variables associated with gaining resources (e.g. money, safe environment) more highly than men. Men valued variables associated with reproductive capacity (e.g. youth) more highly than women.

Conclusion: Women have had limited access to the resources needed to provide for themselves and their offspring. So, they've evolved (through sexual selection) to select mates who can provide these resources. The factor limiting men's reproductive success has been access to fertile women, and so they have evolved to be attracted to women with a high likelihood of reproducing.

Evaluation: There were similar findings across a range of different cultures. However, it wasn't a truly representative study as it was hard to include rural and less educated populations. Cross-cultural research is important as it suggests universality, providing strong evidence for an evolutionary explanation of gender differences in sexual selection.

Buss and Schmitt (1993) went on to develop a more detailed evolutionary explanation for partner preferences.

Sexual Strategies Theory

Buss and Schmitt (1993) came up with the sexual strategies theory. The theory argues that men and women apply various different strategies for choosing partners, depending on the situation. These strategies have evolved to help them meet the different requirements they have of long-term and short-term partners. For example, women try to assess the quality of a short-term partner's genes, whereas men are mostly concerned with a short-term partner's availability and fertility.

Strengths

1) The idea that men and women have different strategies for choosing a partner is supported by Buss (1989).

2) The argument that men use strategies which lead them to choose fertile women as partners is also supported by Singh's findings on waist to hip ratio (see previous page).

Weaknesses

1) There were more similarities than differences between men and women's responses in Buss's (1989) study. Neither resources nor youth were rated as important by men or women — other factors like intelligence and mutual attraction were rated as most important by both genders. Overall there was a much greater difference between cultures than between genders. This doesn't rule out evolutionary explanations for partner preference, but it may suggest that other (e.g. social) factors play a part too.

2) Evolutionary explanations of partner choice don't take into account social determinants of behaviour. For example, in lots of societies women still don't have the same opportunity to provide for themselves as men do. This may have more influence on the differences in partner preference than evolutionary factors.

3) Lots of the evidence for evolutionary explanations of partner preference comes from studies on other animals, and this evidence can't be reliably generalised to human partner preferences.

Attitudes have changed quite a lot since Buss's (1989) study. The results might be quite different if the study was carried out today.

Practice Questions

Q1 What are intra-sexual and inter-sexual selection?

Q2 Outline the evolutionary explanation for partner preferences.

Exam Question

Q1 Discuss how sexual selection is related to human reproductive behaviour. [16 marks]

Research into sexual selection — sounds like a very dodgy excuse to me...

Evolutionary psychology is a tricky one — it's hard to prove that psychological processes like attraction have evolved, so there's lots of debate about how accurate these ideas are. Learn this lot so you'll have plenty to say about it though.

Attraction

There's been lots of research into what people are attracted to when they're starting a romantic relationship, and there are plenty of different theories. The main ones you need to know about are filter theory and the matching hypothesis.

Various Factors Affect **Attraction** in Romantic Relationships

Physical Attractiveness

1) One of the most obvious factors affecting whether a relationship will begin is whether or not people find each other **physically attractive**. Attraction isn't always about **physical features**, but there are various features which have been found to match up with attractiveness. For example:

> **Cunningham (1986)** asked 75 male undergraduate students to rate photos of 50 females for **attractiveness**. He found several features that **correlated positively** with attractiveness — large eyes, small noses, small chins, prominent cheekbones and narrow cheeks.

Generally, a low waist to hip ratio is also considered attractive in women (see p.50).

2) Generally, men are **more likely** than women to report appearance as **important** in attraction (as shown by Buss, see previous page), but both **women and men** consider appearance important for a **short-term partner**.

> **Li and Kenrick (2006)** asked participants to choose between different characteristics they would like in a partner for a **casual relationship**. Both men and women chose **physical attractiveness** as the most important.

Self-disclosure

There's a bit more about this on page 56.

1) **Self-disclosure** is sharing information about yourself, including your views and feelings.
2) **Collins and Miller's (1994)** meta-analysis showed that people tend to **like somebody more** if that person has self-disclosed to them. They also found that self-disclosing to somebody tends to **increase liking** for that person.

Filter Theory Says **Different Criteria** are Important at **Different Stages**

Kerckhoff and Davis (1962) explain the development of relationships using **filter theory**. The theory proposes that there are a series of 'filters' that operate at **different stages** of forming a relationship:

1) Social demographic filter	Initially we form a '**field of availables**' — these are potential people to form a relationship with. This first filter is based on **social** and **demographic** factors such as **age**, **religion**, **living near each other**, and so on.

2) Similarity in attitudes filter	We narrow the set of available people down to a smaller '**field of desirables**' — these are people who a relationship is more likely to **progress** with. This filter is based on sharing **similar attitudes**, **values** and **interests**.

3) Complementarity filter	In the longer term, relationships will progress if both partners are fulfilling each others **needs** (i.e. both partners provide what the other needs). So this filter is based on two people being a good **complement** to each other.

This theoretical model came from **Kerckhoff and Davis's (1962)** study into long-term relationships.

Kerckhoff and Davis (1962) surveyed female **university students** and their male partners, who were **considering marriage**. The survey asked about their personalities, attitudes and their relationship. **7 months later** they conducted a follow-up survey to see if the couple's relationship had progressed towards a **permanent partnership**.

They found that couples who had been together for **less than 18 months** were more likely to have progressed towards a permanent partnership if they had **similar values**. However, among couples who had been together for **more than 18 months**, it was couples who had **complementary needs** (i.e. each partner met the needs of the other) who were more likely to have progressed towards a permanent partnership.

Evidence For
Winch (1958) surveyed 25 couples who had been married for less than 2 years. He found a significantly **stronger correlation** in spouses between **complementary needs** (e.g. needing to nurture others and needing to be nurtured) than between similar needs.

Evidence Against
Levinger et al (1970) replicated Kerckhoff and Davis's study across other universities, but their results didn't support the theory. They found **no significant difference** over time in the correlation between relationship progress and **either** sharing values or having complementary needs.

Attraction

The **Matching Hypothesis** Says People Want an **Equally Attractive Partner**

Walster et al (1966) developed the **matching hypothesis**, which states that people tend to choose partners who are **as attractive** as themselves. Walster et al's (1966) **computer dance study** aimed to test this hypothesis.

Walster et al (1966) — Computer dance study

Method:	A 'Computer Dance' was advertised in a handbook given out to new **university students**, and tickets were sold to **376 men** and **376 women**. The people selling the tickets secretly rated each student for **attractiveness**. The students weren't told they were participating in a study. Instead, they were told that a **computer** would match them with a date for the dance who **shared their interests**. In fact, the participants were paired **randomly** with somebody of the opposite sex, although no men were paired with taller women. During the dance the participants filled in a **questionnaire** about their date. Participants were contacted **four to six months later** to find out if they'd tried to go on any **further dates** with their dance date.
Results:	Participants paired with a **similarly attractive** partner were **not significantly more liked** by their date than those paired with a partner with an attractiveness rating **different** to theirs. Instead, participants who were rated as **more attractive** were more **liked** by their date. More **attractive** participants were also **more frequently** asked out on further dates than less attractive participants, whereas there was **no correlation** between **similarity** in attractiveness in a pair and the **number of times** participants were asked out again.
Conclusion:	The matching hypothesis was **not supported** — the results showed that people **prefer attractive partners**, regardless of their own attractiveness.
Evaluation:	The computer dance was quite different from **usual dating** — the participants didn't **choose** one another, and neither of them had to **ask** each the other on a date. This means that the study has low ecological validity — the results can't really be applied to dating in real life. The way the attractiveness of the participants was judged may mean the results are not that **reliable** — the raters had to judge attractiveness very quickly. The participants were **dressed up** at the dance, and they had **several hours** to judge each other's attractiveness, so their perception might not have matched the rating.

Strengths

1) **Murstein (1972)** asked 99 real couples and 98 fake couples to rate themselves on attractiveness. An independent judge was also asked to rate the couples. For those in a **real relationship** there was a **strong positive correlation** between the attractiveness of the two partners.
2) **White (1980)** studied 123 couples. He found that couples who were only **dating** at the start of the study were more likely to have progressed to a **serious relationship** 9 months later if both partners were **similarly attractive**.

Weaknesses

1) The results of Walster et al's (1966) computer dance study **didn't support** the matching hypothesis.
2) The hypothesis says that matching affects who we choose to **start a relationship** with, but the evidence supporting the theory comes from relationships that have **already started**.

Practice Questions

Q1 Which features did Cunningham (1986) find correlated with female attractiveness?
Q2 What were the results of Kerckhoff and Davis's (1962) study?
Q3 What is the matching hypothesis?

Exam Questions

Q1 Which of these options is **not** a filter described in the filter theory of relationships?

    A Complementarity   **B** Desirability   **C** Social demography   **D** Similarity in attitudes   [1 mark]

Q2 Discuss factors affecting attraction in romantic relationships.   [16 marks]

Computers matching people up for dates? Whatever next...

Who can ever really hope to understand what attracts one person to another? It's a beautiful mystery... Unfortunately, you can't really write that in your exam, so you'll have to make sure you know all about filter theory and the matching hypothesis. As ever, they've both got strengths and weaknesses, so make sure you know those too.

Theories of Romantic Relationships

These pages are gold — you're not just learning psychology, you're getting free relationship advice. Well, not free, unless you stole this book. Either way, there's a whole load of theories about how relationships work for you to get stuck into.

Social Exchange Theory Says People Minimise Costs and Maximise Benefits

1) **Social exchange theory** (Thibaut and Kelley, 1959) suggests that people try to **maximise rewards** (e.g. attention, self-esteem, happiness) from a relationship and **minimise costs** (e.g. time, effort, emotional support).

2) If the relationship is to continue, then the rewards must not be **outweighed** by the costs — we should end up in **profit**. So, relationships are formed using a sort of 'cost-benefit' analysis.

3) But if we are striving to **get more** and **give less**, this may result in an **unequal relationship**.

A problem with this theory is that it's difficult to define what rewards and costs might be as these will differ between people.

Equity Theory Says People Want Balance

1) **Equity theory** suggests that people expect relationships to be **fair and equal**.

2) They want to receive rewards from relationships that are **in balance** with the rewards they provide for the other person.

3) If a relationship is unequal or unfair then it produces **discomfort and distress** in both partners, even if you're the one getting more and giving less.

4) The disadvantaged person may try to **make things fairer** if it seems possible.

Jo had found that sharing her catch with Tom was key to keeping their relationship in balance.

Hatfield et al's research into contentment in marriages **supports** equity theory:

Hatfield et al (1979) asked newlyweds to assess what they and their partner **contributed** to the relationship and their level of **contentment** with the marriage:

- The least satisfied were those who were **under-benefited** (unhappy about giving the most).
- The next least satisfied were those who were **over-benefited** (perhaps they felt guilty about giving the least).
- Equal relationships were the **most satisfactory**.

But there may be **sex differences** in how we feel about unequal relationships. **Argyle (1988)** found that:

- Over-benefited **men** were almost as satisfied as those in equitable marriages.
- Over-benefited **women**, however, were much **less satisfied** than women in equal relationships.

The Investment Model Gives Three Factors that Create Commitment

Rusbult (1980) came up with the **investment model of commitment**.

The investment model says that the **stability** of a relationship over time (i.e. whether it lasts) is determined by how **committed** the individuals are to the relationship, and that commitment **varies** depending on:

1) **Satisfaction** — how well the relationship fulfils the person's **needs**.

2) **Comparison with alternatives** — to what extent the person thinks their needs could be better fulfilled in **another relationship**, or by **not** being in a relationship.

3) **Investment** — how much the person feels they've **put in** to the relationship (emotionally, in terms of time, etc.).

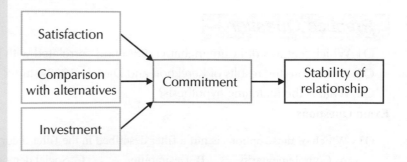

Le and Agnew (2003) did a **meta-analysis** of 52 studies involving 11 582 participants and found a significant correlation between **commitment** to a relationship and **satisfaction**, **quality of alternatives** and **investment**. Commitment level was also found to be a **significant predictor** of whether participants **stayed** in their relationship.

However, some psychologists have argued that these theories are too **simplistic** in trying to describe how relationships are formed — relationships are actually quite **complex**. The theories also don't consider **cultural** and **gender factors**, which may cause people to treat relationships in different ways.

Theories of Romantic Relationships

Duck's *Phase Model* says that *Relationships End* in *Stages*

Duck (1988) developed a **four-phase model** of the ending of an intimate relationship.

1. **Intra-psychic phase** — inside the head of **one person**. One partner becomes **dissatisfied** with the relationship.

2. **Dyadic phase** — between **two people**. The other partner is told about the dissatisfaction.

3. **Social phase** — beyond the couple. The break-up is **made public** to friends and family. **Implications** are discussed (e.g. care of children). The relationship **can still be saved** here (e.g. intervention of family, external marital support).

4. **Grave-dressing phase** — finishing the relationship completely. The ex-partners organise their lives **post-relationship**. They tell their own version of the break-up and of their current relationship with their ex.

Natasha could never seem to find the right moment to move the break-up to the dyadic phase...

One phase in Duck's model clearly leads onto the next as a **threshold point** is reached. For example, the **intra-psychic** phase becomes the **dyadic** phase when the dissatisfied partner **tells their partner** they're unhappy with the relationship.

However, Duck's model doesn't take **individual differences** into account and **research evidence** suggests it doesn't show how **complex** the breakdown of a relationship can be.

Rusbult and Zembrodt (1983) said some people in a relationship breakdown **actively lead** the process (to resolve the problems, or to speed up the ending). Others are **passive** — they believe things will resolve themselves.

Akert (1992) said people who do the breaking up are **less likely** to be upset or to show physical symptoms (e.g. loss of appetite and sleep) — not surprising really.

Duck's phase model is **descriptive** — it doesn't explain **why** relationships might break down. It also doesn't take **cultural differences** in relationships into account.

Practice Questions

Q1 Briefly outline social exchange theory.

Q2 What relationship did Hatfield et al (1979) find between equity and contentment in marriage?

Q3 What are the factors that determine commitment in Rusbult's investment model?

Q4 Describe the grave-dressing phase in Duck's phase model.

Exam Question

Q1 Read the item below and answer the questions that follow.

> William and Kate are having trouble with their relationship. William has recently told Kate that he is unhappy because they don't spend enough time together. They are discussing between themselves what they can do to resolve the problem.

a) Which of Duck's phases of relationship breakdown are William and Kate at? [1 mark]

b) Evaluate Duck's phase model. [4 marks]

People might try and tell you that a relationship is the best kind of ship...

... but that's clearly a lie. The best kind of ship is probably like that one out of Pirates of the Caribbean. It had cannons. And pirates. But I doubt psychologists are cut out for the high seas. Duck might cope, I suppose. Now, make sure you can describe the main theories concerning the maintenance and breakdown of relationships — then we can quack on...

Virtual Relationships

Online relationships are a bit different from face-to-face ones — people are often fairly anonymous online (they don't necessarily have to use their real name, for example), and they can hide aspects of themselves if they want to...

Self-Disclosure **Increases** When People Communicate **Through Computers**

Altman and Taylor's **social penetration theory (1973)** says that intimacy and closeness develop in relationships through a gradual process of **self-disclosure** — sharing information about yourself (see page 52).

Joinson (2001) found that self-disclosure happens **more** when people communicate via **computer** than face to face.

Joinson (2001) — Self-disclosure in computer communication

Method: Undergraduate students were recruited to participate in a **laboratory study**. Participants were paired (mostly in single sex pairs), and asked to discuss an abstract dilemma which stimulated conversation. Transcripts of the participants' discussions were rated on their levels of **self-disclosure**. Raters weren't told which transcripts came from which condition. Only **unprompted** disclosures were included (i.e. not answers to direct questions), and **task-related** disclosures (e.g. an opinion relevant to the task) weren't counted.

> **Experiment 1** — Half of the pairs discussed the dilemma **face to face**, and half discussed it from separate rooms using a **computer chat program**.

> **Experiment 2** — All of the pairs used the chat program, but half of them also had a **video connection**, so could see each other.

Results: In experiment 1, participants in the **computer** condition showed significantly **more self-disclosure** than the face-to-face participants. In experiment 2, pairs who could see one another over **video** had significantly **lower levels** of self-disclosure than pairs without video.

Conclusion: People **disclose more** about themselves when communicating via **computer** than they do face to face, and using **video** reduces the level of self-disclosure in computer communication.

Evaluation: This was a **laboratory experiment**, so the variables were **controlled** and the study can be **replicated**. However, the participants were almost all paired in **same sex** pairs, so the results can't be **generalised** to communication between people who aren't the same sex. In the first experiment, although the raters **weren't** told which transcripts came from which condition, it's likely they could tell which conversations were held face to face and which happened through computer chat. So their ratings may have been **biased**.

Self-awareness *Might Affect* Computer Communication

1) **Self-awareness** means paying attention to yourself, i.e. being **aware** of your thoughts, feelings and behaviour.

> **Public self-awareness** — this is being aware of how you **appear to others**.

> **Private self-awareness** — this is 'looking inwards', i.e. being aware of what's going on inside your head.

2) **Joinson's (2001) study** also included a third experiment where the participants discussed the dilemma through computers in conditions which were designed to induce either **high** or **low** public and private **self-awareness**.

3) Joinson found that the condition designed to create **high private self-awareness** and **low public self-awareness** resulted in significantly **higher** levels of self-disclosure than the other conditions.

4) Chatting via computer usually involves **anonymity** and focussing on your thoughts and feelings to express them in **writing**. Joinson suggested that this is likely to create **low public** and **high private self-awareness**, which may explain why this type of communication results in **more self-disclosure**.

Gating Can **Prevent** Relationships from **Forming**

1) **Gating** is a process that limits how much we **self-disclose** — obstacles known as 'gates' prevent people from sharing information, which means they can't develop **intimacy** and build a **relationship**.

2) Factors that can act as gates, such as **appearance**, **shyness** or **social skills**, are apparent when you meet somebody **face to face**.

3) However, they aren't obvious in **virtual communication**. People often communicate just through typed messages online, so their appearance, body language and so on are hidden.

4) The **absence of gating** in virtual relationships means **self-disclosure** is higher.

Virtual Relationships

The *Absence of Gating* Means *Virtual Relationships* are *Stronger*

Hill et al (1976) studied dating couples who had met **face to face**. They found that **55%** of the couples were still together after 2 years. **McKenna et al (2002)** found that couples who met **online** were **more likely** to stay together.

	McKenna et al (2002) — Relationship formation on the internet
Method:	**Surveys** were sent to randomly selected members of online **special interest forums**, e.g. forums about cats (rather than forums intended for personal ads). The survey asked about how people interacted **offline**, whether they **shared more** with others online, and how **close** the relationships they formed online were.
	Participants were then sent a **follow-up** survey two years later which asked similar questions to see how the feelings and relationships that they had reported in the earlier survey had **changed**.
Results:	People who shared aspects of themselves online which they **didn't** share with others offline reported developing **internet** relationships **more quickly** than 'real-life' relationships. Over **half** of the participants had met an internet friend **face to face**, on average meeting each internet friend **8 times**.
	After **two years**, of the respondents who had started a **romantic relationship** online, **71%** were still in the relationship.
Conclusion:	People can form close, lasting relationships **online**, and these relationships typically form more **quickly**, and are more **stable** and **long lasting** than offline relationships. McKenna proposed that online relationships have a **stable base**, because they begin based on **mutual interests** and **self-disclosure** rather than **outward appearances**. The **absence of gating** allows strong relationships to form quickly.
Evaluation:	The study used a **self-report survey** which may have involved a **biased sample** or produced **social desirability bias** (where people give answers they think will make them look good to others, rather than honest answers). However, this study looked at real-life interaction, so it has high **ecological validity**.

McKenna et al's research (2002) also included a **laboratory experiment**:

1) Pairs of the opposite sex met once either **online** or **in person**, and then a second time in person. The researchers showed that after both meetings, people **liked** each other significantly more if they had **first met online**.

2) For participants who only met face to face, their **quality of conversation** and the level of **intimacy** they reached didn't affect how much they liked each other. This suggests that liking was based on factors other than what was said, e.g. **appearance**.

3) However, liking and conversation quality were **strongly correlated** for participants who had first met online.

4) This supports the conclusion from the surveys that the **absence of gating** online contributes to the stability of online relationships.

Gating was playing havoc with Betty's relationship.

Practice Questions

Q1 What role does self-disclosure play in forming relationships?

Q2 Describe Joinson's study into self-disclosure.

Q3 What is gating?

Q4 What did McKenna et al (2002) find about the stability of online relationships?

Exam Questions

Q1	Explain how the absence of gating may affect virtual relationships.	[4 marks]
Q2	Outline and evaluate research into virtual relationships.	[16 marks]

I told my GF I <3 her, she replied lots of love. I think that's what LOL means...

Lots of this is fairly common sense — people tend to share more online, which makes it easier to form relationships. Relationships are also more likely to get going online because you're less likely to trip up at the first hurdle if it's only your sparkling personality you need to worry about. Not that you need to worry about it, obviously.

Parasocial Relationships

"When I grow up, I wanna be famous" trill countless starry-eyed children. Mass media (like TV) is relatively new, so we've only just begun to look for ways to explain our relationships with celebrities. But there are already a few different theories...

Audiences Can Develop **Parasocial Relationships** With **Celebrities**

1) The relationships that audiences develop with celebrities are very **different** from the relationships formed within **normal social networks**.

2) They are **one-sided**, with one person knowing lots and the other usually knowing nothing about the other party.

3) The term used to describe this type of relationship is **parasocial**.

4) The study of **parasocial relationships** between audiences and celebrities has become a branch of **social relationship research** in its own right.

5) As well as audiences developing relationships with celebrities, many people are **attracted** to the **concept of celebrity** and want to be one themselves.

Their relationship was distinctly one sided but that didn't discourage Molly.

McCutcheon et al Identified **Three Levels** of **Parasocial Relationships**

McCutcheon (2002) created a **Celebrity Attitude Scale (CAS)** based on the findings of a set of questionnaires which asked participants to score 23 items describing different aspects of **celebrity worship**.

Using this scale McCutcheon et al (2002) later identified three **increasingly intensive** stages of celebrity worship, known as the **three levels of parasocial relationships** — they range from being a **harmless fan**, to being a **stalker**:

THREE LEVELS OF PARASOCIAL RELATIONSHIPS

1) **Entertainment-Social** — where the relationship with the celebrity exists as a **source of fun**, shared with others in a social group.

2) **Intense-Personal** — **obsessive thoughts** begin to arise in relation to the celebrity (e.g. "Justin Timberlake is my soul mate").

3) **Borderline-Pathological** — obsessive thoughts begin to give rise to **fully-fledged fantasies** (e.g. "Justin Timberlake is my boyfriend") and **behaviours** (e.g. sending love letters to Justin Timberlake). It is at this stage that **stalking** may begin, which involves a level of pursuit that is intimidating.

Parasocial Relationships Can Be Explained by **Attachment Theory**

1) **Theories of attachment** stem from research by **Bowlby**, who suggested that people form close attachments with their **caregivers**. These bonds influence how they attach and relate to other people in adulthood. (You studied attachment, including Bowlby's research, in Year 1.)

2) In terms of **celebrities**, attachment theory suggests that children who **didn't** form close attachments with their caregivers may later develop **insecure attachments** as adults. They are then **more likely** to be attracted to celebrities. In one-sided relationships, there is little opportunity for **rejection**.

Evidence for:

The results of **Roberts' (2007)** study **support** the idea that there's a link between childhood attachments and parasocial relationships. Roberts asked 200 students (100 males and 100 females) similar questions to McCutcheon et al (2002), and found a **positive correlation** between **insecurely attached** individuals and frequently **contacting celebrities**.

Evidence against:

McCutcheon et al (2006) asked over 250 university students to complete questionnaires which examined their **personality types** and their **views on celebrities**. They found **no relationship** between having an insecure attachment and forming parasocial relationships.

Parasocial Relationships

The **Absorption Addiction Model** Also Explains **Parasocial Relationships**

1) The **absorption addiction model** was created by **McCutcheon et al (2002)**.

2) The model says that people form parasocial relationships when they have a weak sense of **identity** — an individual finds their own life **deficient**, so they follow a celebrity as a source of **fulfilment**.

3) McCutcheon et al outlined **two stages** of the model — **absorption** and **addiction**.

> **Absorption** An individual becomes **absorbed** in following a celebrity — the relationship is a form of **escapism**.

> **Addiction:** In some cases the parasocial relationship becomes **addictive**, and the individual becomes more and more **obsessed** with the celebrity. This can lead to extreme behaviour, like **stalking**. This usually happens as a result of **poor mental health**, or some sort of **crisis**.

4) The **absorption addiction model** is closely linked to the **three levels of parasocial relationships** — the first level (entertainment-social) occurs in the **absorption** stage. If the parasocial relationship becomes **addictive** an individual may move to the second (intense-personal), and sometimes third level (borderline-pathological).

Strengths

1) **Maltby et al (2001)** found evidence that there is a **connection** between **parasocial relationships** and **mental health**. Participants who engaged in parasocial relationships were found to be functioning **less well** psychologically than those who didn't. They also found a **positive correlation** between levels of **anxiety** and **depression** and frequency of more extreme parasocial relationships, which matches the model's predictions.

2) The model explains why **most people** who form parasocial relationships do so at the **entertainment-social** level, and why only a **small minority** develop relationships at the **intense-personal** or **borderline-pathological** level.

Weaknesses

1) This model has been criticised for ignoring the **positive aspects** of being a fan (like being part of a social group), and for **stigmatising** people who form parasocial relationships by linking their behaviour to poor mental health.

2) The studies which are used to support the absorption addiction model don't show that poor psychological functioning **causes** people to form parasocial relationships — they just show that the two things **correlate**.

3) Studies supporting this model have tended to be done in western countries, so the theory is **ethnocentric** (see p.42), and can't be **generalised** to other cultures.

Practice Questions

Q1 What is meant by a parasocial relationship?

Q2 What are the three levels of parasocial relationships?

Q3 Outline one study that supports the attachment theory explanation of parasocial relationships.

Exam Questions

Q1 Outline the attachment theory explanation for the formation of parasocial relationships. [2 marks]

Q2 Outline and evaluate the absorption addiction model of parasocial relationships. [6 marks]

Celeb worship is harmless. My fiancé Justin Timberlake totally agrees...

So attachment theory says people form parasocial relationships because they're safe — you can't be rejected if the person you're forming a relationship with hasn't got a clue who you are. The absorption addiction model argues it's all about escapism, which sounds harmless enough, but being a fan can get out of hand if it becomes an addiction.

Sex and Gender

Gender is the way someone acts and identifies themselves — the behaviours that make a person masculine or feminine. Your gender isn't the same thing as your sex, but there are stereotypical sex-roles associated with men and women...

Sex-Role Stereotypes Are Narrow Views of How Men and Women Behave

1) Your **sex** is whether you are biologically male or female.
2) Your **gender** is the way you act and identify yourself — it's determined by the behavioural characteristics that make a person **masculine** or **feminine**.
3) People who have a **balanced combination** of masculine and feminine characteristics are **androgynous**.
4) **Sex-roles** are the particular behaviours **expected** of men and women — they vary over time and between cultures.
5) **Sex-role stereotypes** are ideas about sex-roles that are **widely held** but tend to be **narrow, inflexible**, and **over generalised**. For example: 'Women should care for children while men bring in the money.'

A study by **Seavey et al (1975)** demonstrated adults showing sex-role stereotypes. Participants were asked to interact with a 3-month-old after the child was introduced as either a girl, a boy or just 'a baby' (i.e. no information about sex given). They found that **participants' behaviour** towards the child **differed** depending on what **information** they were given. For example, **sex-stereotyped toys** were used — i.e. most adults chose a doll to play with when they were told the child was a girl.

People Who Don't Fit Sex-Role Stereotypes Show Androgyny

1) **Bem (1974)** developed a self-report questionnaire known as the **Bem Sex Role Inventory (BSRI)** by asking 50 male and 50 female students to rate **personality traits** (e.g. shyness) as being either masculine or feminine.
2) The most highly rated masculine, feminine and neutral words were then used to form a **questionnaire**, which aimed to measure the mix of **stereotypically** masculine and feminine traits present in an individual.
3) Individuals **rate themselves** for these traits on a scale of 1 to 7. Those who score highly for **both** masculine and feminine traits are said to be **psychologically androgynous**.
4) Bem suggests that androgyny is **advantageous** in society as it means people have the traits needed to cope with a **range of situations**. Those who score highly on only one scale have a more limited range of skills.
5) Several studies suggest that **environmental factors** are the cause of psychological androgyny. For example:

Weisner and Wilson-Mitchell (1990) compared children raised in families that put an **emphasis** on traditional gender roles with children raised in families that actively **downplayed** traditional gender roles.
They found that androgyny was **higher** in children who had been encouraged to **ignore** traditional gender roles.

6) Other researchers have argued that androgyny is more likely to be a **lifestyle choice**. As Bem suggested, psychologically androgynous people have the **advantage** of being able to use the best masculine traits as well as the best feminine traits.
7) However, the BSRI is considered to be a **reductionist** theory, as it reduces femininity and masculinity to a single score. It is also based on **outdated** views, i.e. traits that were desirable in the 1970s.

Practice Questions

Q1 What are sex-role stereotypes?
Q2 Why did Bem consider psychological androgyny to be advantageous?
Q3 What were Weisner and Wilson-Mitchell's (1990) findings on psychological androgyny?

Exam Questions

Q1 Explain what is meant by 'gender'. [2 marks]

Q2 Explain how the Bem Sex Role Inventory is carried out. [3 marks]

Stereotypes are a pain in the neck, but they're hard to get rid of...

There are quite a few fixed ideas about what men and women are like generally (sex-role stereotypes). These aren't usually very accurate though — women often have 'masculine' traits and vice versa. This is what the Bem Sex Role Inventory tests — if somebody is measured as having lots of both sorts of trait they're psychologically androgynous.

Atypical Gender Development

Some people have a male body but feel female, or vice versa — their gender and sex don't match.

People with **Gender Identity Disorder** Feel Their **Sex** and **Gender Don't Match**

1) Some people feel that their **biological sex** doesn't match their **psychological gender** — they feel that they're in the wrong body. For example, somebody born male may feel they're female **mentally** and want to be **treated** as a girl.

2) **Gender identity disorder** occurs when this causes the person **distress**, such as **anxiety**, and they want to **change their sex**.

The DSM calls this gender dysphoria — it's thought that this term has less stigma.

3) Gender identity disorder (GID) can begin in **early childhood**.

4) GID is **different** from cross-dressing (wearing clothes of the other gender). People with GID may cross-dress, but lots of people who cross-dress just enjoy it — they **don't** want to change their sex. Some people with GID live **full-time** as the sex other than their birth sex, and this may involve having surgery to change their physical sex.

Gender Identity Disorder May have a **Biological Explanation**...

1) One explanation for **gender identity disorder** is that the **brain functioning** of these individuals is more typical of the **other sex** (i.e. not their biological sex).

2) Some researchers believe that male and female brains develop **differently** because they're exposed to different levels of **sex hormones** (e.g. testosterone) in the womb. There's more about this on the next page.

3) An individual might develop brain function typical of the other sex if they have **unusual hormone levels** during brain development. For example if a girl's **testosterone** levels are higher than usual.

Strengths

1) **Kruijver et al (2000)** found that the number of **neurones** in a region of the brain called the **BSTc** in male-to-female transsexuals was **similar** to the number in women (typically half as many as in men).

2) **Hare et al (2009)** found that **male-to-female transsexuals** were more likely than non-transsexual men to have a particular version of an **androgen receptor gene**. (Androgens are male sex hormones.)

Weaknesses

1) **Chung et al (2002)** found sex differences in the BSTc didn't appear until **adulthood**, so they may be a **result** of gender developing, not the **cause**.

2) Most girls with **CAH** (see page 63), who produce more testosterone than usual, **don't** develop gender identity disorder.

3) Other factors may also have an effect on gender development, such as **social influences**.

The transsexual people in these studies were mostly people living as the gender other than their birth sex. Some of them had changed their physical sex.

... or a **Social Explanation**

1) **Social learning theory** (which you should remember from Year 1) has also been used to explain **gender identity disorder**. If a child imitates a **role model** of the other sex, or has behaviour associated with the other sex **reinforced** (e.g. through praise), then they may develop a gender that **doesn't match** their sex.

2) **Rekers and Lovaas (1974)** argued, in a case study of a boy who behaved in a stereotypically feminine way, that gender identity disorder could be resolved by **reinforcing 'gender appropriate' behaviours** (i.e. changing gender to match sex).

3) Many psychologists don't agree with this idea, and argue that it **stigmatises** people with an atypical gender identity.

4) **Rekers (1977)** linked his suggestion that individuals' gender identity should be changed to match society's expectations to the (now discredited) idea that **homosexuality** was a disorder that could be 'cured'.

Rekers has been criticised for basing his ideas on religious beliefs rather than scientific support.

Practice Question

Q1 What is gender identity disorder?
Q2 Outline the findings of Kruijver et al's (2000) study.

Exam Question

Q1 Outline and evaluate biological and social explanations for gender identity disorder. [16 marks]

So it might be nature or nurture, or both. Shocker...

There's lots of disagreement about gender identity disorder (including about whether it's a disorder at all). There isn't one single explanation, so make sure you can outline the biological and the social explanations, and evaluate them both.

Biological Influences on Gender

Biological factors influence gender. No surprises there — the title gives that one away. You need to know what these factors are and how they influence gender. Luckily, these two pages are here to help you out. I'm too kind to you.

Biological Psychology Says Gender Differences Result From Sex Differences

1) Biological psychology argues that psychological or behavioural differences between males and females can be explained by differences in **brain development** and **brain activity** between males and females.

2) These biological differences between males and females are caused by **sex chromosomes**, which determine the sex which a foetus develops in the womb, and by **sex hormones** which are secreted by the body.

Males and Females Have Different Sex Chromosomes

1) Women and men both have 22 pairs of matched chromosomes in each cell. The 23rd pair are either **XX** or **XY** — they're the two chromosomes that decide whether you turn out **female** or **male** (known as sex chromosomes).

2) **Females** have a **pair of X** chromosomes — XX. So all ova contain an X chromosome.

3) **Males** have **one X** chromosome and **one Y** chromosome — XY. This means sperm may contain either an X chromosome or a Y chromosome. It's the **Y chromosome** that leads to **male development**.

Sperm and ova only contain one sex chromosome.

4) If an ovum is fertilised by a Y carrying sperm, the offspring will be **XY** (**male**). If an ovum is fertilised by an X carrying sperm the offspring will be **XX** (**female**). Which sperm fertilises the ova is determined by chance.

Testosterone Production Caused by the Y Chromosome Affects Brain Development

1) Early on, the **reproductive organs** of a foetus are **the same** in males and females.

2) There's a **gene** on the **Y chromosome** which causes **male genitalia** to develop and testosterone to be produced. Without this gene, **female genitalia** develop and this testosterone isn't produced.

3) The **testosterone** produced early on in the development of a male foetus also affects **brain development** — there are some **structural differences** between female and male brains. This may explain **gender**.

Testosterone levels day-to-day may also affect brain function (see next page).

4) But differences in male and female brain structure may **not** affect **brain function** — some researchers think the **combined effect** of hormonal differences and structural differences is **similar brain function** in both sexes.

5) **Hyde (2005)** reviewed 46 **meta-analyses** and found there was either **a very small** or **no difference** between the sexes in almost all measures, supporting the idea that men and women are very **similar psychologically**.

Whether or not testosterone is produced is generally considered the **main** way that chromosomes affect gender, but it might not be the only way. Laboratory studies on **animals** have found that some sex differences in early brain development aren't explained by hormone levels during this time, and so they may be **directly caused by genes**.

Chromosomal Variations Have Psychological Effects

Some humans are born with **variations** in the standard sex chromosome pattern — **atypical sex chromosome patterns**.

Studies of people with such variations have shown there are psychological effects of having **different sex chromosomes**. Some of these effects are on aspects of brain function which may have **gender differences** (e.g. spatial ability). This might indicate that gender differences are caused by differing sex chromosomes.

Klinefelter's Syndrome

1) In **Klinefelter's syndrome** males are born with **XXY sex chromosomes** — they have an **extra X chromosome**.

2) Males with this syndrome are **sterile** and tend to be **less muscular** and have **less facial and body hair**.

3) They can have problems using **language** to express themselves and may have trouble with **social interaction**.

Turner's Syndrome

1) In **Turner's syndrome** females are born with only **one complete X sex chromosome** — all or part of their second X chromosome is **missing**.

2) Females with this syndrome tend to be **shorter than average** and their ovaries usually don't function, so they're **sterile** and don't go through **puberty** in the usual way.

3) Girls with Turner's syndrome often do less well at **maths**, and have poorer **spatial ability**.

Biological Influences on Gender

Hormones Can Affect Gender

1) Hormones affect the way that the body and brain **develop**, as well as how they **function** day-to-day.
2) The major male and female specific hormones are **androgens** and **oestrogens**.
3) Both types of hormone are present in males and females, but in very **different amounts**.
4) **Men** produce more **testosterone** (the main androgen) each day than females, and **females** produce more **oestrogens** than males.
5) However, some humans produce **smaller** or **larger** quantities of these hormones than normal.

> For example, sometimes people produce much more **testosterone** than is usual — this happens with a particular form of a syndrome called **CAH**.
> - This form of CAH can cause **early sexual development** in **males**, but doesn't have much of an effect otherwise.
> - The **behaviour** of **girls** with this type of CAH tends to be **masculinised** — they have a preference for playing with boys' toys and enjoy 'tomboyish' activities.
> - **Physically**, girls tend to look more **masculine**. Their **growth** is fast and **puberty** can happen early.
> - In CAH, girls are exposed to high levels of testosterone while they're in the womb, which can cause **physical abnormalities** such as **ambiguous genitalia**. This can make it difficult to tell whether someone is **male** or **female** at birth.

6) Case studies of conditions like this **support** the idea that the effect of **testosterone** on the **brain** is responsible for **gender differences in behaviour**.
7) The role of **oestrogen** has also been studied — particularly in how it can affect and influence female behaviour.

> Oestrogen can lead to **premenstrual tension (PMT)** in some women. This can leave women feeling **emotional**, **irritable** and **aggressive**. Whilst many women manage their experience of PMT, **Easteal (1991)** believed that PMT could be the reason behind crime in some females.

A Stronger Effect of Oxytocin on Women May Explain Gender Differences

1) **Oxytocin** is a hormone that's been associated with **bonding** and **attachment**, and with **social recognition**:

> **Rimmele et al (2009)** found that **increased** oxytocin levels **improved** male participant's ability to recognise if they had **seen a face before**, but it **didn't** improve their recognition of **non-social** images (e.g. objects).

2) Oxytocin is produced by females and males. However, **oestrogens** in the bloodstream **increase the effect** of oxytocin on the brain. So oxytocin may have more impact on the **female brain** than the male brain.
3) It's been argued that this may explain **gender differences** in sociability and **gender roles**, e.g. in parenting.

Practice Questions

Q1 Which chromosome leads to development of male features?
Q2 Describe some of the effects of Klinefelter's syndrome.
Q3 What is the sex chromosome pattern of people with Turner's syndrome?
Q4 Why might oxytocin have a greater effect on women than on men?

Exam Questions

Q1 What is the sex chromosome pattern of individuals with Klinefelter's syndrome?
    A XYY   B XY   C XX   D XXY   E X   [1 mark]

Q2 Discuss the role of hormones in sex and gender development.   [16 marks]

So, your gender is influenced by biology — never saw that one coming...

Ah, hormones. They're always popping up as reasons for this, that or the other. Maybe they're why you're feeling so restless and miserable now. No... wait... that would be the revision. Anyway, biological influences on gender — get learning.

Cognitive Explanations of Gender

The basic idea here is that as children mature they gradually develop an understanding of gender, and which gender they are. The theories you need to know (Kohlberg's theory and gender schema theory) are based on Piaget's ideas about how children's thinking develops, so you might want to have a read up on Piaget (p.70-71) before you get stuck in.

Cognitive Developmental Theory *Says Ideas about Gender* Change *With* Age

1) **Cognitive developmental theory** was first proposed by Piaget.
   It suggests that children's thoughts and views on the world **change** as they develop.

2) Piaget proposed that children pass through several **stages of development** as they mature
   — at each stage their thinking develops and they gain more **complex cognitive abilities**.

3) **Cognitive explanations of gender** use Piaget's theory to explain how a child's ideas about
   gender **change with age** — they propose that children **develop** their idea of gender over
   time, as their **cognitive abilities** and **understanding** of the world improve.

Kohlberg (1966) *Developed a* Theory of Gender Constancy

Kohlberg's (1966) theory of **gender constancy** is part of his wider cognitive developmental theory.
It identifies **three stages** of gender development:

Gender identity — the child becomes aware that they're **male** or **female**, and also begins to **categorise** other people as male and female. Before this stage they're not really **aware** of gender. During this stage children judge gender on **superficial characteristics**, so they think their (or other people's) gender might **change** (e.g. by wearing opposite sex clothes). This stage usually occurs **between the ages of 2 and 3**.

Gender stability — the child realises that their gender will remain **fixed** over **time** (e.g. boys will become men). However, they may think that gender can **change** in **different situations** (e.g. when doing an 'opposite-sex activity'). This stage usually occurs **between the ages of 4 and 6**.

Gender constancy — the child becomes aware that gender remains fixed in **different situations** (e.g. cross-dressing doesn't change gender). At this point the child internalises their gender, because they realise it's **permanent**. They begin to develop their **gender role** by looking to role models of their gender. This usually occurs around **age 7**.

They'd all agreed that staying in the tree was their best chance of avoiding developing gender roles...

Strengths

1) **Thompson (1975)** found that **3-year-olds** were much **more likely** than **2-year-olds** to know their own **gender**.

2) **Slaby and Frey (1975)** used interviews to try and determine if children aged 2 to 5½ had developed gender **identity**, gender **stability** and gender **constancy**. Their results were **consistent** with Kohlberg's theory — almost all of the children had only reached each stage if they'd also reached the previous stages.

3) Slaby and Frey also found that when watching a video of a man and a woman, children in the **later stages** of gender development paid more attention to the person of **their gender** than children in the **earlier stages**. This supports Kohlberg's idea that **gender roles** become important once a child develops **gender constancy**.

4) **Munroe et al's (1984)** study found the same stages in children from **different cultures**, which suggests the stages are **universally generalisable** and therefore, seem to have some **biological basis**.

Weaknesses

1) Kohlberg's theory has been criticised for ignoring the effects of **social influences** and **conditioning**.

2) The theory describes **what** happens, but doesn't explain **why**.

3) **Slaby and Frey's (1975)** study found that some children had developed **gender constancy** before **age six** — earlier than Kohlberg suggested. So the ages Kohlberg gave for each stage may be **overestimates**.

4) Slaby and Frey also found that **boys** were **more likely** to pay greater attention to people of their own gender than girls were. This effect **isn't explained** by Kohlberg's theory.

Cognitive Explanations of Gender

Martin and Halverson (1981) Developed the Gender Schema Theory

1) Martin and Halverson's gender schema theory **combines** cognitive developmental theory and social learning theory to suggest how **gender stereotyping** helps children learn what is and what isn't appropriate for their gender.

2) It proposes that, by the age of **three**, children have developed a **basic gender identity**. They also have a **gender schema** which contains the child's ideas about **gender appropriate behaviour**.

3) Through **observation**, children continue to learn gender appropriate behaviours and **add** them to their schema.

4) A child's gender schema is based on the concept of an **in-group** and an **out-group**:

- Activities, objects and behaviours associated with their **own sex** are seen as **in-group**. Those associated with the **opposite sex** are **out-group**.
- So, for example, a boy might **label objects** such as cars and trousers as in-group and objects like dolls and skirts as out-group.
- Through reference to their **in-group/out-group schema**, children will show a **bias** towards **in-group** behaviours.

5) Having a gender schema can help children to manage all the information that they're exposed to. They can focus on **processing** information related to their **in-group** and **filter out** information related to their **out-group**.

6) However, there are also **disadvantages** — reinforcing stereotypical gender roles can discourage children from showing interest in things related to their out-group. This can limit their opportunities and lead to **discrimination**.

7) As children get older they are capable of **more complex cognition** and understand that their gender doesn't limit them rigidly to in-group objects and behaviours.

Evidence For

1) **Bradbard et al (1986)** found that children were more likely to play with (and remember) unfamiliar toys if they were described as being for their **own gender** rather than for the other. So children do show a bias towards **in-group** activities in their gender schema.

2) **Martin and Halverson (1983)** found evidence that children are more likely to take in information if it fits with their **gender schema**. They showed children drawings of males and females either doing an **activity** stereotypical of **their gender** (e.g. a boy sawing wood), or stereotypical of **the other gender**. Children were more likely to **correctly remember** images where the person's gender **matched** the stereotype for the activity.

Evidence Against

1) **Campbell et al (2002)** found that a child's **awareness** of their own gender and of gender stereotypes had **no effect** on how much they engaged in **gender stereotypical behaviour**. This suggests that having a **gender schema** isn't the **main factor** in developing gender.

2) **Alexander et al (2009)** simultaneously showed a **doll** and a **toy truck** to infants aged **3 to 8 months** old. Boys looked at the truck more than girls did, and girls looked at the doll more than boys did. They seemed to show a preference for **gender stereotypical** toys well **before** the age when Martin and Halverson propose gender identity develops.

Practice Questions

Q1 Briefly describe the cognitive approach to explaining gender development.

Q2 Explain what is meant by gender constancy in Kohlberg's (1966) theory.

Exam Questions

Q1 Which of the following is **not** a stage in Kohlberg's theory of gender development?
A Gender stability **B** Gender identity **C** Gender constancy **D** Gender role [1 mark]

Q2 Describe and evaluate gender schema theory. [16 marks]

In-group, out-group, shake-it-all-about group...

Nothing too scary, just make sure you know all the stages of Kohlberg's theory, and can explain gender schema theory. This stuff's got some interesting implications though. For example, if children only really take in information that fits with their gender schema, then trying to stop people from being restricted by gender stereotypes is likely to be pretty tricky...

Psychodynamic Explanation of Gender

Freud came up with some real corkers... His ideas about gender development might sound a bit off the wall, but you still need to learn them. Luckily that shouldn't be too tricky — there's some pretty memorable terminology in this lot...

Freud Said Gender Develops Through Identification and Internalisation

1) The **psychodynamic explanation** of gender is based on **Freud's ideas** about psychosexual development.

2) Freud thought there were five stages of **psychosexual development** — oral, anal, phallic, latent and genital (see page 4).

The psychodynamic approach is covered on pages 2-5 — it'll help if you're clear on those pages before you tackle this stuff.

3) Freud's **psychoanalytic theory of gender development** says that children develop their gender between age 3 and 5, during the **phallic stage** of development.

4) According to Freud, the child becomes aware of the **difference** between male and female in the phallic stage — in particular they realise male and female **genitalia** is different, and initially think that females have been **castrated**.

5) This leads to **unconscious** desires and anxiety, which children eventually resolve by **identifying** with the parent of their own sex, and then **internalising** that parent — taking on their behaviour and attitudes as their own.

6) Freud called this period of **conflicting** unconscious desires the **Oedipus complex**, which he mostly applied to boys.

7) Later, **Carl Jung** expanded on this by describing the **Electra complex**, which is a similar process for girls.

Boys Go Through the Oedipus Complex

It's pronounced 'ee-duh-puss'.

1) During the **phallic stage**, boys experience conflicting unconscious desires, known as the **Oedipus complex**:

> Boys start to **romantically desire their mother**. They then begin to feel **aggressive** and **jealous** towards their **father** because he's getting in the way of them fulfilling this desire.
>
> They know that their father is more powerful than them, and begin to experience **castration anxiety** — they fear their father because they think he will castrate them if he finds out about their feelings towards their mother.

2) They deal with this by starting to **identify** with their father, and then **internalise** him (incorporate him into their own personality) as their **superego** — this is when the superego develops.

3) This means that they develop a **male gender identity**.

4) Once they've developed their gender they deal with their desire for their mother by **displacing** it onto other women.

This theory has been criticised for suggesting that 'normal' gender development involves becoming heterosexual.

Girls Go Through the Electra Complex

1) While boys go through the Oedipus complex, girls have the **Electra complex**:

> Girls experience **penis envy** — they realise they have no penis, and wish that they had one (because they feel powerless). They start to **desire their father**, because he has one.
>
> They feel **hostile** towards their **mother**, because they blame her for their **castration**, but also **fear** losing their **mother's love** because of their feelings for their father.

2) Eventually, they repress these feelings and start to **identify** with their mother. They then **internalise** her as their **superego**.

3) This means they develop a **female gender identity**.

4) Through developing their gender they **repress** their desire for a penis, and **substitute** it with desire for a **baby**.

Freud's theories aren't always met with acceptance.

Freud didn't agree with calling this process the Electra complex, though it's the accepted term now. He thought the Oedipus complex applied to girls too, but that they switched their desire from mother to father because of penis envy.

Psychodynamic Explanation of Gender

Freud Supported His Theory with His Case Study of Little Hans

1) **Freud (1909)** did a **case study** of a boy (Little Hans) who was afraid of horses (see page 4). Freud's study was based around his correspondence with the boy's **father**, who reported to Freud **conversations** he'd had with Hans.

2) According to his father, Hans developed an interest in his own **penis** (which he called his 'widdler') when he was around **three years old**, and asked whether his **mother** had one.

   Hans isn't his real name. (Probably for the best...)

3) Hans also reportedly **dreamt** that he was married to his mother.

4) When Hans was **three-and-a-half** his mother told him off for touching himself and threatened to **cut off** his penis.

5) Freud thought that Hans had **displaced** fear of his father onto horses, and argued that Hans was especially afraid of white horses with blinkers and black mouths because they **resembled his father** (who had glasses and a moustache).

6) Freud argued that the Little Hans case was evidence for his theory of psychosexual development, because Hans exhibited fear of his father that came from **castration anxiety**, and was part of the **Oedipus complex**.

Freud's Psychoanalytic Theory of Gender Development Has Been Criticised

1) This explanation of gender is based on Freud's **subjective interpretation** of behaviour — the theory can't be **scientifically tested**, so it's difficult to support (or refute) it with research. It could be argued that Freud deliberately came up with interpretations of case studies that **agreed** with his theories, rather than considering other ideas.

2) Freud argued that **everyone** experiences the Oedipus complex. However, the case studies he based his theory on generally involved people who were having **psychological problems**, so it's unclear if it's possible to **generalise** his ideas to the whole population.

3) The idea that girls experience penis envy might have had more relevance in the **early 1900s** when Freud came up with his theory than it does now — back then, being a woman generally meant you had very **little power**, but in most western societies this isn't really the case anymore.

4) Freud's theory implies that children need to be brought up by a mother and father who are in a **heterosexual** relationship together to develop a 'normal' gender identity, but this isn't supported by studies involving children in **non-traditional families**:

   > **Kirkpatrick et al (1981)** looked at the gender development of 40 children aged 5 to 12. Half of the children had **heterosexual mothers** and half had **lesbian mothers**. They found **no identifiable differences** between the gender development of the two groups.

Practice Questions

Q1 Between what ages did Freud think that children develop their gender?

Q2 Briefly explain castration anxiety.

Q3 Describe Freud's case study of Little Hans.

Q4 What did Kirkpatrick et al (1981) find about gender development in non-traditional families?

Exam Questions

Q1 Which **one** of the options below is best described by the following sentence:
The girl incorporates the mother into their personality.
   A Electra complex   B Identification   C Internalisation   D Repression   [1 mark]

Q2 Describe and evaluate the psychodynamic explanation of gender development.   [16 marks]

You laugh, but horses do have a nasty bite on them...

Make sure you can explain the Oedipus complex and the Electra complex, especially how identification and internalisation are involved in resolving them — examiners love it when you use proper terms. It's easy to think this stuff is nonsense, but you need to know it. On the upside, you'll be pleased to hear that 'Hans' grew up to have a successful career in opera...

Social Explanations of Gender

Like most things in psychology, gender is influenced by social factors. These factors include the way that family and friends behave, the media you're exposed to, and the culture you grow up in. Read on...

Social Learning Theory May Explain Gender Development

> You should remember social learning theory from Year 1.

1) **Social learning theory** suggests that we learn by **observing** and **copying** the behaviour of people around us. We particularly imitate the behaviour of people we **identify** with.

2) This learning can be **passive** (when the behaviour is simply watched and copied) or it can be **active** (when the behaviour is reinforced by rewards, or discouraged by punishments).

3) Social learning theory can explain how **gender typical behaviours** are learnt — there are two aspects to this.

4) One aspect is that children identify with and imitate models of their **own gender**. So males copy the behaviour of **other males** and females copy the behaviour of **other females**. For example, girls may imitate the behaviour of their **mothers** — the behaviour becomes part of their idea of the female **gender role**.

5) The other aspect is learning through **reinforcement** — children may experience positive reinforcement (e.g. praise) or negative reinforcement (e.g. less disapproval) for behaviour that's considered **gender appropriate**. This will lead them to adopt **gender typical** behaviour.

6) There is evidence that parents and peers **react differently** to children depending on their gender, which may **reinforce gender typical behaviour**:

Parents

- Rubin et al (1974) found that fathers used words like '**soft**' and '**beautiful**' to describe newborn **daughters** and '**strong**' and '**firm**' to describe **sons**.
- Culp et al (1983) found that women treated babies differently according to how they were dressed — **talking** more to those dressed as **girls** and **smiling** more at those dressed as **boys**.
- Hron-Stewart's (1988) study found that adults were **quicker** to comfort a crying baby **girl** than a crying baby boy, expecting boys to be hardier and braver. Also, mothers were more likely to help a **daughter** complete a task than a son.

Peers

- Maccoby and Jacklin (1987) found that children as young as three prefer **same-sex playmates**. Maccoby (1990) found that when children organise their own activities they tend to segregate themselves according to their **gender**.
- Lamb and Roopnarine's (1979) study of nursery behaviours found that children **encouraged** gender appropriate behaviour and **criticised** gender inappropriate behaviour.

But This Explanation has Weaknesses

1) **Smith and Daglish (1977)** found **no correlation** between how **stereotyped** parents' views of gender appropriate behaviour were and how much their 1-2 year old children showed **gender typical behaviour**.

2) Social learning theory doesn't explain where stereotypical gender roles **came from** in the first place.

The Media May Influence Gender Roles

1) **TV, films, magazines** and **computer games** usually show **gender stereotypical behaviour**.

2) Several studies have shown that the behaviour displayed in these media can influence **gender roles**. For example, **Williams (1986)** showed that the **more TV** a child watches the **more stereotypical** their views on gender are:

> Williams (1986) carried out a two year **natural experiment** in Canada. She looked at the **effect of TV being introduced** to a town (she called it Notel), and compared it to a nearby town that already had TV (Multitel). She found that at the start of the experiment, gender stereotyping was much greater in Multitel than Notel. Williams found that **gender stereotypes** of Notel children **increased** and became more like those of Multitel children after the introduction of TV.

Since the Williams' study was a natural experiment, it had **high ecological validity**. It has also been supported by other studies into the role of media on gender roles. For example, **Leary's (1982)** correlational study suggested that the more TV a child watched, the more likely they were to have stereotypes about different gender roles.

Social Explanations of Gender

There's Been *Cross-Cultural Research* Into *Gender Roles*

1) **Cross-cultural research** has been carried out to identify how gender roles differ between cultures.

2) Cross-cultural research can also help us to understand the **causes** of gender roles — if roles are **similar** in different cultures it suggests a **biological** explanation. However, if they **vary** between cultures a **social** explanation of gender roles is more likely.

> • **Whiting and Edwards (1988)** observed the behaviour of children in the USA, Mexico, Japan, India, the Philippines and Kenya.
>
> • They found that gender behaviour was very **similar to Western stereotypes** and that there were clear differences between **male** and **female** behaviour.
>
> • For example, girls were more **caring** than boys, and boys were more **aggressive** than girls.
>
> • In societies where children were expected to work to contribute towards the family, there were further gender differences. Girls were more likely to look after **younger siblings** and do **domestic work**, whilst boys were more likely to look after **animals** and were less likely to work within the home.
>
> • These findings suggest that **similar** gender roles are found **across cultures**, suggesting that there's a **biological** explanation, supporting the **nature** side of the nature-nurture debate.

3) Other research suggests a social explanation. For example, **Margaret Mead (1935)** carried out a thorough study of gender roles in different cultures. She looked at **three** different tribes in Papua New Guinea and showed that each tribe had a different role for men and women. Not only were the gender roles of each tribe **different** to the Western world, they were also different to **each other**. Her study clearly shows that gender roles do appear to be influenced by our culture and environment, and aren't controlled by our **biology**.

4) However, cross-cultural research is difficult to conduct without involving some form of **ethnocentric bias** (p.42).

Responsibility for *Childcare* May Determine *Gender Roles*

1) Katz and Konner (1981) looked at **80 different cultures** — they found that in **90%** of them **women** had the main responsibility for child rearing.

2) This **gender division** has implications for men and women in terms of **occupation**, **finance** and **mobility**.

3) D'Andrade (1966) looked at information from **224 societies** to investigate what **types of tasks** and jobs were performed by males and females. He found that:

> • **Men** were more likely to **travel further** from the home, and be involved in **weapon making** and **hunting**.
> • **Women** were more likely to **make** and **repair clothes**, **prepare** and **cook food**, and **make objects** for **home**.

4) Segal (1983) suggested that the differences in **activities** associated with gender roles are related to the differences in **involvement in childcare**.

Practice Questions

Q1 What did Rubin et al (1974) discover about the way fathers describe their newborn children?

Q2 What did Maccoby and Jacklin (1987) find from their study on the type of playmates children prefer?

Q3 How can cross-cultural research help us to understand the causes of gender roles?

Q4 Outline the activities associated with males and females in the D'Andrade (1966) study.

Exam Questions

Q1 Outline how social learning theory can explain gender development.	[6 marks]
Q2 Outline the influence of the media on gender roles.	[4 marks]
Q3 Describe and discuss the influence of culture on gender roles.	[16 marks]

A whole town with no TV. In Canada. In 1986. Mad.

It seems everyone's plotting to force us into gender roles and turn us into stereotypes — parents, friends, and the media. There's no getting away from it. I say we fight back. We could start off by getting rid of TVs. We'll just chuck 'em out — it's proven to work and then we'll be free. Except there's still parents, and friends. Hmmm... I'll keep thinking...

Piaget's Theory of Cognitive Development

This bright and shiny new section is all about thinking, and how your thinking develops as you get older. As you might be learning to expect by now, there are a lot of different theories about this. And I bet you want to know all about them. Well, as luck would have it, these pages are all about these theories. It's almost like they were designed just for you...

Piaget Proposed That Cognition Progresses in Stages

Cognition just means thinking.

Piaget said that we're all born with the **basics** to allow **cognitive progression** — reflexes and senses. He reckoned that more **complex** abilities become possible as children move through **stages of intellectual development** as they get older:

Sensorimotor stage (0–2 years)	The child's knowledge is limited to what their **senses** tell them when they're exploring their surroundings. This exploration brings about an understanding of the concept of **object permanence** (if you put a towel over a toy, the toy is still there).
Preoperational stage (2–7 years)	The child has some language now, but makes **logic mistakes** — e.g. cats have four legs, so everything with four legs must be a cat. They typically can't do the **three mountains task** (see below) or **conservation tasks** (see next page). Children at this stage show **egocentrism**, **irreversibility** and **centration** (see below).
Concrete operational stage (7–11 years)	The child's use of logic improves and they can do **conservation tasks**. They no longer show **egocentrism**, **irreversibility** and **centration** but can't yet use **abstract reasoning** (reasoning in their head). They also understand **class inclusion** (knowing that objects can belong to two or more categories at once — for example, that a Labrador belongs to the category 'dog' and the category 'animal').
Formal operational stage (11+ years)	The child is much more advanced now, and can use **abstract reasoning** in **problem solving**. They can also use **hypotheses** and **theoretical principles**, and deal with **hypothetical situations**.

1) Piaget used the idea of **schemas** a lot in his work. A schema contains all the information you **know** about an object, action or concept — e.g. the schema of a human face has two eyes, a mouth and a nose, and the schema of riding a bike contains all the movements you'd need to make.

2) Schemas help you to **organise** and **interpret** information — new experiences either strengthen the schema (are **assimilated**) if they're consistent with it, or change the schema (are **accommodated**) if they're inconsistent with it.

3) Assimilation and accommodation are part of a process that Piaget called **equilibration** — he believed that this process **drives** cognitive development.

4) Piaget reckoned that through equilibration, children try to find a **balance** between assimilation and accommodation. Where possible, new information is assimilated, but when it doesn't fit, accommodation is used to change or alter their existing schemas.

Piaget Used the Three Mountains Task (1956) as Evidence for His Theory

1) Piaget and Inhelder (1956) built a **3-D model** of **three mountains** (well, Piaget was from Switzerland).

2) The mountains had different **landmarks** on them — e.g. one had a cross on it, and another had a house.

3) They put a small doll on one of the mountains and then showed children photos of the mountains taken from **various angles**. The children were asked to pick the photo that matched what the **doll** could see.

4) They found that children at Piaget's **preoperational stage** (2–7 years old) picked the photo taken from their **own perspective**, rather than the one taken from the **doll's perspective**.

5) Piaget and Inhelder concluded that children at this stage were unable to put themselves in the doll's shoes.

Piaget used this and other experiments as evidence that children at his preoperational stage have the following qualities:

1) **Egocentrism** — they can only view the world from their **own viewpoint**. They're not sensitive to the fact that others may have **different** views or thoughts (as demonstrated by the three mountains task).

2) **Irreversibility** — they don't understand that you can undo an action (e.g. that you can reform a sausage-shaped piece of clay into its original ball shape).

3) **Centration** — they focus on small aspects of a task, not the task as a whole.

Piaget's Theory of Cognitive Development

Piaget Showed How *Other Skills* Develop in *Later Stages*

Understanding of conservation

1) **Conservation** is the understanding that a **set quantity** stays the **same**, even if it **looks** different. For example, if liquid is poured from a short, fat glass into a tall, thin glass, the amount of liquid is still the same. Another example is counters in a row — two rows of five counters both have the same number of counters, even if the counters in one row are spaced out so that it looks longer.

2) Children at the **concrete operational stage** can **correctly identify** that the amount of liquid or the number of counters stays the same even after they've been rearranged. But children at the **preoperational stage** will say that the spaced out row contains **more** counters or the tall glass **more** liquid.

3) However, **McGarrigle and Donaldson (1974)** found that if a puppet (Naughty Teddy) 'accidentally' knocked the counters so that the row looked longer, even younger children at the **preoperational stage** said that the number of counters was the **same**. This suggests that they **did** understand conservation.

Understanding of class inclusion

1) **Piaget and Szeminksa (1941)** wanted to investigate children's understanding of class inclusion. They gave children **20 wooden beads** (18 brown and 2 white), then asked the children **three questions** — 'Are all the beads wooden?', 'Are there more brown beads or more white beads?' and 'Are there more brown beads or more wooden beads?'.

2) Children at the **concrete operational stage** (over seven years old) were more likely to answer the third question correctly than children younger than seven. They could distinguish between the **whole class** (wooden beads) and the **subclass** (brown beads) showing they can understand class inclusion.

3) Some psychologists argue that the third question in Piaget and Szeminksa's study is quite confusing. However, a study by **McGarrigle et al (1978)** used a more accessible version of the task involving cows **standing up** or **'sleeping'** (lying down). They found similar results to Piaget and Szeminksa.

There's Evidence *For* and *Against* Piaget's Stages of Cognitive Development

1) There's **cross-cultural similarity** in the stages — studies have suggested that children of all backgrounds progress through the stages in the same way, which provides **support** for Piaget's theory.

2) Piaget **underestimated abilities** at each age — for example, the experiment with Naughty Teddy showed that preoperational children **can** understand the concept of conservation.

3) He said that **practice** and **teaching wouldn't** speed up progression through the stages, but this isn't true — it's been found that teaching **can** help to move children on through the stages.

4) Piaget's **methodology** was also questionable. His use of **observations** and clinical **interviews** were open to **subjective** interpretation.

5) Piaget didn't think that **language** was important in cognitive development. He thought you needed **cognitive development first** in order to allow language to develop. But other theorists, such as **Vygotsky**, have taken a different view on this, as you'll find out on the next page...

Practice Questions

Q1 Name Piaget's four main stages of cognitive development.

Q2 Did McGarrigle and Donaldson's (1974) experiment provide evidence for or against Piaget's theory? Why?

Exam Questions

Q1 Emma's mother pours the same amount of juice into two glasses of different sizes. Emma thinks that the taller, thinner of the two glasses contains more juice. Which concept does Emma not understand?

    A conservation   **B** object permanence   **C** egocentrism   **D** class inclusion   [1 mark]

Q2 Describe and evaluate Piaget's theory of cognitive development.   [16 marks]

Naughty Teddy! You've wrecked my theory...

Piaget's stages were an attempt to explain how children's understanding of the world changes as they develop, and the stages do help to show this. The trouble with any stage theory is that they tend to overestimate any differences between stages, and underestimate differences between individuals within the same stage. Oh well, nothing's perfect I suppose...

Vygotsky's Theory of Cognitive Development

Another highly interesting theory on cognitive development coming up — over to you, Vygotsky.

Vygotsky Reckoned Culture Plays a Big Part in Cognitive Development

1) **Vygotsky** said there were two types of mental function — **elementary** and **higher**. Elementary functions can be thought of as **innate reflexes**, **sensory abilities** and certain types of **memory**. Higher functions include more complex tasks like **language comprehension** and **decision-making**.

2) **Social** and **cultural factors** play a necessary part in moving from one type of functioning to the other — it's the influence of **others** around you that drives cognitive development. Because of this, Vygotsky's theory is known as a **social interactionist theory**.

3) One of Vygotsky's ideas was the **zone of proximal development**. This is the difference between the problem solving a child can do on their **own** and the problem solving they can do with a **more able peer** or **adult**.

4) If your teacher has an idea of what your **potential** is, they can help you reach it by pushing and guiding. So it's **interaction** with the teacher that's important (unlike Piaget's idea that progression happens on its own).

5) Instruction is **social** and driven by the teacher using **language** and **cultural** influences. The intention is to help the child to be **self-regulated** and responsible for their own learning.

Language is Also Important in Cognitive Development

Vygotsky suggests that **language** is a **driving influence** on cognitive development:

1) Children first learn language as a means to **communicate** with caregivers. It's also a tool that allows adults to communicate **social** and **cultural information** to children.

2) As the child grows older they use language not only to communicate but also to **guide** their **behaviour** — they use **self-talk** (talking out loud) to **regulate** and **direct** themselves.

3) This self-talk eventually becomes **internalised** and becomes silent **inner speech**. At this point the child has developed two very different forms of language — **inner speech** and **external oral speech**.

4) **Oral speech** is used socially for **communication**, whilst **inner speech** is a **cognitive tool** that allows individuals to **direct** and **monitor** their **thoughts** and **behaviour**.

5) If someone finds a task difficult they may re-employ **self-talk** to exert greater **control** over their thoughts.

Vygotsky Also Came Up With Stages of Development

Vygotsky's stages **aren't as rigidly defined** as Piaget's — they're broader areas of development (without specified ages) giving an idea of the stages children go through as their thinking matures (**concept formation**).
He came up with these 4 stages after studying how children of various ages went about solving a problem:

1) **Vague syncretic** — **trial and error** methods are used, with **no understanding** of the underlying concepts.
2) **Complex** — use of **strategies** begins but they're **not** used successfully.
3) **Potential concept** — successful strategies are used but only **one at a time**.
4) **Mature concept** — **lots** of strategies used at the same time. Thinking becomes **mature** and **developed**.

Vygotsky's Theory Has Some Support

Vygotsky carried out **very few studies** whilst coming up with his theory. However, other people have carried out studies that have provided evidence that **supports** Vygotsky's theory:

1) **Gardner and Gardner (1969)** found that, with **instruction**, animals can reach **higher levels** of functioning. For example, they taught a chimp, Washoe, sign language and she passed down her knowledge to her adoptive son. This is evidence for the role of **culture** and **language** in learning.

2) **Chi et al (1989)** showed that pretending to **talk to the author** as you read (self-explanation) can help increase understanding. This is evidence for the use of speech in thought.

3) **Berk (1994)** found that children who used **more self-talk** when solving maths problems did better over the following year. This is evidence for the use of **self-talk** in problem-solving.

Vygotsky's Theory of Cognitive Development

Vygotsky's Theory Emphasises Social Interaction

Vygotsky's theory is a **teacher-guided approach** and suggests that **interactions** with others are important in learning. In other words, **other people** are needed to stimulate cognitive development. For example, **scaffolding** is an important concept developed from Vygotsky's theory where other people assist a child's cognitive development:

- **Scaffolding** is when a **teacher**, another **adult** or a **more cognitively advanced child** acts as an **expert** to guide the child.
- They do this by making suggestions or doing demonstrations to provide a **framework** by which the child learns to do a task.
- At first the child might need lots of help, but as they learn **less help** is needed, and they can carry on learning **independently**.
- For scaffolding to work it needs to take place within the child's **zone of proximal development** (see previous page).

Prof. Telfer's trainee teachers suddenly realised he didn't know what he was talking about.

Wood et al (1976) — The effectiveness of scaffolding

Method:	**Thirty** children aged 3–5 were given the task of building a model and were **observed**. A **tutor** gave help to each child according to how well they were doing — the help was either in the form of showing or telling.
Results:	Scaffolding allowed the children to complete a task they **wouldn't** have been able to do alone. The **effectiveness** of the scaffolding was influenced by various factors, e.g. how the tutor **simplified** the task, and how they helped them **identify important steps**. **Showing** was used most when helping **younger** children, whilst **telling** was used more with the **older** children. Also, the **older** the child was the **less** scaffolding was needed for them to complete the task.
Conclusion:	Scaffolding **can** be helpful but consideration needs to be given to **maximise** its effectiveness.
Evaluation:	This study had fairly **good ecological validity**, but there was less control over variables, **reducing reliability**.

Vygotsky's Theory Has Some Weaknesses

Although Vygotsky's theory can be **successfully applied to education**, it has some limitations:

1) Some psychologists think that the theory over-emphasises social and cultural factors in intelligence and **ignores biological factors**.

2) Vygotsky didn't give any suggestions of the **cognitive processes** that might underlie development.

On a positive note, improved teaching methods due to influence from psychological theories can help to better educate children. It's these children who will be entering the workforce next, so better education leads to a more productive workforce and therefore a better economy.

Practice Questions

Q1 What is the zone of proximal development?

Q2 According to Vygotsky, what is inner speech used for?

Q3 Outline two pieces of evidence that support Vygotsky's theory of cognitive development.

Exam Questions

Q1	Briefly outline how a teacher could use scaffolding to help the cognitive development of his pupils.	[2 marks]
Q2	Explain one limitation of Vygotsky's theory of cognitive development.	[2 marks]

It'll take me a week just to learn how to spell ~~Vgyot~~ ~~Vyogt~~ Vygotsky...

I wonder how many different spellings of Vygotsky's name crop up on exam papers... Quite a few, I imagine. If you're like me and struggle to remember how to spell your own name, it's worth taking the time to learn it now. Vygotsky, that is — not your name. If you really can't spell that by now I doubt you'll ever be able to. Sorry to be the one to tell you.

Early Infant Abilities

When one psychologist has come up with a theory, others like to come along and point out why it's not right.
Baillargeon came along and pointed out why she thought some of Piaget's ideas needed a bit of a tweak. Read on...

Baillargeon Looked At Object Expectations

Remember, object permanence means understanding that just because you can no longer see something, it doesn't mean that it's not there.

1) Piaget put forward in his theory of cognitive development that infants develop **object permanence** during the sensorimotor stage. He thought that this was at around **8 to 12 months**.

2) Baillargeon **disagreed** with this — she believed that what Piaget was classing as a lack of object permanence was actually just a **lack of motor ability** to be able to carry out searches for the objects in the studies.

3) From her own studies, she believed that infants develop object permanence at a much **younger** age than Piaget had originally said.

4) Baillargeon suggested that infants are born with very basic expectations about objects. These **innate** abilities would then develop as infants **interact** with the world and learn to more accurately **predict** the outcome of events.

5) Piaget and Baillargeon's theories disagree on how much understanding a child is born with. Baillargeon is a **nativist** — she believes that infants are born with some understanding. Piaget was an **interactionist** — he believed that infants are born with the cognitive ability to understand the world, but that all their understanding is learnt through experience.

Baillargeon Carried Out Violation of Expectation Research

1) Baillargeon's studies were designed differently to Piaget's — rather than requiring the infants to physically search for a hidden object, Baillargeon compared the time that infants spent **looking** at events that were either impossible or possible.

2) Baillargeon's studies became known as **violation of expectation (VOE)** research. Here's the idea:

- VOE research is based on the idea that infants will look at **new** things for **longer** than they'll look at things they've encountered before. Infants become **habituated** to (they respond less to) situations they've seen before.

- In VOE research, the infant is presented with a **new stimulus**. This is shown to them until they look away — looking away shows that they have been habituated to the stimulus and no longer consider it to be new.

- The infants are then shown **two new stimuli**. They're both **similar** to the stimulus that they have just been habituated to. However, one of these stimuli is a **possible event** (something that could physically happen), and one is an **impossible event** (one that seems like it couldn't physically happen in the real world).

- If the infants have object permanence, they'll look at the **impossible event** for **significantly longer**.

One Study Used an Impossible Drawbridge...

Baillargeon found evidence that infants as young as **five months** understood object permanence.

	Baillargeon et al (1985) — The impossible drawbridge study
Method:	**Five-month-old** infants were habituated to a drawbridge that moved through 180°. They were then shown two new stimuli where a box was placed in the path of the drawbridge. In the **possible** event, the drawbridge came to a stop when it came into contact with the box. In the **impossible** event, the drawbridge looked like it passed through the box.
Results:	The infants looked for **significantly longer** at the **impossible event**.
Conclusion:	The infants looked longer at the impossible event because they were surprised. They were aware that the box was behind the drawbridge and knew that the drawbridge **shouldn't** be able to pass through it. The five-month-old infants had **object permanence**.

Early Infant Abilities

... and Another Used a *Truck* and a *Ramp*

	Baillargeon (1987) — Another impossible event study
Method:	**Three-month-old** infants were habituated to a truck rolling down a ramp and then passing behind a screen. The infants then watched the screen being removed, and a box being placed either **beside** the track or **on** the track (where it would **block** the truck from passing). The screen was then put back. In both the possible and impossible events, the truck passed behind the screen and appeared at the other side.
Results:	Infants looked for **significantly longer** at the **impossible event**.
Conclusion:	Infants knew that the box was still behind the screen even though they couldn't see it, and knew that it should have blocked the truck from passing by. Three-month-old infants show evidence of **object permanence**.

Baillargeon's Research Has *Strengths* and *Weaknesses*

Baillargeon's research has provided a lot of **evidence** that very young infants do have knowledge of the physical world — they understand that objects are still there even if they can't be seen. Her studies were **laboratory experiments**, which meant that variables could be **controlled** and the effect of **extraneous variables** reduced. Some other psychologists have used Baillargeon's **VOE methods** in their studies and have produced **supporting results**.

However, some psychologists have **criticised** her work:

1) Some psychologists have suggested that the infants in the studies weren't responding to the fact that the situation was impossible, and that they were just noticing a **difference** from the stimulus they'd been habituated to. These psychologists have suggested that Baillargeon has drawn a conclusion **beyond** what the data showed.

2) The infants are unable to **communicate** their thoughts and so the data relies on how the researchers **interpret** the infants' behaviour. It might be that 'looking time' doesn't indicate surprise, and therefore object permanence, at all.

3) **Rivera et al (1999)** carried out VOE research but found that there was **no difference** in the amount of time that infants looked at a possible versus an impossible event. Other psychologists have also **failed** to **replicate** Baillargeon's findings.

Practice Questions

Q1 When did Piaget think that infants develop object permanence?
Q2 Does Baillargeon hold a nativist or interactionist view of early infant abilities?
Q3 What was Baillargeon's research involving possible and impossible scenarios known as?
Q4 What is meant by habituation?
Q5 Give one criticism of Baillargeon's research.

Exam Questions

Q1	Briefly outline Baillargeon's explanation of early infant abilities.	[4 marks]
Q2	Discuss the use of violation of expectation research.	[16 marks]

Expecting a cuppa at the end of each page...?

Well, you're going to get your expectations violated. Sorry. There's an extra charge for that service. Anyway, the examiners have some expectations themselves. They're expecting you to have learnt this stuff, so there's only one thing for it. Give it another read, and check that you've got all the facts straight. If you haven't, head to the top again.

Development of Social Cognition

Social cognition involves understanding about yourself and others, and being able to see things from other people's perspective. So, for example, I know that I'm awesome and that you're probably not having much fun right now...

A *Sense of Self* Develops During Childhood

Having a **sense of self** includes things like:

- being able to **distinguish** between self and others, and referring to each with **appropriate language**
- having knowledge of our **experiences**, **abilities**, **motivations**, etc.
- having ideas about **body image**

Important stages during development include:

1) **Existential self** — from about three months old we learn to **distinguish** self from non-self, and find out that we exist separately from other things. The development of **object permanence** (see p.70) may help this.

2) **Categorical self** — from about two years old we start to use language to **describe ourselves**, using culturally defined categories, e.g. age, male/female, tall/short, etc. We are also described by **other people** in this way, which can influence our idea of ourself. For example, describing a child as 'clever' or 'naughty' could influence their **self-esteem**.

3) **Identity crisis** — Erikson (1968) claimed that during **adolescence**, when going through body changes and starting to make plans for the future, we may **try out** different roles until we find our true identity.

Having a sense of self also involves being able to see yourself as **others** see you.
This requires some understanding of the minds of others, and being able to see things from **their perspective**.

Theory of Mind (ToM) is About Understanding Other People's Minds

Humans have a unique ability to **cooperate** and carry out **complex interactions**. It's thought this is possible because we have a **theory of mind**. This involves **understanding that we and others have minds** with knowledge, feelings, beliefs, motivations, intentions, etc. We can **explain** and **predict** other people's behaviour by making inferences about their mental states. This includes the knowledge that others may have **false beliefs** about the world.

Problems with ToM have been linked to the **social** and **communication difficulties** associated with **autism**.

> Autism is a developmental disorder. People with autism often have trouble interacting and communicating with others.

Baron-Cohen et al (1985) — The Sally-Anne study

Method:	Three groups were studied — children with autism with an average age of 12 years, children with Down's Syndrome with an average age of 11 years, and 'normal' children with an average age of 4 years. The experiment used two dolls — Sally had a basket, Anne a box. Children were asked to name the dolls (the **naming question**). Then Sally was seen to hide a marble in her basket and leave the room. Anne took the marble and put it in her box. Sally returned and the child was asked, 'Where will Sally look for her marble?' (**belief question**). The correct response is to point to the basket, where Sally believes the marble to be. They were also asked, 'Where is the marble really?' (**reality question**) and 'Where was the marble in the beginning?' (**memory question**). Each child was tested again with the marble in a different place.
Results:	**All** of the children got the **naming**, **reality** and **memory** questions correct. In the **belief** question, the children with Down's Syndrome scored **86%**, the 'normal' children **85%**, but the children with autism scored **20%**.
Conclusion:	The findings suggest that children with autism have an **under-developed theory of mind**, sometimes called **mind-blindness**. They seem unable to predict or understand the beliefs of others.
Evaluation:	Dolls were used in the study so it lacked **ecological validity**. Also, children with autism may in fact have a more highly developed theory of mind and understand that dolls don't have beliefs. Repeating the study by acting out the scenes with **humans** might show an increase in ability on the tasks. However, **Leslie and Frith (1988)** did a similar study with real people and not dolls and found the same pattern of results.

According to evidence, most children develop ToM at around **four** years old. However, the kind of questions asked in Baron-Cohen et al's false belief task may be difficult for younger children to understand. It seems that **three-year-old** children can pass some versions of the test, so ToM may actually develop **earlier**.

There's also disagreement about the **development** of ToM. It may have an **innate** basis, but **nurture** and **experience** are also likely to be important in its development.

Development of Social Cognition

Understanding Others Involves *Perspective-taking*

One aspect of having a ToM is understanding that other people's **perspectives** can differ from your own. Children gradually become more skilful in their **perspective-taking ability**. **Selman (1980)** studied children's perspective-taking ability by analysing their responses to stories presenting dilemmas. For example:

> Selman told children a story about a girl who could rescue a friend's cat by climbing a tree. However, she'd promised her father that she wouldn't climb trees. Selman asked the children if she should be punished if she did climb the tree.

Like all children, Molly had perfected the "who, me?" look. She knew Daddy wouldn't mind about the tree.

From the children's answers, Selman identified **five** levels of **perspective-taking**:

1) **Undifferentiated and Egocentric** — up to about six years of age, children can separate **self** and **other**, but in a physical sense only. They don't perceive any psychological differences, seeing the other person in the same way they see an object.

2) **Differentiated and Subjective** — from five to nine, children understand that other people have **different perspectives** because they have access to **different information** (i.e. know different things). However, only their own perspective is seen as important and they can't take the perspective of the other person.

3) **Second-Person and Reciprocal** — between seven and twelve, children can put themselves in someone else's shoes and view a situation from **another's perspective**. They also realise that other people can do the same.

4) **Third-Person and Mutual** — between ten and fifteen years old, children develop the ability to take the perspective of a **third impartial person** who's viewing an interaction between other people.

5) **In-Depth and Societal-Symbolic** — from about fourteen, children understand that **third-party perspectives** can be influenced by factors such as **social or cultural values**. They can see a situation from a variety of different perspectives, e.g. moral, legal, etc.

As children go through these stages they become better able to understand that other people have different perspectives, and can use information to put themselves in other people's shoes.

Selman's ideas about perspective-taking can have **practical applications** in **education**. For example, using **multi-cultural** materials and having **class discussions** can expose children to different perspectives. This may help to promote their perspective-taking ability.

Practice Questions

Q1 Explain what is meant by 'existential self', 'categorical self' and 'identity crisis'.

Q2 How does Baron-Cohen et al's false belief task show whether or not a child has a theory of mind?

Q3 How did Selman study perspective-taking ability?

Q4 Give one way that Selman's theory can be applied to education.

Exam Questions

Q1 Describe and evaluate research that supports theory of mind as an explanation for autism.   [8 marks]

Q2 Outline Selman's theory on the development of social cognition.   [6 marks]

Actually, I took the marble while your back was turned and swallowed it...

One of my friends at school definitely went through that identity crisis thing. He started out as an emo kid, suddenly went really sporty and obsessed with football, and then for a term he seemed to think he was a rapper. He also spent nearly a whole year dressing like a cowboy. I think he's settled down now though — last I heard he was an accountant.

The Mirror Neuron System

Here comes the science bit — all about the biological basis for social cognition. I knew you'd be thrilled. Enjoy.

Social Cognition Has a Biological Basis

1) **Neurons** in the cerebral cortex are organised into **four** main areas: the **frontal**, **temporal**, **parietal** and **occipital** lobes.

2) Different processes, such as **visual perception**, involve one or more of these lobes. Some areas of the brain seem to have very specialised roles in **cognition**.

3) It seems likely that many of our sophisticated **social** abilities, such as **theory of mind** (see page 76), also involve complex brain mechanisms — these may have **evolved** as our brains and intelligence grew. Abilities like this could have been stimulated by our complex **social living**.

4) Attempts have been made to **connect** findings from neuroscience and social psychology and combine them into more complete theories — this is known as **social neuroscience**.

Mirror Neurons Respond to the Actions of Others

Mirror neurons are brain cells that are involved in **performing** an action, such as holding a cup. However, they're **also** active when you **observe** someone else doing the same action. So, whether you're actually holding a cup, or only observing someone else holding a cup, particular mirror neurons will be **active**.

	Di Pellegrino et al (1992) — Recording neuron activity
Method:	**Electrodes** were inserted into individual neurons in the **premotor cortex** of macaque monkeys. When the monkeys reached for food, the **activity** in the neurons was recorded.
Results:	The neurons were **active** when the monkeys reached for food, but also, unexpectedly, active when they observed **someone else** reach for food.
Conclusion:	This was the **first** study to provide evidence for the existence of **mirror neurons**. Although the function of mirror neurons is not yet clear, they may help in understanding observed behaviour.
Evaluation:	The experiment was **not** designed to study mirror neurons, so the information gathered about them was **limited**. Also, it involved inserting electrodes into animals' brains, which raises **ethical issues**.

It's hard to record the activity of individual neurons in the brains of **humans**. So, studies have been done using brain scanning techniques such as **functional Magnetic Resonance Imaging** (fMRI, see page 14), which analyse **brain activity** during particular kinds of behaviours. For example, Iacoboni et al (1999) found that there are areas of the **frontal** and **parietal cortex** that are active when people carry out and observe actions.

Mirror Neurons May Be Important for Social Cognition

Neurons that are active both when **you** do something and when you see **other people** do the same thing may help you **understand** the behaviour of others.

	Fogassi et al (2005) — Mirror neurons and intentions
Method:	The activity of **41 mirror neurons** in 2 macaque monkeys were recorded as they observed a person pick up an apple as if to eat it, or pick up the apple and place it in a cup.
Results:	**Different** groups of neurons responded to the two outcomes (eat or place). Also, some neurons fired **after** the apple was picked up but **before** the second action (eat or place) was carried out.
Conclusion:	Different patterns of response link with different **behavioural objectives** and some neurons seem to predict the **intention** of actions. So, mirror neurons may help to **understand** and **predict** the behaviour of others.
Evaluation:	Animals may behave differently under lab conditions, meaning the experiment has **low ecological validity**. Also, the experiment was carried out on monkeys so it's difficult to **generalise** the results to humans — neurons in humans may not respond in the same way.

Experiments with **humans** using **fMRI** show that brain areas that are active when we feel particular emotions (e.g. happiness or pain) are also active when we see others feel the same emotion. This supports suggestions that mirror neurons may be involved in **empathy**.

The Mirror Neuron System

There's a Lot of **Debate** About the **Role** of Mirror Neurons

1) The **function** and **importance** of mirror neurons is not yet fully understood. For example, they may be involved in **imitation** — but macaque monkeys (which have mirror neurons) have a **limited ability** for imitation learning.

2) A connection between mirror neurons and **theory of mind (ToM)** has also been debated. However, mirror neurons are found in monkeys that **don't** seem to have ToM in the same way that humans do. Also, **fMRI research** shows that ToM tests activate brain regions that **aren't** generally thought to be part of the mirror neuron system. It may be that mirror neurons can be involved in **learning by imitation**, but that the development of ToM involves **more** than this.

3) More needs to be learnt about the **development** of mirror neurons. **Falck-Ytter (2006)** reckoned that mirror neurons start to develop during the **first year** of life. However, **Meltzoff and Moore (1977)** found that human infants can imitate facial expressions **soon after birth**. This could either suggest that mirror neurons have an **innate** basis, or else that imitation **doesn't** necessarily involve mirror neurons.

Social Neuroscience Has Raised *Important Issues*

Jake and Milo still couldn't understand human social cognition. But at least they had each other.

1) **Social neuroscience** is **inter-disciplinary** — it involves both **biological** and **social** concepts and theories. These different types of theories may **mutually inform** each other — biological research can help understand social processes better, and vice versa. This means we can understand behaviour at different levels of explanation.

2) This approach may bring important **insights** into human **social cognition** (e.g. the basis of **empathy**). Also, some conditions associated with developmental problems (e.g. **autism**) might be better understood.

3) Animal experiments involve invasive methods, e.g. inserting electrodes into the brain — this raises **ethical issues**.

Practice Questions

Q1 What are mirror neurons?

Q2 How have mirror neurons been studied in animals and in humans?

Q3 Who first identified mirror neurons?

Q4 Outline a piece of evidence supporting the idea that mirror neurons may be involved in empathy.

Q5 Why is social neuroscience a particularly valuable new field of research?

Q6 What ethical issues could be associated with mirror neuron research?

Exam Question

Q1 Outline and evaluate research on the role of the mirror neuron system. [16 marks]

OK, he's picking up the cup — ready neurons... aim... and fire...

This is an interesting little topic to end the section with — it's fairly new stuff and nobody knows quite what's going on yet. There are new ideas springing up and being shot down all over the place. And to think, if a monkey hadn't happened to look over and see someone picking up some food, these pages might never have existed.

Diagnosing Schizophrenia

*A lot of people think that schizophrenia involves having multiple personalities, but it **really really doesn't**, so don't make this mistake in the exam or else you'll look like a right banana. And nobody wants to look like a right banana.*

Schizophrenia Disrupts the Mind's Ability to Function

'Schizophrenia' literally means 'split mind'.

1) **Schizophrenia** is a **thought process disorder**. It's characterised by **disruption** to a person's **perceptions**, **emotions** and **beliefs**.

2) The onset of schizophrenia can be **acute** (a **sudden** onset, where behaviour changes within a few days), or **chronic** (a **gradual** deterioration in mental health that develops slowly over time).

3) **Males** and **females** are **equally** affected. In **males**, schizophrenia usually develops in their **late teens** or **early 20s**, while **females** tend to develop it 4 or 5 years **later**. Overall, **0.5%** of the population is affected.

4) It's thought that schizophrenia **isn't** a **single disorder** but that there are various **subtypes** — however, there still **isn't** an agreed **definition**.

Schizophrenia has Lots of Different Clinical Characteristics

People with schizophrenia can experience a **range** of possible **symptoms**:

1. Perceptual symptoms

- **Auditory hallucinations** — **hearing** things that **aren't there**. People often hear **voices** saying **abusive** things.
- Auditory hallucinations are the **most common** type of hallucination in schizophrenia, but there are **other types** of hallucination too. Sometimes people **see**, **feel**, **smell** or **taste** things that aren't there.

2. Social symptoms

- **Social withdrawal** — not **taking part** in or **enjoying** social situations.
- People might be **aloof** or **avoid eye contact**.

3. Cognitive symptoms

- **Delusions** — **believing** things that **aren't true**. People can have **delusions** of **grandeur** (where they believe they're more **important** than they are, e.g. that they're the king) or of **paranoia** and **persecution** (where they believe people are out to **get them**). Some people with schizophrenia also experience **delusions** of **control** — they believe that their **behaviour** is being **controlled** by **somebody else**. For example, **thought insertion** is when someone feels that thoughts are being put into their head. **Thought withdrawal** is when they believe that someone is **removing** their thoughts. They might also believe that **people** can **read** their thoughts — this is **thought broadcasting**.
- **Language impairments** — **irrelevant** and **incoherent** speech. People often show signs of **cognitive distractibility**, where they **can't maintain a train of thought**. They might also **repeat sounds others say** (echolalia), speak **nonsense** or **gibberish** (word salad), speak in **nonsensical rhymes** (clang associations), experience **speech poverty** (give **very brief replies** in conversation and show **no** extra, spontaneous speech) and **invent words** (neologisms).

4. Affective / emotional symptoms

- **Avolition** — a **lack** of **drive**, **motivation** or **interest** in achieving **goals**.
- Lack of **interest** in **hygiene** and **personal care**.
- Lack of **emotion** — **not reacting** to typically emotional situations. This is also called **emotional blunting**.
- **Inappropriate emotions** — **reacting** in an **inappropriate** way, e.g. laughing at bad news.

5. Behavioural symptoms

- **Stereotyped behaviours** — continuously **repeating** actions, which are often **strange** and **don't** have a **purpose**.
- **Psychomotor disturbance** — **not** having **control** of your **muscles**. People may experience **catatonia**, where they sit in an **awkward position** for a **long time**. In this state people will sometimes **stay** in whatever position they're **put** in (so if you lift their arm over their head it'll stay like that **until** you move it **back**). **Catatonic stupor** involves lying **rigidly** and **not moving** for **long periods** of **time**. People are **conscious** during these episodes and can **remember** what was going on **around** them, although they **don't** seem **aware** of it at the **time**.

Diagnosing Schizophrenia

Schizophrenia has **Positive** and **Negative** Symptoms

The symptoms experienced by people with schizophrenia can be split into **two** types — **positive** and **negative** symptoms. Positive and negative symptoms **don't mean** they're 'good' or 'bad' symptoms. They refer to whether experiences and behaviours are **extra** (positive) or **lacking** (negative).

Positive Symptoms

This is where people **experience** something, feel that something is **happening** to them, or **display** certain **behaviours** — they are **extra** experiences and behaviours that are **not** normally there.

They include:
- **hallucinations**
- **delusions**
- **jumbled speech**
- **disorganised behaviour**

Negative Symptoms

This is where people **don't** display 'normal' behaviours — these symptoms are a **lack** of experiences or behaviours which **are** normally there.

They include:
- **speech poverty**
- **lack of emotion**
- **avolition (becoming disinterested)**
- **lack of ability to function normally**

Positive symptoms are also known as Type 1 symptoms, and negative symptoms are also known as Type 2 symptoms.

The **DSM** Classifies Mental Disorders

1) The **DSM** is the American Psychiatric Association's Diagnostic and Statistical Manual of Mental Disorders (you'll probably remember the DSM from Year 1).

2) It contains a list of **mental health disorders**, outlining the symptoms themselves and how long these symptoms should be present for, to result in a **diagnosis**.

3) It aims to give diagnosis of mental disorders **reliability** and **validity**:

Reliability
Reliability is how far the classification system produces the **same diagnosis** for a particular set of symptoms. In order for a classification system to be reliable the **same diagnosis** should be made **each time** it's used. This means that **different clinicians** should reach the **same diagnosis**.

Validity
Validity is whether the classification system is actually measuring what it **aims to measure**.

- **Descriptive validity** — how similar individuals diagnosed with the disorder are.

- **Aetiological validity** — how similar the cause of the disorder is for each sufferer.

- **Predictive validity** — how useful the diagnostic categories are for predicting the right treatment.

4) For a person to be diagnosed as having schizophrenia, the DSM states that they must show **at least two** of:
- delusions
- hallucinations
- disorganised speech
- disorganised or catatonic behaviour
- any negative symptoms

At least one of their symptoms must be from the first three of these (delusions, hallucinations or disorganised speech).

Their symptoms have to have been present for **at least six months**, with at least **one month** of active symptoms.

Diagnosing Schizophrenia

There can be *Problems* with the *Reliability* and *Validity* of *Diagnoses*

Problems with reliability

1) Schizophrenia diagnosis may be affected by **cultural bias**. For example, **Harrison et al (1984)** showed that there was an **over-diagnosis** of schizophrenia in **West Indian** psychiatric patients in Bristol. No research has found any cause for this, so it suggests that the **symptoms** of **ethnic minority** patients have been **misinterpreted**. This questions the **reliability** of the diagnosis of schizophrenia — it suggests that patients can display the **same symptoms** but receive **different diagnoses** because of their ethnic background.

2) **Cultural bias** has also been shown to stem from the medical staff themselves. **Copeland et al (1971)** found that **69%** of **American** psychiatrists in the study diagnosed a particular patient (shown in a video) as having schizophrenia compared with only **2%** of British psychiatrists asked to diagnose the same patient.

3) Reliably diagnosing schizophrenia can also be difficult due to **gender bias**. Loring and Powell (1988) conducted a study where 290 psychiatrists were asked to diagnose the same two patients. When they were told the patient was male, **56%** diagnosed the patient as having schizophrenia. If they were told the patient was female, this dropped to around **20%**, despite symptoms being **identical**. This gender bias wasn't as clear if the psychiatrists were female. So, gender bias comes not only from the gender of the **patient**, but also from the gender of the **practitioner**.

Problems with validity

1) **Rosenhan (1973)** conducted a study where people with no mental health problem got themselves admitted into a **psychiatric unit** by saying they heard voices — they became **pseudopatients**. Once they'd been admitted they behaved 'normally'. However, their behaviour was still seen as a **symptom** of their **disorder** by the staff in the unit. For example, one pseudopatient who wrote in a diary was recorded as displaying 'writing behaviour'. This questions the **validity** of the **diagnosis** of mental disorders — once people are **labelled** as having a disorder, all of their behaviour can be **interpreted** as being **caused** by the **disorder**.

2) **Symptom overlap** can also cause problems with the validity of diagnosis. Lots of the **most common** symptoms in schizophrenia are also found in **other disorders**. For example, **avolition** is also a symptom of depression. This makes it hard to determine which disorder the patient may have.

Comorbidity Can be a Problem Too...

- **Comorbidity** can also be an issue in making a **reliable** and **valid** diagnosis of schizophrenia.
- Comorbidity means having **two or more** conditions at the same time. For example, patients with **schizophrenia** may also have **depression**. Having **more than one** condition makes it really **difficult** for healthcare professionals to diagnose schizophrenia as a **distinct** mental illness.
- It could be that some of their symptoms belong to one known disorder, but that the others belong to an **untreated** mental disorder which **hasn't** been **recognised** yet.

Practice Questions

Q1 When does schizophrenia most often develop in males and females?
Q2 What are delusions?
Q3 What is meant by avolition?
Q4 What is the difference between positive and negative symptoms of schizophrenia?

Exam Question

Q1 Describe how schizophrenia is diagnosed, and evaluate the issues surrounding its diagnosis.   [16 marks]

Word salad — like crunchy alphabet spaghetti...

Like so many things in psychology, schizophrenia is incredibly hard to define. People can show a variety of symptoms, which can be classified in different ways. Learning this is a bit of a pain now, but at least it means you should have loads to say in the exam, and you can't really ask for more than that. Well, apart from a holiday in the Caribbean...

Explanations of Schizophrenia

Different people have different ideas about what causes schizophrenia. This was mostly a sneaky little ploy dreamt up by psychologists and examiners to make your revision harder. OK, that's not strictly true, but it does feel like it sometimes.

Schizophrenia Could be Caused by Biological Factors

> Concordance rates show the chance that both people in a pair have a disorder, given one of them does.

Genetic Factors

Being **genetically related** to someone with schizophrenia can significantly **increase** a person's **chances** of developing it. **Family** and **twin** studies have looked at **concordance rates**:

Gottesman (1991) reviewed about 40 twin studies and found that with **identical (MZ) twins** there was about a **48%** concordance rate (i.e. there is a **48% chance** that one MZ twin will have schizophrenia if the other does). With **non-identical (DZ) twins** the concordance rate was about **17%**. This is significant because, if it's assumed that MZ and DZ twins share the same amount of environmental influences, it means the reason for increased concordance is the **genetic difference** — MZ twins share **100%** of their genes, compared to DZ who share **50%**.

Evidence for...

1) **Shields (1962)** found **MZ twins** raised in **different families** still showed around **50%** concordance.

2) **Adoption studies** found that if children are **adopted** because one or both of their **biological parents** has schizophrenia, the **chance** of them developing it stays the **same**. It suggests that **genetics** are more significant than the **environment**.

Evidence against...

1) No study has found a **100%** concordance rate between MZ twins, so schizophrenia **can't** just be caused by **genes**. **Shared environment** may cause higher concordance rates in **family** studies because children **imitate** 'schizophrenic' **behaviours**.

2) This means **other factors** need to be considered, e.g. biochemical or psychological factors.

Biochemical Factors

Post-mortems and **PET scans** have shown that people with schizophrenia have abnormally high levels of the neurotransmitter **dopamine**. These findings led to the development of the **dopamine hypothesis**, which states that **synapses** that use **dopamine** as a **neurotransmitter** are **overactive** in the brains of people with schizophrenia.

Evidence for...

1) **Antipsychotic** drugs **reduce** the **symptoms** of schizophrenia by **blocking** dopamine receptors. This suggests that it's the **overactive** dopamine receptors **causing** the symptoms.

2) Drugs like **amphetamines**, which **increase dopamine function**, can sometimes cause **schizophrenia-like** symptoms in people without schizophrenia.

Evidence against...

1) **Antipsychotic** drugs only work on the **positive symptoms** of schizophrenia, e.g. hallucinations. This means increased dopamine function **doesn't** explain **negative symptoms** like social withdrawal.

2) The **link** with dopamine is **correlational**, so it doesn't show **cause and effect**. It may be that increased dopamine function is a **symptom** of schizophrenia, rather than a cause of it.

Neurological Factors

> A neural correlate is something within the brain that can be linked to a behaviour or condition.

Neural correlates, such as **abnormal brain structure**, could explain schizophrenia.

Evidence for...

1) **Johnstone et al (1976)** compared the **size** of the **ventricles** (hollow areas) in the brains of people with schizophrenia with the brains of those without schizophrenia. They found that the people with schizophrenia had **enlarged ventricles**, which suggests that **schizophrenia** is **linked** to a **reduction** in the **temporal** and **frontal lobe** volume.

2) **Buchsbaum's (1990) MRI scans** on the brains of people with schizophrenia found **abnormalities** in the **prefrontal cortex**.

Evidence against...

1) **People without schizophrenia** can also have **enlarged ventricles**, showing the relationship isn't that simple.

2) These findings are **correlational**, so they don't show **cause and effect**. It may be that abnormal brain structure is a **symptom** of schizophrenia, rather than a cause of it.

Explanations of Schizophrenia

Evolutionary Explanation

- Some **evolutionary** explanations of schizophrenia suggests that there must have been an **advantage** to having schizophrenia for it to remain in the population.
- One evolutionary idea is that people diagnosed with schizophrenia today share **similar characteristics** to **shamans** of the past.
- They were likely to lead people to **split off** from a group when it got too big, starting new cultures.

Evidence for...	There is such a **strong genetic link** to schizophrenia, that there **must** be some form of evolutionary explanation.
Evidence against...	There is little **evidence** and the theory is **difficult** to **prove**.

The evolutionary explanation for schizophrenia is generally discredited.

Schizophrenia Could be Caused by Psychological Factors

Family Dysfunction

- Psychologists have suggested that conditions in **dysfunctional families** could cause schizophrenia.
- One idea is that a **cold** and **dominant** 'schizophrenogenic' mother could **create conflict**, causing **schizophrenia**.
- Another idea is Bateson's (1956) **Double Bind Theory**, which suggested that **faulty communication** in families could lead to **contradictory messages** for children and cause schizophrenia.
- **Expressed emotion (EE)** environments contain high levels of **hostility** and **criticism** towards the person with schizophrenia. EE has been found in dysfunctional families and **correlates** with **relapse** in people with schizophrenia. For example, **Vaughn and Leff (1976)** found that people with schizophrenia were **more likely** to **relapse** once discharged from hospital in environments of **high EE**.

Evidence for...	Other research investigating the role of the family on schizophrenia **supports** the theory of family dysfunction. For example, **Lidz et al (1958)** investigated families and proposed that **dysfunctions** such as emotionally distant parents and unequal marriages could have an impact on the children in the family, ultimately leading to schizophrenia.

Evidence against...	The theory **ignores** the **biological evidence** for schizophrenia and puts the **blame** on the **family** and **parents**. Most of the studies into the effects of family dysfunction were also retrospective — the families were only studied **after** the disorder had developed, and so it could have been the condition itself that had disrupted family life.

Research into family dysfunction as a cause of schizophrenia has been criticised for having poor methodology, so it's generally discredited as a theory.

Cognitive Explanations

- **Cognitive** psychologists argue that schizophrenia is caused by **dysfunctional thought processing**.
- This leads to **delusions**, **thought interference**, **language impairment** and **memory problems**.

Evidence for...	1) **Neufeld (1978)** compared the cognitive processes of people with schizophrenia with a **control** group. Participants with schizophrenia took **longer** to **encode stimuli** and showed **short-term memory problems**. This suggests their ability to process information was impaired.
	2) **Meyer-Lindenberg et al (2002)** found that people with schizophrenia did worse in a **memory** and **reasoning** task, showing **reduced activity** in the area of the brain associated with this.

Evidence against...	1) **Biochemical** research suggests that **cognitive** problems are **caused** by **increased dopamine function**, rather than faulty information processing. So the faulty information processing may be a **result** of increased dopamine levels, meaning it's a **symptom**, not a **cause** of schizophrenia.
	2) Cognitive explanations don't exclusively **explain** the cause of schizophrenia — they might need to be linked to **biological explanations**.

Explanations of Schizophrenia

Socio-cultural Factors

The **social causation hypothesis** states that people with **low social status** are more likely to suffer from schizophrenia than people with higher social status. It's thought that factors like **poverty** and **discrimination** cause **high stress levels**, and that this can cause schizophrenia.

Evidence for...	**Harrison et al (2001)** found that people who were born in **deprived areas** were more likely to develop schizophrenia. This suggests that factors like **poverty**, **unemployment** and **crowding** have an **impact** on schizophrenia.
Evidence against...	These results are **correlational**, so they **don't** show **cause and effect**. The **social drift hypothesis** suggests that there are more people with schizophrenia in deprived areas because having schizophrenia gives them a **lower social status**, e.g. because they might be unemployed.

The Diathesis-Stress Model Combines Biological and Psychological Factors

1) The **biological approach** to schizophrenia has been **criticised** for being a **reductionist** theory.

2) It attempts to explain schizophrenia by reducing it down into the **simplest**, **smallest components** possible, such as **genetics**, **neurotransmitters** and **parts of the brain**.

3) An **interactionist approach** does the **opposite** — it assumes that processes interact with each other to cause behaviour.

4) For instance, to explain schizophrenia, an interactionist approach looks at a **combination** of **biological** and **psychological** factors:

Interactionism is a holistic approach — you can read more about holistic approaches on page 45.

The **diathesis-stress model** proposes that people who are **biologically vulnerable** to developing a mental disorder may be **more likely** to develop it if they are subjected to certain social or **environmental stressors**.

Lots of **research** has been conducted in this area. The fact that **concordance rates** in twin studies (see page 47) aren't 100% indicates that there does seem to be some **genetic link**, but that other factors must play a role as well.

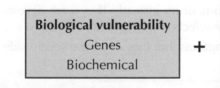

Biological vulnerability
Genes
Biochemical

+

Environmental stressor
E.g. Job worries
Family Problems
Money worries

→ **Schizophrenia**

Practice Questions

Q1 Outline the role that dopamine might have in causing schizophrenia.

Q2 Outline how family dysfunction could explain schizophrenia.

Q3 Give an example of an environmental stressor that could cause schizophrenia according to the diathesis-stress model.

Exam Questions

Q1 Read the item below then answer the question that follows.

> Rosie has just had a PET scan. It showed that she has enlarged ventricles, which has reduced the volume of her temporal lobe. Doctors have also identified abnormalities in her prefrontal cortex.

Use the biological approach to explain why Rosie may be experiencing symptoms of schizophrenia. [2 marks]

Q2 Briefly outline how the diathesis-stress model explains schizophrenia. [4 marks]

Q3 Discuss psychological explanations for schizophrenia. [16 marks]

Explain schizophrenia? I can barely even spell it...

So there isn't just one definite idea about what causes schizophrenia — surprise surprise. At least these pages are useful though. When you're evaluating one explanation of schizophrenia, you can use all the other explanations as evidence against it — so you could use the evidence for genetic factors as evidence against cognitive explanations. Or whatever.

Treating Schizophrenia

There are a number of different treatments for schizophrenia, and most people benefit from having a combination of a few of them. Lots to learn here. First up, antipsychotics...

Schizophrenia Can be Treated Using Biological Therapy

Therapy using drugs is also called chemotherapy.

1) The **biological** approach to treating schizophrenia involves **drug therapy**.

2) Treatment is based on the **dopamine hypothesis** (p.83) — the theory that schizophrenia is linked to increased dopamine activity in the brain. **Antipsychotic drugs (neuroleptics)** work by **blocking dopamine receptors**.

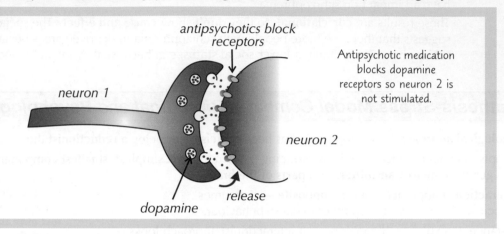

antipsychotics block receptors

Antipsychotic medication blocks dopamine receptors so neuron 2 is not stimulated.

neuron 1

neuron 2

dopamine

release

3) There are two types of antipsychotics — **typical** and **atypical**.

4) **Typical antipsychotics** were developed in the 1950s. Although they are still used to treat schizophrenia today, they are less widely used due to their side effects. This is because they mainly appear to treat only the **positive symptoms** and their side effects can be **severe**. These side effects include **dry mouth**, **blurred vision**, **dizziness**, **muscle spasms** or **cramps** and **tremors**.

5) Whilst **typical** antipsychotics act upon **dopamine** receptors, **atypical** antipsychotics act on both **serotonin** and **dopamine** receptors.

6) Nowadays, people are most often prescribed **atypical antipsychotic drugs** instead. They were developed in the **1950s** and introduced in the **1970s** as a result of the adverse **side effects** of typical antipsychotics.

7) **Atypical antipsychotics** can treat both **positive** and **negative symptoms**, but they can have severe side effects too.

Advantages

- Drug therapy is more effective at reducing **positive symptoms**, e.g. hallucinations.

- It's **successful** for a large number of patients with schizophrenia, meaning that more people can live in the **community** rather than being institutionalised.

- It's the most **widely-used** and **effective** form of treatment for schizophrenia. Almost all other treatments are used **alongside** drug therapy.

When you're evaluating a treatment for schizophrenia, you can use the advantages of another treatment as a disadvantage of the one you're evaluating.

Disadvantages

- Drug therapy **isn't** very effective for treating **negative symptoms** like social withdrawal.

- There are **ethical issues** surrounding the use of drug therapy. Some people argue that drug treatment is a **'chemical straitjacket'** — it **doesn't** really **help** the patient, it just **controls** their **behaviour** to make it more socially acceptable and easier to manage.

- Most people will experience some **short-term side effects** when taking antipsychotic drugs, e.g. drowsiness, blurred vision, dry mouth, constipation and weight gain.

- **Long-term side effects** include increased risk of **diabetes** and **tardive dyskinesia** (involuntary repetitive movements that continue even after they've stopped taking the medication).

- **Clinical trials** have shown that as many as **two-thirds** of people stop taking antipsychotic drugs because of the side-effects. However, **newer** antipsychotic drugs seem to have **fewer long-term side effects** than the **older** ones.

- It treats the **symptoms** of schizophrenia but **not** the **cause**. Symptoms often **come back** if people stop taking antipsychotic drugs. This leads to the **'revolving door phenomenon'**, where patients are constantly being discharged and re-admitted to hospital.

Treating Schizophrenia

Schizophrenia Can be Treated Using Psychological Therapies

Cognitive Behaviour Therapy

1) Cognitive behaviour therapy (CBT) is based on the assumption that patients can be helped by **identifying** and **changing** their 'faulty cognitions'.

2) One of the main **techniques** of CBT is based on Ellis's **ABC model**. Cognitive restructuring can occur by patients identifying their **activating event** (A), **exploring** their **beliefs** (B) and **recognising** the **consequences** (C).

3) People with schizophrenia are encouraged to **reality-test** their **hallucinations** and **delusions**, e.g. to question and try to accept and ignore the voices they hear. This is with the aim of **reducing** their levels of **distress**.

4) They are pushed to **challenge** their **beliefs** and to **question** where the voices may have **originated** from.

5) Patients are encouraged to use strategies such as **positive self-talk** to help themselves.

6) They do **role-play exercises** and **homework** to test out their 'faulty thinking' and are helped to see the **consequences** of thinking differently.

7) Through this they can gradually realise where the 'faults' in their **thought patterns** are, and can begin to **change** them.

> You came across Ellis's ABC model when looking at depression in Year 1.

Chadwick et al (1996) — A study of CBT

Method: Chadwick et al (1996) reported the case of Nigel, a man with schizophrenia who believed he had the **ability to predict** what people were about to say. Nigel himself asked to prove his 'power' to Chadwick's team and so they showed him over 50 video tapes of different scenarios, paused at certain intervals. Nigel was asked to predict what was going to happen next.

Results: Nigel **didn't** get one prediction **correct**.

Conclusion: Nigel concluded, through this **reality testing** form of CBT, that he didn't in fact hold any 'special power'.

Evaluation: Although this is a case study, and therefore can't be generalised to a wider population, it does show that CBT **can be successful** in certain situations.

Advantages

- **Sensky et al (2000)** found that CBT was **effective** in treating patients with schizophrenia who **hadn't responded** to **drug treatment**. It was helpful with **positive** and **negative** symptoms, and patients **continued** to **improve** 9 months after treatment had ended.
- CBT puts patients **in charge** of their own treatment by teaching them **self-help strategies**. This means there are **fewer ethical issues** than with other therapies (e.g. drug therapy).

Disadvantages

- CBT only treats the **symptoms** of schizophrenia — it **doesn't address** the **cause** of the disorder.
- It's difficult to **measure** the effectiveness of CBT because it relies on **self-report** from the patient, and the **therapist's opinions**. This makes it **less objective**.
- Patients can become **dependent** on their therapist.
- The patient has to have a level of **self-awareness** and to voluntarily **participate**. This can be difficult when a patient has symptoms such as a **lack of awareness** or an **inability to engage** with others.
- CBT can be a very **time-intensive** treatment and so **drop out** rates can be high when people have severe symptoms.
- The style of CBT doesn't work for everyone — **individual differences** mean some people don't respond well to being **confronted**.

Treating Schizophrenia

Family Therapy

1) Family therapy, or **family intervention**, has developed over the past 40 years. It is based on the idea that **family dysfunction** can lead to an **increased risk** of relapse in people with schizophrenia (see page 84).

2) The **aim** of family therapy is to **reduce conflict** and **high emotion** amongst family members.

3) This can happen by **helping** the family **form alliances**, **reduce** the **burden of care**, **limit** outbursts of **anger** expressed by individual family members and **encourage** people to set **realistic goals**.

4) Family therapy is often used alongside **other treatments**, mainly **drug** treatments.

Advantages	• Family therapy has experienced some **success**. **Pilling et al (2002)** found family therapy **reduced** the rate of readmission in some patients with schizophrenia.
	• It is particularly **useful** in patients who **lack insight** into their own condition or who **can't** coherently explain their thoughts.
Disadvantages	• Getting **informed consent** from all members of the family can be difficult. There are also issues surrounding **confidentiality** which need to be addressed.
	• Families need to be **engaged** and **open** to changing behaviour — **not** every family will be.

Token Economies Can be Used to Manage Schizophrenia

1) **Behavioural** treatments for schizophrenia are based on **operant conditioning** — learning through **reinforcement**.

2) **Token economies** can help encourage people in **psychiatric institutions** to perform **socially desirable behaviours**, e.g. getting dressed and making their beds. Patients are given **tokens** which reinforce these behaviours — they can then **exchange** these for something they want, like sweets or cigarettes.

Ayllon and Azrin (1968) — Token economy in a psychiatric ward

Method:	45 female patients with schizophrenia received tokens for 'good' behaviours (e.g. making their beds). These could later be exchanged for **rewards**. Tokens were taken away for bizarre behaviour. Naturalistic observation was used to assess the effectiveness of this procedure in changing behaviour in the hospital ward.
Results:	The women, who had been institutionalised for an average of 16 years and displayed bouts of screaming, incontinence, aggression and low social skills (e.g. eating by shoving their faces into the food), showed a massive **improvement** through the incentive of receiving privileges.
Conclusion:	Token economies can exert control over behaviour to give patients back a sense of dignity.
Evaluation:	The participants were all women, so the results **can't be generalised** to the real world.

Advantages

• Token economy programmes can produce **significant improvements** in **self care** and **desirable behaviour**, even with **chronic institutionalised people with schizophrenia**.

• This means they work **best** within **institutions** — people who stay in institutions often **lose** the **motivation** to care for themselves, something token economies directly address.

• For example, **Paul and Lentz (1977)** compared the use of a **token economy system** with **standard hospitalisation**. They found that the people with schizophrenia whose disorder was managed using **token economies** showed the **greatest improvement** in behaviour.

Disadvantages

• Token economies don't have high **ecological validity** — they don't **transfer** into the **real world**. Once people are away from institutions they often don't continue showing desirable behaviour, because there's **nothing** to **reinforce** it.

• The patients' behaviour might be **superficial** — they might only produce desirable behaviour if they're going to receive a token.

• There are **ethical issues** surrounding the use of **behavioural therapy**. It could be argued that it **doesn't** really **help** the patient, it just makes their behaviour more acceptable to other people. Depriving patients of rewards may be seen as infringing on their **human rights**. However, it may be justified if the outcome is that the patients get back their independence.

Treating Schizophrenia

An *Interactionist Approach* Can Be Used To *Treat* Schizophrenia

1) The **interactionist approach** uses a combination of approaches to explain behaviour (see page 46). It is also called the **biopsychosocial approach**.

2) Because it is a **holistic** approach, it emphasises that the treatment should be holistic too. So treatment should involve **biological**, **cognitive** and **behavioural** therapies.

3) Medication only seems to treat the **symptoms** and not the **cause** of schizophrenia. Also, lots of patients don't take it regularly due to **forgetting**, or **stop** taking it altogether due to the **unpleasant side effects**. Therefore, the interactionist approach suggests that **other treatments** should be used alongside medication.

Advantages
- Since not **one treatment** seems to work exclusively to treat or manage schizophrenia, it makes sense to use a **variety** of treatments.
- Using psychological therapies alongside drug therapies not only allows the patient to **manage** their **behavioural symptoms**, but also provides them with the **skills** to tackle their condition and challenge any '**faulty cognitions**'.

Disadvantages
- It is **difficult** to know which treatment is **working**.
- People with **severe symptoms** of schizophrenia are more likely to need **higher** levels of medication. These patients often have a **lower** willingness to try new things, or **learn** new social skills.
- Therefore, the **treatments** need to be **appropriate** and **flexible** to the needs of the patient at the time.
- It can get very **complicated** and **time consuming** — patients may be required to take **medication**, undergo **family therapy** and **cognitive therapy**, and also have forms of **social support**.

Practice Questions

Q1 Outline some disadvantages of drug therapy in the treatment of schizophrenia.

Q2 Outline one advantage of CBT in the treatment of schizophrenia.

Q3 Describe how Chadwick et al (1996) investigated the use of CBT in patients with schizophrenia.

Q4 How can token economies benefit patients with schizophrenia?

Q5 Give one disadvantage of the interactionist approach to treating schizophrenia.

Exam Questions

Q1 Outline one difference between typical and atypical antipsychotics in the treatment of schizophrenia. [2 marks]

Q2 Read the item below and then answer the question that follows.

> Jim is 16. He has a younger brother and lives with his Mum and Dad. Jim has just been diagnosed with schizophrenia. His doctor strongly believes his condition has developed as a direct result of the continuous conflict between Jim and his mother. Jim's family are now undergoing family therapy to help Jim manage his condition.

Outline the use of family therapy as a treatment for Jim's schizophrenia. [4 marks]

Q3 Outline how token economies can be used in the management of schizophrenia. [4 marks]

Q4 Discuss why the interactionist approach could be considered important in treating schizophrenia. [16 marks]

Chemical straitjackets — might be a bit itchy...

Well, at least after reading about all the things that can go wrong with your brain it's nice to know there are treatments. Not as nice as walks in the rain or a cuddle or pink wafers, no, but quite nice all the same. I'd love a cuddle right about now. If you're in a similar predicament then take a moment to hold this book close to you and have a little snuggle.

Explanations for Food Preferences

Would you rather have a large cream cake, or the mouldy left-over sprouts found at the back of the fridge? I know which I'd go for... but psychologists claim there are reasons we might prefer certain foods. Read on to find out more.

There Are **Evolutionary** Reasons For **Food Preferences**

People need food to **survive** and throughout history it's been a driving force for **evolution**. This can help explain why so many people would rather have a chocolate eclair than a slice of grapefruit.

Why we like sweet stuff...

- **Harris (1987)** found that **newborn babies** have a preference for sweet things and dislike bitter things.
- These preferences and dislikes are **universal**, suggesting a **genetic** (therefore evolutionary) explanation.
- Early mammals were **frugivores** (ate mainly fruit). Sweet food now triggers the release of the pleasure-inducing brain chemical **dopamine**, which acts as a reinforcer.
- Most **poisons** have a strong bitter taste — so our dislike of this type of taste could be a **survival reflex**.

Why we prefer food that's bad for us...

- **Burnham and Phelan (2000)** suggest that a preference for **fatty foods** would have helped our ancestors survive in times of **food scarcity** — these foods are full of energy-giving **calories**.
- Even though food is no longer scarce, we're still programmed to stuff ourselves with burgers and cakes when they're available, in order to **build up fat reserves** in case there's ever a shortage. Again, **dopamine** may act as a reinforcing reward.

Why we like our meat spicy...

- **Sherman and Hash (2001)** analysed almost 7000 recipes from 36 countries and found that **meat** dishes contained far more **spices** than **vegetable** dishes. They hypothesised that this was because spices have **antimicrobial** properties — meat is more vulnerable to being infested with bacteria and fungi than vegetables are.
- This may also explain why people in **hot climates** tend to eat **more** spicy food — microbes grow faster in warmer conditions.

For the ultimate dopamine hit Jessie liked to take her sugar neat.

Why we're careful about what foods we eat...

- **Taste aversion** happens when we **associate** the taste of a food that has made us ill with the feeling of illness. This is thought to have an evolutionary basis, as it prevents us from eating foods that make us unwell.
- Food **neophobia** is where we're reluctant to eat foods that we've not encountered before — we're more likely to eat food we know is safe. **Birch et al (1987)** found that preferences for food **increased** as familiarity with the food increased.

You should be familiar with social learning theory from Year 1.

Social Influences Can Also Explain **Food Preferences**...

- Social learning theory involves **observation**, **imitation**, **identification** and **vicarious reinforcement**. These processes can all result in the development of food preferences and eating behaviours in people.
- **Brown and Ogden's (2004)** study provided support for the social learning theory of eating behaviour. They found that the snacking habits of children were **significantly correlated** to the snacking habits of their parents. This seems to provide evidence for **observation**, **identification** and **imitation**.
- Role models don't just have to be parents. **Lowe et al (2004)** found that when children watched videos featuring characters who enjoyed eating fruit and vegetables, they were more likely to eat healthily after watching the video than before.
- The **media** can also influence food preferences. **Hastings et al (2003)** concluded that food advertising directly affected which types of food children selected in a supermarket.

Explanations for Food Preferences

... and So Can *Cultural Influences*

In the UK today we tend to assume that you have to be **skinny** to be **beautiful**.
But that's actually quite a **recent** idea.

1) Throughout human history, being **voluptuous** (curvy) was considered an attractive trait in a potential partner — it signalled **health** and access to **plentiful resources** in times of scarcity. People were proud to gorge themselves on food and drink because it signalled their **wealth** and **status**.

2) However, in the last 40 years the '**supermodel**' and '**size zero**' figure has become popular in Western culture. Highly profitable diet, exercise and surgery industries have sprung up as a result of this popularity.

3) In many other places big is **still** seen as best though — for example, in many **African** cultures plump females are regarded as wiser and more fertile, in **Asian** cultures weight is often still linked to affluence and success, and **Pacific Islanders** (Hawaiians/Samoans) equate large physical size in both genders with beauty and status.

Food is also an important part of many **religions**:

> 1) Some **fast** to show devotion (e.g. **Muslim** Ramadan).
>
> 2) Some **feast** to celebrate important events (e.g. **Christian** Christmas).
>
> 3) Some **forbid** certain foods (e.g. **Judaism** — pork isn't eaten).
>
> 4) Some incorporate food in **rituals** (e.g. **Catholicism** — communion wafers).

Different cultures attach different **meanings** to foods, and eating forms a major part of many **celebrations** and **ceremonies** worldwide. Imagine birthdays without cake, or Christmas without sprouts...

Practice Questions

Q1 Why do evolutionary psychologists argue that humans have a preference for spices?

Q2 What is meant by taste aversion?

Q3 Outline how food preferences could be influenced by a role model.

Q4 Explain why a fuller figure has traditionally been considered attractive in many cultures.

Q5 Explain how religion might influence food preferences.

Exam Questions

Q1 Complete the sentence below.
Neophobia is a reluctance to eat:
    A salty foods   **B** sweet foods   **C** unknown foods   **D** spicy foods   [1 mark]

Q2 Read the item below then answer the question that follows.

> Gretal's favourite actress is the new advertising face of a healthy eating campaign, 'Fruit Matters'. 'Fruit Matters' encourages people to eat three pieces of fruit each day. Before Gretal saw the campaign, she ate one piece of fruit a day. Now she has started eating three pieces of fruit each day.

Describe how Gretal's food preferences may have occurred as a result of social influence.   [4 marks]

Q3 Briefly outline the role of cultural influences on eating behaviour.   [4 marks]

Q4 Discuss evolutionary explanations for food preferences.   [16 marks]

Knobbly ones, hairy ones, disconnected ones. Knees can be scary...

Oh wait... neophobia is something else. Either way... it kinda makes sense when you think about it. If you're presented with a dodgy snack that appeared from goodness-knows-where, would you really eat it? Well — even if you would, I think you'd be downright bonkers (as would evolutionary psychologists). So leave it be and learn these pages.

Controlling Eating

Interestingly enough, there are biological reasons for why you feel hungry or full at different times. And here they are...

Neural Mechanisms Control Eating and Satiation

Satiation just means feeling full.

hypothalamus

1) The **hypothalamus** is a gland in the brain responsible for **homeostasis** (keeping conditions in the body constant).
2) It helps to **regulate** things like temperature, circadian rhythms and intake of food and drink.
3) The **ventromedial hypothalamus (VMH)** and the **lateral hypothalamus (LH)** are parts of the hypothalamus that are thought to be involved in **food regulation**.

Ventromedial just means the bit at the bottom in the middle, and lateral means the side parts.

The Ventromedial Hypothalamus (VMH) is involved in Satiety

1) Satiety is the **unconscious physiological process** that **stops** you eating.
2) The **VMH** provides the signal to stop eating when it picks up **hormonal messages**. For example, when food is being digested the level of the hormone CCK in the bloodstream is high. This stimulates receptors in the VMH.
3) Experimental **electrical stimulation** of the VMH has been shown to **reduce food intake**.
4) Malfunctions in the VMH may cause **obesity**. This was demonstrated by Baylis et al (1996).

The VMH is also called the ventromedial nucleus.

Baylis et al (1996) — VMH lesioning in rats

Method:	Two **symmetrical lesions** (injuries) were made in the VMH of eight male and five female rats. Their body weight was later compared with **age-matched controls**.
Results:	The rats with lesions in their VMH had become **obese**, while the control rats had not.
Conclusion:	Lesions in the VMH cause **hyperphagia** (overeating) and obesity, so the VMH must play a role in satiation.
Evaluation:	This was a very **small sample** using only one breed of rat, so the findings can't be generalised. Also, **other tissues** surrounding the VMH might have been damaged when the lesions were created, so it might not necessarily be just the VMH that is involved.

The Lateral Hypothalamus (LH) is involved in Hunger

1) When the body's blood sugar level drops, homeostatic responses kick in to help restore the **equilibrium**.
2) **Receptors** in the LH detect the drop in blood sugar. This then causes neurons to fire that create the sensation of hunger.
3) The person is driven to eat, and blood glucose levels increase. Receptors then send a hormonal message to the **VMH** to give the sensation of fullness (see above).

The LH is also called the lateral nucleus.

Damage to the LH can reduce food intake. For example, chemical lesions are known to produce **aphagia** (failure to eat). However, as with VMH studies, there may be **methodological problems** muddying the water.

Winn et al (1990) — LH lesioning in rats

Method:	The toxin **NMDA** was used to make **lesions** in the LH of rats. A small dose (lesions in **LH only**) and a large dose (lesions spread to **adjacent areas**) condition was used, and there was also a **control group**.
Results:	Rats that had the small dose of NMDA showed **no changes** in their eating behaviour after a brief recovery period. However, rats that had the large dose showed **long-term deficits** in their eating behaviour.
Conclusion:	Damage to the **hypothalamus** impairs feeding responses, but the LH may **not** have as much of an effect as previously thought.
Evaluation:	This research is useful as it shows that the localisation of brain function is **more complex** than originally thought. However, this was an **exploratory study** to test whether NMDA was an effective toxin for use on the hypothalamus and wasn't originally intended to investigate hunger. Therefore, all the relevant variables may not have been controlled, reducing the **reliability** of the results.

Controlling Eating

Hormones Tell You When You're Hungry or Full

Ghrelin tells your brain when you're hungry

- **Ghrelin** is a **hormone** that's released into the bloodstream from the stomach and small intestine.
- When **food is eaten**, the stomach **stops** releasing ghrelin.
- Ghrelin level then **rises over time**, until the next meal.
- The **more** ghrelin is released, the **hungrier** you are.

Anna and Matteo bonded over the croissants and their shared release of ghrelin.

	Cummings et al (2004) — The role of ghrelin in eating behaviour
Method:	**Six** male participants were asked to record their hunger level every **30 minutes** after they were given lunch. Their **ghrelin level** was monitored every five minutes using blood samples. The participants chose when to eat dinner, and were told to request their dinner when they felt **hungry enough**.
Results:	Immediately after they had eaten lunch, ghrelin levels **fell** in all of the participants. It was at the lowest level about 70 minutes after they'd eaten, then began to rise again until the participants ate dinner. There was a **positive correlation** in most of the participants between **hunger level** and the **amount of ghrelin** in their blood (the hungrier they were the higher their ghrelin level).
Conclusion:	Ghrelin does seem to **signal** appetite and hunger in humans.
Evaluation:	This experiment used a **small sample size** and only used **male participants** so the results can't be generalised to a wider population. Although the results only provide a **correlation** rather than a cause and effect relationship, they do support other findings linking ghrelin to eating behaviour.

Leptin tells your brain when you should stop eating

- Leptin works in a **different** way to ghrelin.
- It is a hormone made by fat cells that tells the brain when the body is **full**.
- When a certain amount of **fat** is stored in your body, **leptin** is released to tell you to stop eating.
- Lots of studies into the role of leptin in **obesity** have involved mice. **Halaas et al (1995)** looked at mice who were missing the gene that makes leptin.
- They concluded that these mice **didn't** have any **satiety signals** telling them to stop eating and so they were **obese**.
- Halaas et al found that when they were given **injections** of leptin, they appeared to be able to **control** their eating and their **weight** returned to a **normal** level.
- Lots of studies into leptin have been carried out on **animals**, which means these findings **can't** reliably be **generalised** to humans. However, some research has been carried out on **humans**. E.g. **Montague et al (1997)** found that two obese cousins both had **faulty** leptin production genes. There's more about this on p.97.

Practice Questions

Q1 Name the two parts of the hypothalamus involved in controlling eating behaviour.

Q2 What did Winn et al conclude in their 1990 study?

Q3 Outline the results found by Cummings et al (2004) in their investigation into ghrelin.

Q4 Describe the role of leptin in eating behaviour.

Exam Questions

Q1	Complete the following sentence. The release of ghrelin signals:				
	A satiety	**B** hunger	**C** high fat stores	**D** excess leptin	[1 mark]
Q2	Discuss the neural mechanisms involved in the control of eating behaviour.				[16 marks]

Grumbling stomach in the middle of an exam? We've all been there...

But it's just your ghrelin talking. It can be a bit awkward right in the middle of somewhere really quiet — like in a library, or during the middle of your Psychology lesson. But, next time it happens, explain to people that it's just your hormones. Then demand lots of chocolate to stop it grumbling. It always works. Beautiful...

Anorexia Nervosa

Lots of people are worried about their weight, but for some this preoccupation leads to really serious health problems. Eating disorders, like anorexia nervosa, are more common than you might think.

*Anorexia Nervosa Leads to Significant **Weight Loss***

Anorexia nervosa is one of the most common eating disorders in the UK. The NHS claim that about **1 in 250 females** and **1 in 2000 males** will suffer from anorexia nervosa at some point in their lives. It usually occurs between 16-17 years old. It involves a dramatic reduction in the amount of food eaten, leading to significant **weight loss**.

Eating disorders involve abnormal patterns of eating that are harmful to the affected person.

The **DSM** (the main diagnostic manual for mental disorders) describes **three** main characteristics of anorexia:

Restriction of energy intake — when a person consistently consumes **fewer** calories than they require, it results in a significantly **low** body weight.

Intense fear of gaining weight — people with anorexia nervosa are very **fearful** of gaining weight or getting fat even though they're seriously **underweight**. As a result, they often carry out behaviours to **avoid** gaining weight, such as extreme dieting or excessive exercise.

Body-image distortion — people with anorexia nervosa have **distorted self-perception**. They believe they're **overweight** even when very **thin**, **judge** themselves based largely on their weight, and don't accept the **seriousness** of their low weight.

*There Are **Biological Explanations** For Anorexia Nervosa*

Genetic Explanations Have Been Suggested

	Holland et al (1988) — Concordance rates in twins
Method:	**Concordance rates** were studied in 45 pairs of twins. At least one twin of each pair had been diagnosed as having anorexia nervosa — the study examined how often the other twin also suffered from the disorder.
Results:	The concordance rate was **56%** for **identical** (MZ) twins and only **5%** for **non-identical** (DZ) twins.
Conclusion:	Anorexia has a **genetic basis**.
Evaluation:	Identical twins share 100% of their genetic material, so **other factors** must also be involved in causing anorexia nervosa as the concordance rate was only **56%**. The higher concordance in MZ twins could be due to **environmental** rather than genetic factors, as looking the same may lead to more shared experiences.

Neural Causes Have Also Been Investigated

1) Researchers have suggested that anorexia nervosa may be due to **damage to the hypothalamus**, specifically the **lateral hypothalamus** (an area of the brain involved in controlling hunger — see page 92). **Lesion studies** show that damage to this area can produce **aphagia** (a failure to eat) in animals, and recent research suggests that people with anorexia have **reduced blood flow** to this area. But it hasn't yet been proven whether this is a **cause** or an **effect** of the disorder.

2) People with anorexia often also have **abnormally high levels** of the neurotransmitter **serotonin** and this causes abnormally high levels of **anxiety**. Serotonin production is stimulated by biological components (amino acids) in **food**, so starvation may actually make people with anorexia feel better. But again, it's not clear whether these serotonin levels are a **cause** or an **effect** of the disorder.

Like all biological arguments these explanations have strengths (e.g. they're supported by scientific evidence), and limitations (e.g. they place little emphasis on the effect of people's social environment, relationships, etc.).

Anorexia Nervosa

There Are Also **Psychological Explanations** For Anorexia Nervosa

1) Family Systems Theory

1) Some studies have found that the parents of people with anorexia are often **high achievers**, have **high expectations** and may be **controlling**.

2) **Minuchin et al (1978)** explored the influence of the **family** on the development of anorexia nervosa within children. They applied a '**family systems**' approach to anorexia nervosa.

> Family systems theory is the idea that disorders (e.g. anorexia nervosa) are a product of, and can be treated through, the whole family and not just the individual.

3) Their theory states that families of people with anorexia nervosa show:

- **Enmeshment** — families have a very **strong emotional connection**, with no real **role boundaries**. This means individual members don't have their own **clear identities**.

- **Overprotectiveness** — the child feels they cannot become an **autonomous** (independent) individual because of the enmeshment, and because the family is **overcontrolling** and **overprotective**.

- **Rigidity** — the family upholds very **strict** beliefs, especially in showing **loyalty** towards one another.

4) Minuchin et al (1978) explain that families might **appear** to be **functional**, but they are often over-protective, rigid and **cannot** manage **conflict**.

Strength of the family systems theory

Kramer (1983) conducted a study investigating the family characteristics of people with **eating disorders** compared to a **control group**. Their findings showed that those with eating disorders did have **higher levels** of **family dysfunction** than people with normal eating behaviour.

Limitations of the family systems theory

1) The family systems theory could be seen to **blame** the family for the eating disorder. **Changing** the way a family **functions** could be **harmful** to the patient's health and wellbeing.

2) Cases of anorexia nervosa can start when a young person has **left home**, or even in **adulthood**. But the family systems theory only explains the development of anorexia nervosa in young people still at home.

2) Social Learning Theory

1) Social learning theory states that the environment influences behaviour through **modelling**, **observation**, **imitation** and **reinforcement** (make sure you're clear on social learning theory — you covered it in Year 1).

2) In Western societies, culturally-defined beauty comes partly from being **slim** (page 91).

3) People often **imitate** those they admire. For example, young girls frequently look up to celebrity **role models**.

4) These role models may **control** their appearance, or appear to be **successful** by being slim.

5) Other role models may include **family members** and **peers**, all of whom may appear to be **successful** if they are slim.

6) This may lead to the girls **observing** and **imitating** the role model's behaviour. **Vicarious reinforcement** comes from seeing their role model being **praised** for their figure and attracting attention. They then **adjust** their own behaviour to try to **achieve** the same **rewards**.

7) Family and friends can **reinforce** the behaviour, by initially complimenting the person on their thinner figure. However, the girl may then continue to **lose more weight**, leading to the development of anorexia nervosa.

Anorexia Nervosa

Research into the role of the media in anorexia nervosa can be used to support social learning theory.

Keel and Klump (2003) — The role of media influences

Method: A review of studies looking at anorexia nervosa and the **role of media** influences was conducted. The review looked at studies conducted all over the world to get an idea of how **culture** might affect the results.

Results: Anorexia nervosa was found in **all** countries, but the **more** Westernised the influences were in a country, the **higher** the rates of anorexia nervosa.

Conclusion: Western media may have a role in determining anorexia nervosa prevalence rates, but because it's present in all countries, there must be **other** factors too.

Strength of social learning theory

Social learning theory helps to explain why the number of people diagnosed with eating disorders has **increased** over the years — the media and advertising are becoming a lot more **noticeable** within our society.

Limitation of social learning theory

All Western women are **subject** to the **same pressures** from the media, but they **don't** all get eating disorders. So social learning theory **can't** be the **only explanation** for anorexia nervosa — other factors must be involved, for example, **genetic** or **neural** factors.

3) Cognitive Theory

The **cognitive theory** of anorexia nervosa suggests that those with the disorder have a **distorted perception** of themselves as well as a set of **irrational beliefs** about their appearance and behaviour.

For example, people with anorexia may:

- Believe that they are **fat**, even though they are **underweight**.
- Form **thoughts** about themselves based entirely on their **appearance**.
- Hold a set of **irrational beliefs** about **food** and **dieting behaviours**.
- Form **thoughts** about their **sense of self** based on how well they can **control** their eating.

Evidence of this sort of thinking has been found in people with anorexia. For example, **Gardner and Moncrieff (1988)** found that **people with anorexia** were more likely than a control group to state that an **image of themselves** had been **distorted**, whether or not the image had actually been altered.

Strength of cognitive theory

It considers **mental processes** which are often overlooked in other theories.

Limitation of cognitive theory

It fails to take **individual differences** into account by assuming that all people with anorexia nervosa process stuff in the same way.

Practice Questions

Q1 Explain how Holland et al's (1988) study provides evidence for a genetic explanation of anorexia nervosa.

Q2 How does cognitive theory explain the cause of anorexia nervosa?

Exam Question

Q1 Read the item below then answer the question that follows.

> Donna's parents have very high expectations of her, and make sure that she follows a strict study schedule, so that she meets these expectations. Her family have a very strong emotional bond and Donna and her younger sister are often being mistaken for each other, as they're so alike. Last year, Donna was diagnosed with anorexia nervosa.

Describe how Donna's anorexia could be explained by the family systems theory. [6 marks]

Anorexia nervosa isn't as recent a problem as you might think...

...in fact, it was first diagnosed in 1868 by William Gull. And although it's most common in teenage girls, it can affect all kinds of different people from all walks of life. It could be caused by a mixture of the factors listed on these pages.

Obesity

It might seem odd to consider obesity as an eating disorder — but overeating to the point of being clinically obese certainly counts as an abnormal eating pattern that's harmful to the person affected. And that's why it's in here.

Obesity *is When Someone Has an* Abnormally High Body Mass Index

1) A person is **obese** if they're carrying too much adipose (fatty) tissue. People are generally classed as obese if their **BMI** (body mass index) is **30 kg/m² or higher** (though BMI is also affected by how muscular you are).

2) Obesity is generally caused by a person **taking in more calories** (food) than they **burn off** (by exercise), but there are some genetic conditions and medications that can increase the risk of obesity.

3) It's estimated that by **2050** over half of the people in the UK will be obese.

4) The most effective way to treat obesity is with a **sensible diet and plenty of exercise**. However, increasingly people are turning to quick fixes — 'miracle' pills or surgery such as stomach stapling, gastric band fitting or gastric bypass surgery.

Body mass index is a measurement of height relative to weight. A normal BMI is between 18.5 and 25.

Exercise is one way to combat obesity, but that still didn't excuse Kristy's outfit.

Obesity *Can Have* Biological Explanations

There could be a genetic link... Some studies have shown that there is a **genetic** element to obesity.

Stunkard et al (1986) — Adoption studies and obesity

Method:	The weight of 540 **adult adoptees** from Denmark was compared with that of both their **biological and adoptive parents**. The adoptees were split into 4 weight classes — thin, median, overweight and obese.
Results:	There was a **strong relationship** between the weight of the adoptees and their biological parents. There was **no relationship** between the weight of the adoptees and their adoptive parents in any of the classes.
Conclusion:	Genetic influences have an important role in determining adult weight, whereas **environment** seems to have **little effect**.
Evaluation:	This finding is **supported** by other biological versus adoptive relative research, and even by some **twin studies**. However, it's probably too **reductionist** to say that genetics alone are responsible for obesity. Also, the participants were all from Denmark, so the results **can't be generalised** to other cultures.

Montague et al (1997) investigated two obese children and found that they both had a defective '**ob gene**'. This is the gene which produces **leptin** (see page 93). If the body **doesn't have enough** leptin, it won't know when to stop eating, resulting in **obesity**.

Montague et al (1997) — Leptin's role in obesity

Method:	Two severely obese children (male and female cousins) were studied — a large proportion of their total body weight was made up of **adipose (fatty) tissue**.
Results:	A **mutation** on the part of their DNA responsible for controlling their supply of **leptin** was found — they didn't produce enough leptin. Leptin is a protein produced by adipose tissue to signal that **fat reserves** in the body are **full**.
Conclusion:	Their leptin deficiency had caused the children's obesity. They did not have enough of this chemical to **suppress appetite** in the normal way.
Evaluation:	A number of trials in which obese patients were given doses of leptin have had **very little success**, so leptin deficiency may **not** explain obesity in the **population as a whole**.

... or there could be a neural explanation

Obesity is a result of **eating behaviour**, and it might have a neural explanation. Eating behaviour is controlled by the **hypothalamus** (as you'll have read all about on page 92) and animal studies which have involved creating **lesions** in the **VMH** (the 'satiety centre') have led to the development of **obesity** in these cases. **Hetherington and Ranson (1940)** found that lesioning the VMH in rats led to **excessive overeating**, leading to **obesity**.

Obesity

Psychological Explanations Might Also Explain Obesity

The Boundary Model

The **boundary model** was developed by **Herman and Polivy (1983)**. Their model proposed that:

- **Biological processes** drive people's need for food.
- Feeling **hungry** means that you'll always eat at least the **minimum amount** of food needed by your body.
- **Eating food** will bring about a feeling of **satiety** to **stop** you eating too much.
- **Social**, **environmental** and **psychological** factors all affect the size of the **range** between hunger and satiety.

The **boundary model** shows the minimum level of food needed to **eliminate hunger** and the maximum level of food needed to **feel full**. **Biological pressures** usually ensure we eat enough food to **stay within** this range.

Restraint Theory

Restraint theory is the idea that when someone tries to **not** eat, they end up eating more.

The boundary model shows two **biological** boundaries (**hunger** and **satiety**).
Restraint theory proposes that dieters also have a **cognitive** boundary.

Restraint theory states that:

- A **restrained eater**, or dieter, will eat until they **reach** their **cognitive diet boundary**.
- But — if they cross their cognitive diet boundary, they reach a stage of **disinhibition**.
- **Disinhibition** means they 'give up'. At this point, the dieter thinks there **isn't any point** in trying to restrict anymore, and so they'll eat until they're **full**, or even beyond.
- Dieters can lose the ability to recognise **hunger** and **satiety cues**, and so their range may be **bigger**.

If dieters regularly eat **over** their **biological boundary**, this could lead to **obesity**.
Herman and Mack (1975) illustrated **restraint theory** in their study of dieters.

Herman and Mack (1975) — Disinhibition in restrained eaters

Method:	In a study with an independent measures design, samples of **dieting** and **non-dieting** students were placed in three 'pre-load' conditions — drinking either one or two glasses of milkshake or nothing at all. They were then given unlimited supplies of ice cream.
Results:	The non-dieters ate **less** ice cream the more milkshakes they had drunk. The dieters ate **more** ice cream the more milkshakes they had drunk.
Conclusion:	Drinking the milkshake had damaged the dieters' determination — they gave in to total indulgence after failure, showing **disinhibition**. This is known as '**the counter-regulation effect**'.
Evaluation:	These findings **support** what we already know about dieting (the 'diet starts tomorrow' mentality). **Follow-up studies** have found that many people have an 'all-or-nothing' mentality to dieting — if they break the diet they tend to see it as immediate failure and so eat as much as they like.

Obesity

But Restraint Theory **Can't** Explain it All

- Restraint theory proposes that **dieting** and **restricting** food intake can lead to **overeating**. But, this doesn't explain why some dieters are **successful**. There's a bit more about this below.
- People with **anorexia nervosa** can also have episodes of **overeating**, but they aren't obese.
- Similarly, people with anorexia nervosa **restrict** their eating. But again, this **doesn't** tend to lead to obesity.

Dieting Doesn't Always Lead to **Weight Loss**

It's not as easy as just going on a diet and watching the weight drop off. Whether a person **succeeds** in losing weight depends on things like motivation, willpower, genetics, lifestyle and medical conditions (e.g. diabetes or thyroid problems). Other factors include:

Support and Encouragement

1) Eating is often a part of **social interaction**, so many experts think dieting should be too.
2) Informing friends and family of weight loss goals should help reduce the **temptations** of food and encourage **positive reinforcement** (and punishment) from others. Lots of dieters also join a weight loss group or diet with a friend or partner to maintain **motivation**.
3) But this approach doesn't work for everyone — some people find constant monitoring by others stressful and use **secretive binge eating** as a defence mechanism.

They were meant to be on a diet, but Mike sensed that his wife's resolve had slipped.

Wing and Jeffrey (1999) recruited participants to a **4 month weight loss program** either **alone**, or **with 3 friends or family members**. Participants recruited with friends and family were instructed to use **social support** to help them during the weight loss program (i.e. to encourage each other). **6 months after the end** of the program **66%** of the participants with **social support** had kept off **all of the weight** they lost, compared to **24%** of participants who were recruited **alone**.

Physiological Changes Due to Dieting

1) Your body has evolved to cope with **chronic food shortages** by lowering your metabolic rate (how fast energy is burned) to protect fat stores in times of **starvation**. Extreme dieting triggers this response.
2) People who go on an extreme diet and then return to normal eating end up with **more excess calories** than before, which are then converted to fat. Also, people often **overeat** after a diet, causing more weight gain.
3) They may then start **another**, even more restrictive diet to undo the weight gain. But this will just reduce their metabolic rate **further**, and so the pattern of **'yo-yo'** dieting continues.

Practice Questions

Q1 Why did Stunkard et al (1986) reject environmental factors as causes of obesity?

Q2 Outline the boundary model.

Q3 What is restraint theory?

Q4 Describe Herman and Mack's (1975) experiment into the disinhibition of restrained eaters.

Exam Questions

Q1	Briefly outline the genetic explanation for obesity.	[2 marks]
Q2	Outline how disinhibition can lead to obesity.	[4 marks]
Q3	Discuss explanations for the success and failure of dieting.	[16 marks]

So it could be my genes stopping me fitting into my jeans...

Hmmm, this section has given me some food for thought and no mistake. Eating can be a complicated business and trying to explain it isn't straightforward either. As usual, a single, simple explanation just won't cut it. Terribly sorry.

Stress as a Bodily Response

I'm sure you all know what stress is. It's having 3 hours left to revise before an exam, or having to visit your girlfriend or boyfriend's parents. We all feel it — but this is Psychology, so it needs a proper scientific explanation.

Stress is a Response to **Stimuli** in the **Environment**

Stress is one of those annoying words with two meanings... How helpful.

1) It can be the environmental **stimulus** that triggers a stress response, e.g. a giant cockroach dancing towards you. In other words, it's the thing that causes you to act stressed.

2) But it can also be the **response** to the stimulus — our reaction, e.g. running for the hills.

However, the white-coated ones have agreed to explain stress as '**the response that occurs when we think we can't cope with the pressures in our environment**'. This is shown in the diagram below:

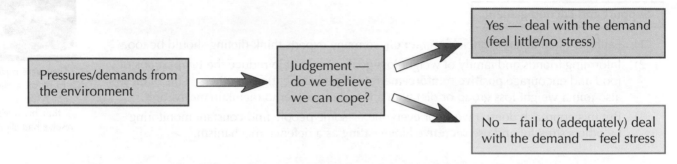

So, stress is the response that occurs when we think the demands being placed on us are greater than our ability to cope. These are our **own judgements** — so we could **over** or **underestimate** the demands, or our ability to cope.

Whether the stress is justified or not doesn't matter — if we **think** we can't cope we get stressed. And when we get stressed something physically changes in us.

The **Hypothalamus** is the Bit of the Brain that **Responds to Stress**

The evaluation of whether something is a **stressor** occurs in the **higher brain centres** — the **cerebral cortex**. When there's an environmental stressor, these higher areas send a signal to the **hypothalamus**.

The hypothalamus has many functions — including controlling the **physiological activities** involved in stress. It triggers **two processes** in the body, depending on whether the stressful event is immediate or not:

The Activation of the **Sympathomedullary Pathway**...

> This is the 'fight or flight' response you met in Year 1.

1) When the body experiences immediate stress, the **hypothalamus** triggers activity in the **sympathetic branch** of the **autonomic nervous system** (you'll have seen the different bits of the nervous system in Year 1), and the sympathetic branch becomes more active.

2) **Adrenaline** and **noradrenaline** are then released into the bloodstream from the **adrenal medulla**. The adrenal medulla is the **central** part of the **adrenal gland**, which is near the **kidneys**.

3) This affects the body in many ways, such as decreasing digestion and increasing breathing.

Stress as a Bodily Response

... Followed by the Activation of the **Hypothalamic Pituitary-Adrenal System**

If the stress is **long-term**, then the sympathomedullary response will start to use up the body's **resources**. So, a second system produces a **countershock response** — which supplies the body with more fuel. It's like putting your body on red alert.

1) The hypothalamus also triggers the release of **CRH** (corticotropin-releasing hormone).

2) CRH stimulates the **anterior pituitary gland**.

3) This then releases a hormone called **ACTH** (adrenocorticotropic hormone).

4) ACTH travels through the body and then stimulates the **adrenal cortex**, which is the **outer** part of the **adrenal gland**.

5) The adrenal cortex then releases **cortisol**, which increases blood sugar by converting **protein** to **glucose**, giving the body **energy**.

6) This energy is needed to **replace** what was used up by the body's initial reaction to the stress, e.g. running away.

7) In the long term, high cortisol levels can damage the **immune system**, and have a negative effect on **memory**.

ACTH

Cortisol

① Hypothalamus releases CRH.

② Anterior pituitary gland releases ACTH.

③ ACTH stimulates adrenal cortex.

④ Cortisol is released into the bloodstream to convert protein into glucose, providing energy.

Hans Seyle also described the body's physiological response to stress. You can read about this on the next page.

Changes in the Body Can Be Seen as Having *Survival Value*

1) During our evolution many threats to us would have been from **predators** or other **physical dangers**.

2) To successfully respond to them, we'd have required **energy** to fight or run away — the **'fight or flight'** response.

3) However, in **modern society** stressors are more likely to be **psychological** than physical and are more **long-term**, e.g. the stresses of working at a desk, commuting, noisy neighbours, etc.

4) Therefore the physical stress response is not really needed, and in the long term it may actually be harmful to our bodies — the next two pages explain how.

5) Some stress can be positive and exhilarating — this is known as **eustress**, e.g. a parachute jump might lead to this kind of arousal.

Practice Questions

Q1 What is stress?
Q2 Which part of the brain triggers activity in the sympathomedullary pathway in response to stress?
Q3 What does the adrenal medulla release in response to immediate stress?
Q4 Where is cortisol released from?

Exam Questions

Q1	Outline the role of the sympathomedullary pathway during stress.	[6 marks]
Q2	Outline the response of the hypothalamic pituitary-adrenal system to stress.	[6 marks]

Well, as bodily responses go, I guess stress isn't so bad...

Stress is a natural reaction in response to anything which threatens you. In the past, it would have been a lion chasing you. Now it's more likely to be a deadline or late train. So next time you see someone getting stressed, try telling them, "relax, it could be worse — at least you're not being chased by a lion" — that'll soon calm them down.

Stress and Physical Illness

The last couple of pages made it blindingly obvious that stress isn't just something in your head — it's a physical response. These pages cover what stress can do to your physical state in the long run.

Hans Selye *Explained Stress as a* Three-Stage Response

In the 1930s, Hans Selye was researching the effects of hormones when he noticed that rats would become ill (e.g. develop stomach ulcers) even when they were given harmless injections (can't have been that 'harmless').

He concluded that the **stress** of the daily injections **caused the illness** and suggested that all animals and humans react to stressors through a **three-stage physiological response**.

Selye (1936) called this the **general adaptation syndrome (GAS)**.

1) **The Alarm Stage** — when we perceive a stressor, our body's first reaction is to **increase arousal levels** so that we're ready to make any necessary **physical response**. These mean we're able to run away (the 'fight or flight' response) if we're faced with a big-toothed hairy monster.

2) **The Resistance Stage** — if the stressor remains for a long time, our bodies can **adapt** to the situation and we seem to be able to cope in a normal way. For example, if we start a high-pressure job we would initially be unable to cope and go into the alarm stage, but after time we would seem to adapt. However, physiologically, **arousal levels** would still be **higher** than normal to cope with the situation.

3) **The Exhaustion Stage** — after **long-term exposure** to a stressor our bodies will eventually be **unable** to continue to cope with the situation. Alarm signs may return and we may **develop illnesses**, e.g. ulcers, high blood pressure, depression, etc. Selye called these 'diseases of adaptation'.

Comment — the stages Selye identified are **supported** by a lot of scientific research. However, the GAS theory describes a single type of response, and so **neglects** the fact that the body's reaction to stress does vary. E.g. how much adrenaline is released depends on how the stressor is perceived by the person (how frightening it is, etc.). Also, a certain **bacterium** has been found to be involved in the formation of ulcers. It could still be the case, though, that stress **weakens** the immune system, making ulcers more likely.

Long-Term Stress *Can Affect the* Cardiovascular System

The **cardiovascular system** is just a fancy name for the **heart** and **blood vessels**. A **long-term stress response** may have a direct effect on this system. For instance, increased stress levels can lead to an increase in blood pressure. This in turn can increase the risk of various **cardiovascular disorders**.

For example, high blood pressure can lead to **arteriosclerosis** (hardening of the blood vessels) and **coronary heart disease** (restricted blood flow to the heart). These disorders may lead to potentially fatal conditions, such as **thrombosis** (blood clots), **heart attacks** and **strokes** (decreased blood flow to the brain, which can cause loss of brain function). **Krantz et al (1991)** conducted a study to investigate the effects of stress on the heart:

Krantz et al (1991) — Stress and the heart

Method:	In a **laboratory experiment**, 39 participants did one of three stress-inducing tasks (a maths test, an attention test and public speaking). Their **blood pressure** and the extent to which the vessels around their heart **contracted** (low, medium or high myocardial ischaemia) was measured. Participants were instructed not to take any prescribed heart medication prior to the study.
Results:	Participants with the greatest myocardial ischaemia showed the highest increases in blood pressure. A small number of participants who showed mild or no myocardial ischaemia only had a very moderate increase in blood pressure.
Conclusion:	Stress may have a **direct influence** on aspects of body functioning, making **cardiovascular disorders** more likely.
Evaluation:	Although these effects occurred in stressful situations, it can't be said that stress **caused** them. Also, it wasn't shown whether the effects also occur at other times. They might sometimes happen even if the person feels relaxed — and therefore couldn't just be linked to feeling stressed. Not everybody showed the same reaction, which suggests that **individual differences** between the participants may also have played a role. The **ecological validity** of the study was reduced because it took place under **laboratory conditions** that weren't fully representative of real-life stress. However, the findings of the study are supported by **Williams (2000)** — it was seen that people who got angry easily or reacted more angrily to situations had a higher risk of cardiovascular disorders.

Stress and Physical Illness

Stress Can Also Affect the *Immune System*

The immune system is made of cells (e.g. white blood cells) and chemicals that **seek and destroy bacteria** and **viruses**. When someone experiences stress over a long time (a **long-term, chronic stress response**) their immune system stops functioning properly. This is called **immunosuppression**. Loads of studies have tested whether chronic stress makes us more vulnerable to infection and illness.

Brady et al (1958) — Stress and the development of ulcers

Method:	**Monkeys** were put in pairs and given electric shocks every 20 seconds for 6 hour sessions. One monkey of each pair (the 'executive') could push a lever to postpone each shock. The other could not delay them.
Results:	The 'executive' monkeys were **more likely** to develop illness (ulcers) and later die.
Conclusion:	The illness and death was not due to the shocks but due to the **stress** that the executives felt in trying to avoid them. In the long term, this stress **reduced** the immune system's ability to fight illness.
Evaluation:	The experiment has **ethical** issues — the experiment was very cruel and would not be allowed today. Also, we can't **generalise** results from monkeys to humans. Furthermore, we know that people with **little control** over their own lives (such as those with low-level jobs and the long-term unemployed), can experience **high levels** of stress, which this research cannot explain.

Immunosuppression Happens in *Humans* Too

Research on humans (fortunately much more ethical than the monkey study) has also supported the theory that stress can **reduce** the effectiveness of the immune system. Take the following study, for example:

Kiecolt-Glaser et al (1995) — Stress and wound healing

Method:	In a study with an **independent measures** design, a punch biopsy was used to create a small wound on the arms of 13 women who cared for relatives with Alzheimer's disease (a very stressful responsibility). A **control group** of 13 people also took part.
Results:	Wound healing took an average of 9 days longer for the carers than those in the control group.
Conclusion:	Chronic, long-term stress **impairs** the effectiveness of the immune system to heal wounds.
Evaluation:	**Sweeney (1995)** also found that people caring for relatives with dementia took longer than a control group to heal their wounds. However, for both studies the two groups may have **varied in other ways** apart from the stress of being a carer. The effects on the carers could be due to poor diet, lack of sleep, etc, and not just the stress they experienced. The study only contained a small number of participants — for more reliable results it should be repeated with a larger number.

Practice Questions

Q1 What conclusion did Krantz et al (1991) make from their study into cardiovascular disorders?

Q2 What were the results of the Brady et al (1958) study?

Q3 Who were the experimental group in the Kiecolt-Glaser et al (1995) study?

Exam Questions

Q1 Which of following is **not** a stage of the general adaptation syndrome?

    A resistance   **B** stress   **C** alarm   **D** exhaustion   [1 mark]

Q2 Discuss the role of stress in illness.   [16 marks]

No more exams thanks — can't be doing with ulcers...

If you think about it, it kind of stands to reason that being really stressed out all the time will have some effect on your body. It can affect your heart and your immune system, and generally just isn't very good for you. So try not to stress out — it's really not worth it. Take a deep breath, take in the lessons for life on these pages and chill out.

Stress and Life Changes

There are loads of sources of stress — for some unfortunate individuals it's the thought of peanut butter sticking to their teeth, but for normal folk, it's the major life changes which can make things stressful.

Life Changes *are a Source of Stress*

- Throughout our lives, we all experience **major life events** — like the death of a close relative, getting married or moving house. These events, and the adjustments they cause us to make, can be a major source of stress. When psychologists want to find out what level of stress these events cause, they look at health, because it's likely to be linked to stress.

- **Holmes and Rahe (1967)** developed a measuring scale to investigate the relationship between life changes and stress.

Holmes *and* Rahe *Studied* Life Change Stress *and* Illness

1) **Holmes and Rahe** assumed that both **positive** and **negative** life events involve change, and that change leads to experiencing stress.

2) To test this assumption, they studied approximately **5000** hospital patients' records and noted any **major life events** that had occurred before the person became ill.

3) It was found that patients were **likely** to have experienced life changes prior to becoming ill, and that **more serious life changes** seemed to be more **linked to stress and illness**.

When José got his car stuck in a ditch, he wasn't best pleased to a get a cold the very next day.

They *Ranked* Life Events *on the* Social Readjustment Rating Scale (SRRS)

1) **Holmes and Rahe (1967)** made a list of 43 common life events and asked loads of people to give each one a score to say how stressful it was.

2) They called the numbers that made up each score the **Life Change Units (LCU)**. The higher this number of LCUs, the more stressful it was.

3) Then they **ranked** the events from most stressful to least stressful and called this **self-report scale** the **Social Readjustment Rating Scale (SRRS)**. Examples are shown in the table to the right.

Life Event	Rank	Score (LCU)
Death of a spouse	1	100
Divorce	2	73
Retirement	10	45
Change in School	17	37
Christmas	42	12

Retirement, stressful? Pah, I can't wait...

Further Correlational Research *Supported Their Findings*

See above for a reminder of what LCU scores are.

Rahe et al (1970) — LCU score and illness

Method:	In a **correlational study**, more than 2500 American Navy seamen were given a form of the SRRS to complete just before they set sail on military duty. They had to indicate all of the events that they had experienced over the previous six months.
Results:	There was a significant correlation between LCU scores and illness. Higher LCU scores were found to be linked to a higher incidence of illness over the next seven months.
Conclusion:	The stress involved in the changes that life events bring is linked to an increased risk of illness.
Evaluation:	The results are **not representative** of the population and can only be **generalised** to American Navy seamen. Also, the results don't explain **individual differences** in response to stress. There are also limitations associated with using correlational research. You can't assume a **causal relationship** between the variables — the correlation might be caused by a third unknown variable. As well as this, there are problems with using the SRRS to rank stressful events (see the next page).

Stress and Life Changes

There are Some **Issues** with the SRRS

1) People can have positive **and** negative life events

The SRRS doesn't separate **positive and negative life events**. Stress and illness might be more linked to negative life changes. For example, a wedding might be stressful, but positive overall, while the death of a spouse might have a very negative stressful effect.

Long-term, minor sources of stress, such as everyday **hassles** (see next page), are not considered.

2) Holmes and Rahe's research was biased

Most of the research conducted by Holmes and Rahe involved male participants, meaning it is **gender biased** (page 40). It's also **ethnocentric** (page 42) so it can't be **generalised** to everybody. For example, people who don't celebrate Christmas won't find it stressful.

3) The findings relied on self-report

The questionnaires used within the SRRS rely on **self-report**. So the findings may be **unreliable** as people may not always remember events and things that happened to them accurately.

4) The research is correlational, not experimental

Correlational studies aim to establish if two variables are **related** to each other. They're useful because they allow us to investigate **relationships** between stress and lots of other variables. For example, it's likely that our stress levels are the result of many **interrelated factors**, rather than one single factor.
On the other hand...

Experiments aim to establish if a change in one variable **causes a change** in another. They have an advantage if we want to find out exactly what is **causing** stress.

Several of the life changes within the SRRS could be **related** to each other. For example, a big change in **job conditions** or getting **fired** are likely to affect a person's **financial situation**. **Pregnancy** or a change in **personal habits** and **living conditions** may affect **personal health**. This means that life changes could be both the cause **and** effect of stress.

Despite criticisms the SRRS was useful for showing that changes in life may link to stress and illness.

Practice Questions

Q1 What did Holmes and Rahe investigate as a cause of stress?

Q2 What does SRRS stand for?

Q3 Which research method was used in the Rahe et al (1970) study?

Q4 Suggest some life changes that could be related to each other.

Exam Question

Q1 Describe and evaluate the Social Readjustment Ratings Scale. [16 marks]

The sauces of stress — feels like you're always playing ketchup...

As a quick break, make your own SRRS by putting these stressful situations in order: 1) meeting your girl/boyfriend's parents, 2) walking into a job interview and realising your fly's undone, 3) feeling a spider run across your face in bed, 4) getting peanut butter stuck the roof of your mouth (don't try it if you can help it, trust me), 5) knowing that what you're writing will be read by thousands of cynical A-Level students and you can't think of anything funny to write.

Stress and Daily Hassles

For some people, it's the more niggly things that cause stress. Psychologists call these daily hassles. These are things like having a busy commute everyday, not having enough sleep, having to put up with really noisy neighbours...

Daily Hassles are Everyday Events that are Stressful...

Some psychologists have suggested that stress is related to more **mundane events** than the major life events put forward by Holmes and Rahe. Examples of these daily problems, which they named **hassles**, include:

- Having too many things to do
- Misplacing objects
- Getting stuck in traffic

...But Uplifts Can Reduce Stress

- In addition to investigating the impact of hassles on daily life, psychologists have looked at the effects of **uplifts** (things that make you feel good) in predicting peoples' stress levels.
- Whilst hassles include the ongoing strains of daily living, **uplifts** may be things like **doing well at school**, **spending time** with your partner or **socialising** with friends.

Hassles and Uplifts Scales Can be Used to Measure Life Stresses

Hassles and uplifts scales have been developed to assess how the hassles and uplifts people experience affect their stress levels, and therefore their health.

	Kanner et al (1981) — Stress and daily hassles
Method:	**100 adults** completed a questionnaire each month which asked them to choose which **hassles** they had experienced that month from a list of 117. They then had to **rate** each hassle to show how severe it had been for them. They were also asked to complete a 135-item uplifts scale asking about positive experiences they'd had in the last month. Both scales were repeated for 9 months.
Results:	Certain hassles occurred more frequently than others, such as worrying about weight, family health and the rising cost of living. They found that those with high scores were **more likely** to have physical and psychological health problems. They also found that scores on the uplifts scale were negatively related to ill health. Events on the uplifts scale may reduce stress, or protect us from it.
Conclusion:	Daily hassles are **linked** to stress and health, with a stronger correlation than that found with the SRRS (see page 104).
Evaluation:	The weaknesses of **correlational methods** are relevant here — it isn't possible to establish a cause and effect relationship between the variables. Using questionnaires resulted in **quantitative data**, which is useful for making comparisons, but they don't allow participants to explain why certain experiences are stressful to them, so potentially useful data is missed. They rely on **honesty** in order for the results to be valid — participants may not be completely truthful about admitting mundane daily events that they find stressful. They also rely on the participants' **recall** being accurate.

Other studies have also **supported** Kanner et al's findings:

In a study by **Bouteyre et al (2007)**, 223 first year Psychology students at a French university completed a hassles scale and a scale ranking depression. It was found that **41%** of students experienced depressive symptoms and that there was a positive correlation between hassles and depressive symptoms. This suggests that the **hassles** associated with the initial transition period at university could be a **risk factor for depression**.

Learning to punt was just another hassle for Norman when he started University.

Stress and Daily Hassles

DeLongis et al developed a Combined Hassles and Uplifts Scale

DeLongis et al (1988) developed a 53-item combined hassles and uplifts scale (the Hassles and Uplifts Scale). Each item (e.g. 'family') was rated as to how much of a **hassle** or **uplift** it was to the person that day.

Participants were then asked to complete a questionnaire measuring major life events alongside the 'Hassles and Uplifts Scale'. The researchers found **no relationship** between **life events** and **illness** — but a relationship between hassles and subsequent next day illness was observed. They concluded that the **everyday hassles** had a **bigger impact** on stress levels and health than the less frequent **major life changing events**.

There are Some Issues with the Hassles and Uplifts Scale

1) The research is correlational, not experimental

Just like the SRRS, the Hassles and Uplifts Scale **can't** show a **cause-and-effect** relationship. Also, hassles can influence someone's health, but health can also influence how people perceive daily activities and events — making them seem **more stressful** when ill than when seen in normal health.

2) Other resources should also be considered

The Hassles and Uplifts Scale doesn't consider the **social resources** available to each individual (i.e. money, health, work, etc.). **Moos and Swindle (1990)** have shown that the impact of **ongoing** and **chronic sources of stress**, such as an **unfulfilling job**, can be moderated by various social resources.

3) Everyone is different

Individual differences mean that everyone treats events and situations in a different way. Some people might be able to cope better with daily stresses, but be more affected by major life events. Some people are just **naturally better** at dealing with stress than others.

Cultural differences can also influence how people see daily hassles and uplifts, meaning the scale is **ethnocentric**, as it's based on Western views and lifestyles. **Social support** can affect peoples' perceptions of stress (see pages 114-115).

4) The findings relied on self-report

The Hassles and Uplifts Scale relies on **self-report** which can make the findings **unreliable**. People taking part may **lie** to suggest they are coping better than they really are.

Cynthia didn't need any experiments — she knew exactly what was causing her stress.

Practice Questions

Q1 Give an example of a daily hassle.

Q2 What are uplifts?

Q3 Describe the method used by Kanner et al (1981).

Q4 What conclusion did DeLongis et al (1988) make from their study?

Exam Question

Q1 Briefly outline and evaluate one study which used the Hassles and Uplifts Scale. [4 marks]

My momma always said, life is like a box of daily hassles and uplifts...

...you never know what you're gonna get. You could get stuck in a queue at the self-checkouts where the person in front is paying with a bag of coppers, or you could win a tenner on the lottery. So — try not to get worked up over the little things and focus on the uplifting things. Gee — I feel like a proper motivational psychologist now.

Stress at Work

I could say my job is stressful... writing witty, engaging intro lines for A-Level students across the country. But — I'm sat here, with a steaming mug of tea, listening to the wind outside thinking (rather smugly) that it's not that bad really...

The **Workplace** is a Massive Source of Stress

Unfortunately, most people need to work. Some aspects of the **work they do**, **where they work**, or **who they have to work with**, become a source of stress. This is important because if a person is very stressed at work they may be more likely to get ill. Stress in the workplace comes from **five** key areas.

1) **Relationships at work** — relationships with bosses, colleagues and customers may be stressful. E.g. we might feel **undervalued** and that we **lack support**.

2) **Work pressures** — having a large **workload**, perhaps with **strict deadlines**.

3) **The physical environment** — workplaces may be very noisy, overcrowded, or too hot or cold (aren't we fussy...). Work may also involve health risks or unsociable working hours.

4) **Stresses linked to our role** — worrying about **job security** or our **prospects for promotion**. Also, the range of our responsibilities may be unclear, and we may experience conflict, e.g. trying to please our bosses and the people who work for us.

5) **Lack of control** — we may not have much **influence over the type and amount of work** we do, or where and when we do it. There's more about this below.

Stress is not only bad for the individual, but also for their employer and the economy, because they will take more days off sick.

A **Lack of Control** in the Workplace is Stressful

Feeling that we don't have much influence over the **type of work** we do and our **workload** (how much work we have to do) can lead to stress. This can be seen in **Marmot et al's (1997)** study:

Marmot et al (1997) — Illness in the workplace

Method: Over **7000** civil service employees working in London were surveyed. Information was obtained about their grade of employment, how much control they felt they had, how much support they felt they had, etc.

Results: When the medical records of these employees were followed up **5 years later**, those on lower employment grades who felt less control over their work (and less social support) were found to be more likely to have **cardiovascular disorders**. Participants on the lowest grade of employment were four times more likely to die of a heart attack than those on the highest grade.

Conclusion: Believing that you have little control over your work influences work stress and the development of illness.

Evaluation: The study only looked at '**white collar**' work (office-type jobs), so the results may not apply to other jobs. **Smoking** was found to be common in those who developed illnesses. So, perhaps those who felt less control at work were more likely to smoke — and the smoking caused the heart problems rather than stress. Other **factors** (e.g. diet and exercise) may be linked to job grade and could be causing illness rather than the perceived lack of control.

Frankenhaeuser (1975) also investigated the link between lack of control and stress in the workplace using urine samples and blood pressure. These are **physiological measures** of stress (see next page).

Frankenhaeuser (1975) — Stress levels in sawmill workers

Method: Frankenhaeuser studied **2 groups** of workers at a sawmill. One group had the repetitive task of feeding logs into a machine all day. The job was very noisy and the workers were socially isolated. They didn't have much control over their work as the machine dictated how quickly they should feed the logs in. The other group had a different task which gave them more control of their workload, and more social contact. Stress levels were measured by testing **urine samples** and **blood pressure**.

Results: The workers who had minimal control and social contact had **higher levels** of stress hormones in their urine. They were more likely to suffer from high blood pressure and stomach ulcers.

Conclusion: A **lack** of control and social contact at work can lead to stress.

Evaluation: This was a field experiment, so it has high **ecological validity**. The findings are **supported** by Marmot's study. However, it doesn't take individual differences into account — some individuals may just be more prone to stress. The results could have been affected by extraneous variables, such as how much the workers were paid.

Stress at Work

Physiological Measures of Stress Can be Taken

Stress affects the **body** in different ways, and as Frankenhaeuser's study showed on the previous page, **stress levels** can be measured using **physiological tests**.

1) **Heart rate** — A **chest strap** containing a **transmitter** measures **electrical activity** and indicates heart rate. **Increased** heart rate is a sign of **stress**.

2) **Blood pressure** — This is measured by putting an inflatable cuff on the arm which restricts blood flow. As it deflates, the pulse rate in the arm indicates blood pressure levels. **Stress** is associated with **high blood pressure**.

3) **Hormone levels** — **Blood** and **urine** can be tested for stress-related hormones. For example, **increased** levels of **adrenaline** and **cortisol** indicate **higher** levels of **stress**.

Having sweaty hands was not an option for Tim and Josh.

4) **Skin conductance response** — This measures the **electrical resistance** of the skin, which is affected by **moisture level** (sweat). An **increased** skin conductance response is associated with **stress**.

There are Strengths and Weaknesses of Using Physiological Measures

Strengths
- Physiological tests are **objective** — it's not possible to lie, and the results **won't** be **influenced** by the participant or the researcher.
- The test results can indicate appropriate **treatments** for the stress — e.g. if someone has an **increased heart rate**, they can be put on drugs called **beta blockers** to slow their heart down.

Weaknesses
- The tests might not be measuring stress. Other behaviours such as **poor diet**, **poor sleeping patterns** and **alcohol consumption** can also cause changes in these measurements. Each of these behaviours can be used as **coping mechanisms** when people are **stressed**. So it could be that **physiological changes** are caused by one of these **stress-related behaviours**.
- Technology isn't always 100% accurate.

Practice Questions

Q1 Give one reason why the workplace might be a source of stress.

Q2 Who were the participants in Marmot et al's (1997) study?

Q3 Name two different physiological measures of stress.

Exam Questions

Q1 Outline and evaluate physiological measures of stress. [8 marks]

Q2 Discuss the workplace as a source of stress, including the effects of workload and control. [16 marks]

Hormone-filled urine and sweaty hands — no wonder work is stressful...

Being prepared for your exams will hopefully make you much less stressed. So... you could liken CGP to a giant stress ball. Just give the book a squeeze and all your stresses will disappear. Well, maybe learn the stuff first. Better to be safe than sorry. You can thank me when you've picked up your results and dried off your sweaty palms.

Stress — Individual Differences

By now you hopefully know all about how stress affects the body. But that doesn't mean stress affects everyone in the same way. If you stick two people in a pit and drop spiders on them, it's unlikely they're going to react in exactly the same way. Psychologists call different personal reactions 'individual differences'.

Different **Personalities** Can Lead to Different Stress Levels

Psychologists love sticking people into groups. One theory about personality is that you can split everyone into three groups called '**Type A**', '**Type B**' or '**Type X**'. Type A people are competitive and ambitious. Type Bs are non-competitive, relaxed and easy-going. Type Xs have a balance of Type A and Type B behaviours. **Friedman and Rosenman (1974)** tested how these different types of personality affect the likelihood of CHD (coronary heart disease) — one of the most obvious effects of stress.

	Friedman and Rosenman (1974) — Type A personality & illness
Method:	Approximately **3000**, 39-59 year old American males were assessed to class their personality characteristics into Type A, Type B or Type X using interviews and observation. At the start of the study **none of them** had CHD (coronary heart disease).
Results:	Eight years later, **257** of them had developed CHD. 70% of these were classed as **Type A** personality. This includes being 'workaholic', extremely competitive, hostile to others, and always in a rush. Participants classed as Type B were less competitive and less impatient. They were found to have half the rate of heart disease of Type A. These results were found even when the extraneous variables of weight and smoking were taken into account.
Conclusion:	Type A personalities seem to be at a **higher risk** of stress-related illnesses, such as CHD.
Evaluation:	Having only three personality types seems a bit **simplistic**. The study doesn't prove that personality characteristics can **cause** stress and illness. It could be the other way round. For example, Type A personality may develop as a **response** to being under stress (from work etc.). Also, the **sample** used in the study was quite limited — middle-aged, male Americans. This means that it may not be possible to **generalise** the results to the rest of the population. In addition, participants may not have been completely **honest** in their interviews so that their characteristics appeared desirable to the researcher (**social desirability bias**).

Later research also identified **Type C** personalities — mild-mannered, easy-going people who may not react well to stressful situations, and suppress their emotions. These people seem to have a higher risk of **cancer**.

Kobasa (1979) Identified **Hardiness** as an Important **Individual Difference**

Kobasa described people as being **hardy** or **non-hardy**. There are three main characteristics of hardy personalities:

1) Hardy personalities are very involved in what they do, and show a high level of **commitment**. This means that they work hard at relationships, jobs and other activities in life.

2) They view change in a positive rather than a negative way, seeing it as an opportunity for **challenge**. Hardy personalities enjoy a challenge and see it as an opportunity to develop themselves.

3) They have a strong feeling of **control** over their life and what happens to them. This is known as having an **internal locus of control**.

In comparison, **non-hardy** personalities view any life experiences in a much more **negative** way, and feel that they're **unable to cope** with situations. They feel that **external agencies** have control over what happens to them and that it isn't worth trying to become more powerful. They **give up** easily and don't see any value in trying to change what's happening around them.

It's difficult to **quantify** what's meant by a hardy personality, making it difficult to **measure** and test. We should also avoid making assumptions about **cause and effect** — it could be that some people have hardy personalities because of a lack of stress in their lives, rather than low stress being the result of personality. Levels of hardiness could **fluctuate** and may decrease when the person is experiencing lots of stress, such as after a bereavement.

Stress — Individual Differences

Research has Shown a Relationship Between **Stress** and **Hardiness**

There is evidence suggesting that people with a hardy personality are less likely to suffer from illness as a result of stress. For instance, a study by **Maddi et al (1987)** looked at employees of a US phone company that was reducing its workforce. During the downsize, **two-thirds** of the workforce suffered from stress-related health problems. However, the other **one-third** of the workforce **thrived** during the period. It was found that these people were much more likely to have a **hardy personality**.

Lifton et al (2006) measured the hardiness of **1432 students** at five US universities. Students who displayed **hardy personalities** were significantly **more likely** to successfully **complete** their degrees. A large number of students who dropped out had low hardiness scores.

Stress can also be Related to **Gender**

There are some differences in the way men and women behave, so psychologists (who don't miss a trick) thought that maybe these differences could affect what kinds of things men and women find stressful, and how they cope. They looked at how **biological**, **social** and **cognitive** differences between males and females influence their response to stress.

<u>Biological Explanation</u> — through evolution, men in their role of 'hunter-gatherer' may have developed a stronger 'fight or flight' response than women, who had the role of caring for the kids. In this way, males and females may have developed different physiological responses to stress.

Taylor et al (2000) suggest that women produce a calmer response to stress due to a hormone. Oxytocin is released in response to stress and has been shown to lead to maternal behaviour and social affiliation. Taylor called this the 'tend and befriend' response (instead of the 'fight or flight' response) and thought it might make females more likely to seek social support to help them cope with stress.

<u>Social Explanation</u> — to fulfil their Western stereotypical social role, men are expected to be less open about their feelings than women. This means they're less likely to discuss stressful experiences with others and may use harmful coping methods instead, e.g. smoking and drinking.

Carroll (1992) found that women do generally make more use of social support to deal with stress. However, coronary heart disease has increased in women — but this could just be because a change in social roles means that it's now more acceptable for women to drink and smoke.

<u>Cognitive Explanation</u> — **Vogele et al (1997)** claim that women are better able to control anger and therefore respond more calmly to stressful situations. Men may feel that anger is an acceptable way to respond, and feel stress if they cannot show it. These cognitive differences could be the result of biology or the roles we are taught to follow, or a bit of both.

Practice Questions

Q1 Explain the differences between Type A and Type B personalities.

Q2 Give a criticism of Friedman and Rosenman's (1974) research.

Q3 What are the three characteristics associated with a hardy personality?

Q4 What did Vogele et al (1997) claim about stress?

Exam Questions

Q1	Discuss gender differences in coping with stress.	[8 marks]
Q2	Describe and evaluate research into personality types and stress.	[16 marks]

We are all individuals, we are all individuals, we are all individuals...

This is an important thing to remember throughout Psychology. People are divided into groups to show how different things affect people — but there are also individual differences, which means that when put in the same situation, people will often react differently. This seems obvious but it's easy to forget if you get wrapped up in all the theories.

Stress Management

Biological methods of stress management help people cope with stress by changing the way their body responds to it. You need to know about drug treatments and biofeedback...

Drug Treatments *Work in* Two Ways

1) They **slow down** the activity of the **central nervous system** (CNS). Anti-anxiety drugs called **benzodiazepines** (BZs) increase the body's reaction to its own natural anxiety-relieving chemical **GABA** (gamma-aminobutyric acid), which slows down the activity of neurones and makes us feel relaxed.

OR...

2) They **reduce** the activity of the **sympathetic nervous system** (SNS).

The SNS increases heart rate, blood pressure and levels of the hormone **cortisol**. High levels of cortisol can make our immune system **weak** and also cause heart disease. The group of drugs called **beta blockers** reduce all these unpleasant symptoms.

Biofeedback *Uses Information About* What's Happening *in the Body*

Biofeedback gives people information about **internal physical processes** that they wouldn't otherwise be aware of, e.g. muscle tension. The idea is to give them more **control** over these internal processes and the ability to **alter** them. There are **four** main steps involved:

1) The person is attached to a machine that monitors and gives **feedback** on internal physical processes such as **heart rate**, **blood pressure** or **muscle tension**.

2) They are then taught how to **control** these symptoms of stress through a variety of techniques. These can include **muscle relaxation** — muscle groups are tensed and relaxed in turn until the whole body is relaxed. This teaches people to notice when their body is becoming tense. Other techniques include actively clearing the mind using **meditation**, or **breathing control** exercises.

3) This feeling of relaxation acts like a **reward** and encourages the person to repeat this behaviour, so that it becomes a habit. It's a type of **behavioural (operant) conditioning**.

4) The person learns to use these techniques in **real-life** situations.

Trisha didn't need biofeedback — she had stress totally sorted.

Budzynski et al (1973) investigated the role of biofeedback in stress management:

Budzynski et al (1973) — Biofeedback and tension headaches

Method:	The sample was **18 participants** who volunteered in response to a newspaper advert about headaches. The participants were screened to make sure they only suffered from tension headaches and were then divided into **three groups**. **Group 1** received **relaxation training** twice a week for 8 weeks. Their muscle tension was monitored by an EMG monitor which fed back information by making clicks. They were told that **more clicks** meant **more muscle tension** and **worse headaches**. They were encouraged to **relax** so that the clicks slowed down. **Group 2** received the **same relaxation training**, however they weren't told that the clicks reflected their level of muscle tension and a fake soundtrack of clicks was played to them. **Group 3** were the **control group**. They didn't have any relaxation training. Participants who'd had relaxation training were also told to **practise** the techniques at home.
Results:	At the end of the study and three months afterwards, **Group 1** had the **lowest muscle tension** and **fewer headaches**. They also showed **lower levels** of hysteria, **depression** and were **less preoccupied** with their **health** than they were before the study. Participants who'd **practised** the relaxation techniques at home showed **more improvement** than those who hadn't.
Conclusion:	Biofeedback can **reduce stress related illnesses** such as tension headaches.
Evaluation:	The presence of a **control group** and **Group 2** showed that it was the actual feedback that was important, not just the presence of feedback. However, the sample size is small, making **generalisation** difficult. Also, the results can't be generalised to other stress-related symptoms.

Stress Management

Biological Methods of Stress Management Have Strengths and Weaknesses

Both drugs and biofeedback are **effective**:

Drugs are **quick** and **effective** in reducing dangerous symptoms such as high blood pressure. **Kahn et al (1986)** found that benzodiazepines were superior to a placebo (sugar pill) when they tracked around 250 patients over an 8-week period.

Attanasio et al (1985) found that biofeedback helped teenagers and children with stress-related disorders to gain **control** over the symptoms of **migraine** headaches. They also showed an increase in **enthusiasm** and a more positive attitude.

Placebos are pills that do nothing at all. They're used to test if any effect happens just because people think they're being treated.

BUT both treat **symptoms** rather than the underlying causes of stress:

Drugs only help with the **symptoms**, and only so long as the drugs are taken.

Biofeedback also aims to **reduce** symptoms, but using relaxation techniques can also give the person a sense of **control** and have more **long-lasting** benefits.

Drugs have **side effects**, biofeedback **doesn't**:

Drugs can have minor **side effects** such as dizziness and tiredness, or more serious effects such as blurred vision and changes in sex drive. **Withdrawal symptoms** when people come off medication, such as increased anxiety, seizures, tremors and headaches, can be distressing. Benzodiazepines can be **addictive** and people develop **dependency** on them, so they are generally limited to a maximum of 4 weeks use.

There are no side effects of biofeedback — just **relaxation**. This method's advantage is that it's **voluntary** and not invasive.

Drugs are **easier** to use than biofeedback:

Drugs are relatively **easy** to prescribe and use.

Biofeedback needs specialist **equipment** and expert **supervision**. Some argue that the benefits of biofeedback could be gained from other relaxation techniques, and so this is an unnecessary expense.

Practice Questions

Q1 What is GABA?

Q2 Describe the method Budzynski et al (1973) used in their study on biofeedback and tension headaches.

Q3 Give one problem of using drugs to deal with stress.

Q4 Briefly describe the findings of Kahn et al's (1986) investigation into drug treatments.

Q5 Why is biofeedback a more expensive form of treatment than drugs?

Exam Questions

Q1 Describe how drug therapy can help in the management of stress.	[4 marks]
Q2 Outline and evaluate the use of biofeedback in enabling people to manage and cope with stress.	[16 marks]

Stress management — it's more than squeezing a stress ball...

This ridiculously stressed and hectic lifestyle we choose to live is turning us all into ill people. I can't understand it myself — personally I choose the more Caribbean attitude to time management. I'm quite confident I'll never need to take BZs or try some biofeedback. But then again, I might get into trouble for not finishing this book on time.

Stress Management

The end is in sight — the last two pages on stress. So sit back, relax, and learn how to manage your stress before the exams. And then you can give yourself a brand new book to read and a nice bath to keep you stress-free and happy.

Stress Inoculation Therapy Can be Used to Manage Stress

1) **Cognitive techniques** aim to manage stress by identifying and **altering** the **thought processes** that cause stress.

2) **Meichenbaum (1985)** developed a cognitive stress management approach called **stress inoculation therapy (SIT)**.

3) SIT introduces **minor** levels of stress to individuals, which allows them to **psychologically adjust** and **prepare** for stressful situations.

4) There are **three phases** to SIT:

- **Conceptualisation** — identify fears and concerns with the help of a therapist.
- **Skills acquisition and rehearsal** — train to develop skills like positive thinking and relaxation, in order to improve self-confidence.
- **Application and follow-through** — practise the newly acquired skill in real-life situations, with support and back-up from the therapist.

Alfie's mum made him practise SIT every day.

5) Meichenbaum (1985) found that SIT works both with **short-term stressors** such as preparing for public speaking, and **longer-term stressors** such as medical illness, divorce or work-related stress.

There are **strengths** and **weaknesses** to SIT:

- Because SIT requires people to acknowledge their stress and understand the cause of it, it can result in **longer lasting** coping.
- However, **cognitive methods** don't suit all individuals — they must be determined to stick to the technique.
- Meichenbaum's (1985) research was based on white, middle-class people, and so **can't be generalised** to others.
- The procedures in SIT are **lengthy** and require considerable **insight** and **commitment** of **time** and **effort**.

Social Support Can Play a Big Part in How Stress is Managed

1) From page 103, you know that stress can **suppress** the **immune system**.

2) It's been suggested that **social support** (e.g. from families, friends, help groups) can **reduce stress**, and so reduce the impact on the **immune system**.

3) If this is the case, we would expect people with **strong social support** to be **less likely** to become **ill** and **more likely** to **recover** from illness than those without a good social support system.

Waxler-Morrison et al's (1991) study can provide **evidence** for this:

	Waxler-Morrison et al (1991) — The role of social support
Method:	This was a **natural experiment** investigating the effect of **social support** on **survival chances** of women with breast cancer. Data on social support (e.g. number of supportive friends, extent of contact with friends, size of social network, etc.) was collected from **133 women** with breast cancer using **questionnaires** and **interviews**. The women's **medical records** were followed over 4 years.
Results:	They found that women with **better social support** had **better survival rates**. Types of support that were relevant included being married, having a job, having contact with friends, and getting support from friends.
Conclusion:	**Social support** may be helpful in **reducing stress**, as the women with good social support networks were **more likely** to **survive** breast cancer. This could be because they were less stressed and so their **immune system** was working more efficiently than women without a good support system.
Evaluation:	It's important not to **assume causality** — social support is associated with survival but doesn't necessarily cause it. Further investigation is needed to find the precise relationship between social support and cancer survival. The fact that the study only included women reduces the **reliability** of the conclusions that can be drawn from the results.

Stress Management

There are **Different Types** of Social Support

1) **Instrumental** Support

- Sometimes people need **practical help** — this is called **instrumental support**. It might include going to get someone's **groceries**, doing the **cleaning** or providing **money**, **childcare** or other **resources**.
- Instrumental support **reduces the stress** of those who are **overwhelmed** in terms of worrying about time, money, responsibility, etc.

2) **Emotional** Support

- Giving people a **hug**, a **pat on the back**, or even just listening and **empathising** are all types of **emotional support**.
- These actions make people feel **loved**, and give them **comfort** and **reassurance**.
- Emotional support usually comes from close **friends** and **family** members and **reduces emotional distress**.

3) **Esteem** Support

- When others show **esteem support**, they provide **expressions of encouragement** to build up someone's confidence. They might **reinforce** peoples' strengths and remind them of all the things they are good at.
- For example, **life coaches** rely on esteem support to make people believe in their own abilities, enhancing their individual **self-worth**.
- People then feel much more **able to cope** with stressful situations.

Stress didn't feature highly in Poppy's merry world.

Practice Questions

Q1 What did Meichenbaum (1985) develop?

Q2 Outline some limitations of stress inoculation therapy.

Q3 Name one social factor that increases breast cancer survival chances according to Waxler-Morrison et al (1991).

Q4 What is esteem support?

Exam Questions

Q1 Describe how stress inoculation therapy works. [6 marks]

Q2 Read the item below then answer the questions that follow.

> Rachel and Dominic have recently married. Dominic has just started a new job and Rachel travels a lot through work. They have bought a house and were about to move in when a pipe burst and flooded the kitchen. They now need to redecorate before they can move in, but neither of them has much time to do so.
>
> Luckily, both Rachel and Dominic's parents have loaned them some money and are going to help redecorate.

a) Identify the type of social support that Rachel and Dominic's parents are providing. [1 mark]

b) Discuss the role of social support in coping with stress. [16 marks]

Worth keeping hold of your friends then — you might need 'em one day...

Ahhhh, so the old saying could be true — love really is the best medicine, and having lots of friends could help you survive cancer. That's good to know. Also good to know — the fancily named stress inoculation technique for managing stress. Not quite as heart-warming, but just as necessary seeing as you've got exams coming up soon.

Biological Explanations of Aggression

Aggression is a tendency that humans share with almost all species of animal, as anyone who's tried to give a cat a bath will know. It's a response that can be partially explained by biology. Not sure that'd go down well as an excuse though...

There Are **Genetic Influences** Underlying Aggression

> Aggression is behaviour intended to harm — including physical and psychological harm.

1) Species of various animals have been **selectively bred** to produce highly **aggressive** individuals — e.g. Doberman dogs were originally bred by humans to behave aggressively towards intruders so they can be used as guard dogs.

2) This ability to select the most aggressive dogs and breed them together to give **new generations** with the **same** aggressive tendencies suggests that there are specific **genes** that determine levels of aggression.

3) In humans, evidence for a genetic component to aggression comes from **twin studies** and **adoption studies**, where **criminality** is used as a measure of aggression.

Christiansen (1977) — Twin study into aggression

Method:	An analysis of criminality in 3586 pairs of **twins** born between 1881 and 1910 in a region of Denmark was done, in order to find **concordance rates**. Of this sample, **926** individuals were registered by the police for **criminal activity**. Identical **(MZ)** and **non-identical (DZ)** twins were compared for the rate at which **both** twins of the pair were registered.
Results:	**Male MZ twins** showed **35% concordance** for criminality, compared to the **12% concordance** shown between **DZ twins**. **Female MZ** twins showed **21% concordance** compared to **8%** for **DZ** twins.
Conclusion:	Twins of criminals are more likely to **also** be criminals if they share all of their twin's genes (MZ), rather only some of their genes (DZ). So there's a **genetic component** to aggressive behaviour.
Evaluation:	Genetics can't be the only factor, as the concordance rate for MZ twins (who share all of their genetic material) wasn't 100%. By studying **all** the twins born in a specified time frame, this study gives a **representative** rate of concordance. However, as with all twin studies, **environment** might account for the different concordance rates — because they look the same, MZ twins may be treated **more alike**, and have more shared experiences.

The **MAOA Gene** Has Been Linked to **Aggressive Behaviour**

1) Monoamine oxidase A (**MAOA**) is an **enzyme** involved in processing neurotransmitters, including **serotonin**, in the brain. Serotonin is thought to be involved in **aggression** (see page 118).

2) The **MAOA gene** controls production of MAOA.

3) Some versions of the gene, which result in **lower levels** of MAOA (and therefore lower serotonin activity — i.e. less serotonin being processed in the brain), have been linked to **aggressive behaviour**.

4) The link between this gene and aggression was discovered by researchers studying a **Dutch family**:

> **Brunner et al (1993)** studied an **extended family** in the Netherlands, where several male family members showed patterns of behaviour involving **impulsive aggression**, including violent crime.
>
> They identified a **fault** in the **MAOA gene** of the individuals who showed impulsive aggression, which wasn't present in other male family members. The individuals with this fault were **deficient in MAOA**.

Salem had miaow deficiency.

5) Studies on **mice** have found a similar relationship between MAOA gene variations and aggression.

> **Cases et al (1995)** found that **adult male mice** who were **missing the MAOA-producing gene** had specific behaviour patterns, which included **heightened aggression**.
>
> This is known as a **knockout study** — animals are bred so that they are missing a **specific gene** (the gene is knocked-out), and are then studied to observe the **effect** of the gene.

Biological Explanations of Aggression

The **Genetic Explanation** for **Aggression** Has **Strengths** and **Weaknesses**

Strengths

1) **Twin studies, adoption studies** and **knockout studies** suggest there is a genetic element to aggression.

2) **Caspi et al (2002)** found that men with a 'low MAOA activity' gene were not significantly more likely to engage in **anti-social behaviour** (including violence). However, there was a significant effect in men who had been **maltreated as children**. This suggests that genetics **interact** with environmental factors to influence aggression levels.

Weaknesses

1) The genetic explanation **ignores social** and **environmental** factors, which may play a part too.

2) **Walters' (1992) meta-analysis** found only a **weak correlation** between genetic factors and crime. This effect was **weaker** for more recent and better designed studies.

The **Limbic System** is an **Area of the Brain** That's Been Linked to **Aggression**

1) Different areas of the **brain**, including the **temporal lobe** and the **limbic system**, have been linked to different forms of aggressive behaviour.

2) One part of the limbic system, the **amygdala**, has been found to have a particularly strong connection to aggression.

> The limbic system is a group of brain structures mostly associated with emotion and memory.

3) Animal studies have shown that **electrical stimulation** of different parts of the amygdala can either **cause** or **reduce** aggression. **Lesions** to the amygdala have been found to cause cats to **attack**, but caused dogs to become **more submissive** and **less aggressive** — they needed **more stimulation** to provoke a response.

4) There is some evidence for the role of the amygdala in **human** aggression too. **Charles Whitman**, a sniper who killed 14 innocent people and wounded 31 others, left a note that pleaded for his brain to be examined after death for possible dysfunction. An autopsy showed that he had a **temporal lobe tumour**, pressing on his amygdala.

An **amygdalotomy** is a procedure which involves **disconnecting** the amygdala from the rest of the brain. Studies have shown that, following the procedure, many patients experience a **loss of emotion** and become a lot **less aggressive**.

Mpakopoulou et al (2008) conducted a review looking at studies investigating aggression in patients **before and after** an amygdalotomy. Of the 13 papers they looked at, they found that overall, **aggressive behaviours** in those who'd had an amygdalotomy had **decreased** between 33 and 100% with no impact on the patients' learning or intelligence.

amygdala

Practice Questions

Q1 How can selective breeding support the genetic explanation of aggression?

Q2 What does the MAOA gene do?

Q3 What is a knockout study?

Exam Questions

Q1 Outline the role of the limbic system in aggression. [4 marks]

Q2 Discuss the genetic explanation for aggression. [16 marks]

Pardon me for being aggressive — it was not me, it was my amygdala...

Not quite as snappy as the original, but I still have high hopes that it'll catch on. So, plenty to take in here — as well as the amygdala stuff there's genetics. There's lots of evidence that genes play a part in aggression, but it's not as simple as an 'aggression gene' — certain genes may make aggression more likely, but social factors probably play a part too.

Biological Explanations of Aggression

I imagine when you got to the end of those last two pages you were deeply disappointed they'd finished. Luckily, there are two more lovely pages of biological explanations here, just waiting for you to get stuck in. I'm too good to you.

Turnover of **Serotonin** May Affect **Aggression**

Serotonin is important in the limbic system (previous page), so these explanations are linked.

1) **Serotonin** is a neurotransmitter which is thought to **inhibit aggressive behaviour** — **low serotonin** in the brain (or reduced serotonin activity) is thought to be linked to **aggression**.

2) The level of **serotonin activity** in the brain is measured by **turnover** — this is how much serotonin is produced and then **broken down**.

Animal Studies

There's lots of evidence from **animal studies** that **low serotonin turnover** is linked to **increased aggression**.

> **Higley et al (1996)** studied a group of 49 **rhesus monkeys** over 4 years. They determined each individual's **serotonin turnover**. Monkeys with **lower serotonin turnover** were observed to be **more aggressive**. After 4 years, 11 monkeys had died or were missing. All of the monkeys in the **highest serotonin turnover** group **survived**, and the 4 monkeys who had died as a result of **aggressive encounters** were all in the **lowest serotonin group**.

> **Valzelli and Bernasconi (1979)** bred mice with **low serotonin turnover**. They found that, when isolated, these mice were **more aggressive** than mice with normal serotonin turnover.

Diet Manipulation Studies

1) Other studies have used **controlled diets** to attempt to manipulate brain serotonin levels in **healthy participants**.

2) Serotonin is made from an **amino acid** called **tryptophan**. A diet **low** in tryptophan, but **high** in other amino acids, is thought to **reduce brain serotonin** levels.

> **Moeller et al (1996)** found that healthy male subjects showed **increased aggression** 5 or 6 hours after they were given a **tryptophan-free** mixture of amino acids. The researchers proposed that this aggression was likely to have been caused by **decreased serotonin levels** in the participants' brains.

3) Similar research has linked this effect of serotonin on aggression to the **amygdala** (see previous page).

Studies **Linking Serotonin** with **Aggression** Have **Limitations**

There's plenty of evidence that serotonin is **related** to aggression, but scientific support which shows how serotonin **causes** aggression in humans is lacking. There are several weaknesses in the evidence available:

1) Animals studies show a **strong link** between low serotonin turnover and aggression, but this doesn't mean the link is **causal**. Also, findings from animal studies can't be generalised to **humans**.

2) Studies using diet are better **controlled**, and usually involve **healthy participants**. However, they don't **directly** link serotonin to aggression — it's just **thought** that this is why a controlled diet can affect aggression.

3) **Laboratory studies** have low ecological validity. **Natural experiments** have higher ecological validity, and these studies tend to support a **more complicated** relationship between serotonin and aggression. For example, lots of studies have used convictions for **criminal offences** as a measure of aggression:

> **Virkkunen et al (1987)** studied serotonin turnover in 20 **arsonists**, 20 **violent offenders** and 10 **healthy volunteers**. Serotonin turnover was **significantly lower** in the arsonists than in the other groups. However, serotonin turnover **didn't** correlate with the **severity** of the arsonists' offences. Virkkunen et al proposed that this showed a link between serotonin and **impulsive** behaviour, rather than **aggressive** behaviour.

4) However, results from studies of **convicted criminals** may not be **generalisable** to the population as a whole.

Biological Explanations of Aggression

Testosterone *May Also Be Involved in Aggression*

1) Testosterone is an **androgen** (male sex hormone) — it's responsible for the development of **male characteristics**, and may also affect the brain.

2) Men produce much **more** testosterone than women, and men are statistically more likely to engage in **violence** than women. For example, a very **high proportion** of people arrested for violence against another person in the UK are men.

3) It's been argued that this indicates testosterone is related to **aggression**.

4) Studies involving people **convicted of violence** have supported this suggestion.

> **Dabbs et al (1987)** measured testosterone levels in the saliva of 89 male **prison inmates**. Those with a **higher testosterone** concentration were more likely to have been convicted of **violent crimes**. Almost all of those with the **highest levels** had been convicted of violent crimes, and almost all of those with the **lowest levels** had been convicted of non-violent crimes.

Jeff wasn't the aggressive type, but if he ever saw that hairdresser again...

5) However, there's a problem with establishing **cause and effect** — this data is only **correlational**. Another factor could be causing aggressive behaviour, or it could be that being aggressive raises levels of testosterone.

6) **Van Goozen et al (1994)** studied the effects of testosterone **directly**. This avoided having to depend on correlational data, which made it easier to establish cause and effect.

	Van Goozen et al (1994) — Aggression in transsexual participants
Method:	In a **repeated measures** design, 35 female-to-male and 15 male-to-female transsexuals completed **questionnaires** to assess **proneness to aggression**. They completed the questionnaires before and after receiving hormone treatment to 'change' their sex. Female-to-male transsexuals were given testosterone (an androgen) and male-to-female transsexuals were given anti-androgens. Treatment lasted 3 months.
Results:	**Female-to-male** transsexuals reported an **increase** in aggression proneness, whereas **male-to-female** transsexuals reported a **decrease**.
Conclusion:	Levels of **testosterone** determine the likelihood of displaying **aggressive behaviours**.
Evaluation:	By controlling levels of testosterone **experimentally**, the **direction** of cause and effect between testosterone and aggression can be established. However, **self-report** measures of aggression were used, which are subjective and so may not be valid. The participants may have been conforming to **stereotypes** of their new gender roles by expressing an increase or decrease in aggression.

Practice Questions

Q1 What is serotonin?

Q2 Give an example of a diet manipulation study investigating aggression.

Q3 What is testosterone?

Q4 Give one weakness of evidence from studies of criminals for the role of testosterone in aggression.

Exam Questions

Q1 Briefly outline and evaluate the findings of one study investigating the role of testosterone in aggression. [3 marks]

Q2 Describe and evaluate the role of serotonin in aggression. [16 marks]

All this brain chemistry stuff is enough to make anyone lose their temper...

There are some tricky bits here, but don't let all the jazzy biology words throw you — the key ideas are pretty simple. Serotonin and testosterone are probably both involved in aggression, but it's not totally clear that either of them cause it — lots of the evidence is correlational, and studies often focus on criminals, so the results may not apply to everyone.

Ethological and Evolutionary Explanations

Aggression often (though not always) serves a purpose. That doesn't give you licence to go stomping around throwing things about though — it's not big and it's not clever. Speaking of clever, you'd best get on and learn this stuff...

The **Ethological Explanation** for **Aggression** is Based on **Animal Behaviour**

Ethology is the study of naturally occurring **animal behaviour**, which can include human behaviour. Ethologists usually look at a particular type of behaviour (e.g. aggression) **across species**.

Lorenz proposed a theory of aggression based on **animal behaviour**, which he applied to humans too. He defined aggression as **fighting instinct** directed at members of **your own species**.

Lorenz Believed That Aggression is an **Innate Response**

> *Aggression as an adaptation is covered more on the next page.*

1) Lorenz argued that aggression has evolved as an **adaptive response** — an individual will be more likely to pass on their **genes** if they're able to gain the **upper hand** in competition for food, mates or territory.

2) He described aggression as an **innate tendency** that's triggered by **environmental stimuli**:

- The urge to engage in **aggressive** behaviour builds up **continuously** over time — the **more time** that has passed since the last release of aggression, the more an animal feels **internal pressure** to be aggressive.
- Eventually a **stimulus** (an external event or situation) will **trigger** aggression.
- As the internal pressure to release the aggression **builds up**, the **strength of stimulus** needed to trigger this **decreases**. If the pressure is **very high** then aggression might be triggered **spontaneously**.
- The stimulus triggers an **innate releasing mechanism** — this is a proposed 'innate pathway' in the brain (i.e. a brain network that we're born with), which sets off a **fixed action pattern**.
- A fixed action pattern is an **instinctive behaviour** which is identical **across a species**. For example, babies instinctively grab things they're offered and hold on tightly.

3) Aggression in this form (a fixed action pattern set off by a specific stimulus), has been observed in **red-bellied sticklebacks** (a species of fish).

- During breeding season the **male sticklebacks** develop **bright red bellies**. In males, seeing the **bright red** of another male's belly stimulates an **innate releasing mechanism**, which triggers specific **fighting behaviour** (the **fixed action pattern**) directed towards the rival.
- **Tinbergen (1947)** found that this response was triggered more by **unrealistic models** with **red undersides** (such as diamond shapes with no features) than by real sticklebacks with no red belly.
- This supports the suggestion that the behaviour is **instinctive**, and set off by a **specific trigger**.

4) Lorenz also believed that most aggression is **ritualised**, i.e. it's released relatively **harmlessly**.

- A behaviour won't be passed on through genes if it gets an animal **killed** before it produces offspring. If animals were **routinely killed** during everyday power struggles or mating contests, it's likely the species would become **extinct**. So, there are **ritual behaviours** in place to stop confrontations being fatal.
- For example, wolves end a fight by the loser exposing his jugular vein as a sign of **submission**. This puts the winner in prime position to kill their rival, but in fact the winner takes no further action.
- Lorenz claimed that **sport** was an example of harmless ritualised aggression release in **humans**, and argued that sport was an important method for **reducing aggression** in society.

The **Ethological Explanation** for **Aggression** Has **Strengths** and **Weaknesses**

Strengths

1) Aggression **does** occur as a fixed action pattern in some animals, e.g. sticklebacks.

2) This theory could explain why humans **kill each other** relatively often — without weapons human fighting isn't usually lethal, so we haven't evolved to **back down**. Now that we have access to weapons, fights are more likely to kill.

Weaknesses

1) This theory doesn't explain aggression which isn't an immediate response to an environmental stimulus, for example **premeditated murder**.

2) **Arms et al (1979)** found that watching aggressive sport **increased aggression** in participants, rather than dispersing it.

Ethological and Evolutionary Explanations

Evolutionary Explanations *Say* Aggression *is an* Adaptive Response

Evolutionary psychology explains aggression as a strategy that has evolved as an **adaptive response** to problems. The argument is that using aggression helped individuals to **survive** and **reproduce** in the past — so aggression is a trait that modern humans have **inherited**.

Evolutionary psychologists have outlined various **adaptive functions** which aggression may have served in the past:

1) To **gain status** or **dominance** in a group.
2) To **gain resources** from others (e.g. territory, mates).
3) In **defence** (against losing resources or status, or being injured or killed).
4) To **deter infidelity** in long term mates.

Evolutionary explanations have been criticised because they don't explain cross-cultural or individual differences in aggression, and they don't take social factors into account.

Sex Differences *in Aggression* May Have Evolved

1) **Wilson and Daly (1985)** studied murders in Detroit and found that the majority of **perpetrators** and **victims** were **young men**. 29 of the cases they looked at were murders that had resulted from '**escalated showing off disputes**', and **only one** of these murders resulted from a dispute between **women**.

2) **Evolutionary psychologists** argue that **men** (and **young men** in particular) are more aggressive because they faced the most **competition** for mates in the past. The main limit on men's reproduction was access to **fertile mates**, so competing successfully for mates was important.

This is related to intra-sexual selection (see page 50).

3) Women, however, were mainly limited by their access to **resources**. Evolutionary psychologists argue that these different pressures have led to different **psychological responses** evolving in men and women.

Buss et al (1992) — Sex differences in jealousy

Method:	This was a **cross-cultural questionnaire study**. Participants were presented with the **hypothetical scenario** that someone they were in a serious, committed romantic relationship with had become interested in someone else. They were asked what would distress them more — imagining their partner forming a deep **emotional attachment** to that other person, or enjoying passionate **sexual intercourse** with the person.
Results:	Across all studies, **more men** than women reported **sexual infidelity** to be most upsetting. On average, **51%** of the men versus **22%** of the women chose this to be more distressing than **emotional infidelity**.
Conclusion:	Men's jealousy is innately triggered by the threat of uncertainty over the **paternity** of children produced within the relationship. However, women are more threatened by **emotional involvement** as it could mean being left for another woman, and so reducing the resources available to her children.
Evaluation:	The fact that the evidence was **consistent** across **different cultures** suggests that these different responses are **innate** rather than learned. However, the fact that the questionnaires were based around a **hypothetical** situation, and the responses available to the participants were **multiple choice**, means that the **validity** of the results is questionable — they may not accurately reflect what participants would actually do if they found themselves in that situation.

Evolutionary theories are very difficult to provide evidence for (or against) — they're effectively impossible to test on humans.

Practice Questions

Q1 What is an innate releasing mechanism?
Q2 How did Buss et al (1992) explain sex differences in jealousy?

Exam Questions

Q1 Briefly outline evolutionary explanations for human aggression.	[6 marks]
Q2 Describe and evaluate the ethological explanation of aggression.	[16 marks]

Forget infidelity — it's people with no exams that make me jealous...

The thing to remember about evolutionary arguments is that they're not saying that people think to themselves 'I'll be aggressive so I'm more likely to pass on my genes'. They're saying that because this behaviour had that effect in the past, it was more likely to be inherited. And it still affects people's behaviour today, even if they're not aware of it. Spooky.

Social Explanations of Aggression

Just when you thought there couldn't possibly be any more explanations for aggression... Next up, social psychological explanations. These theories are all to do with how we interact socially with our environment.

The **Frustration-Aggression** Model Says Aggression **Comes From** Frustration

1) **Dollard et al (1939)** proposed the **frustration-aggression hypothesis**, a social psychological explanation for aggression.

2) They argued that aggression is **always** a result of frustration (defined as interference with attempts to reach a goal), and that frustration **always** leads to aggression (this could be aggressive behaviour, or just feeling aggressive).

3) The **strength** of this aggression is determined by the **degree of frustration**, which depends on how much you **want** to reach the goal, how **close** you were to achieving it, and how much you've been **set back** by the interference.

4) **Fear of punishment** may **inhibit** aggressive behaviour towards the source of the frustration. If this aggression is weaker than the fear it will be **displaced** onto something (or someone) other than the cause of the frustration.

Strengths	Weaknesses
1) **Buss (1963)** found that frustration can **increase** the occurrence of aggression — students in groups who had been **frustrated** (e.g. by being prevented from winning money) were slightly **more aggressive** than the control group. 2) **Harris (1974)** studied people's responses when a confederate pushed in front of them in a **queue**. People displayed **more aggression** when they were **close to the front** of the queue than when they were near the back. This supports the suggestion that being **frustrated** causes **more aggression** the **closer to your goal** you are.	1) **Berkowitz (1965)** argued that frustration alone **isn't enough** to trigger aggression — **environmental cues** to release aggression are also needed. There's more about this below. 2) The suggestion that frustration **always** leads to some form of aggression is widely disputed. Evidence for this claim is **contradictory**. For example, **Buss (1966)** found **no link** between frustration and aggression (contradicting his earlier work). 3) It could be that frustration only leads to aggression if the frustrating behaviour is seen as an **attack**. **Mallick and McCandless (1966)** found that participants responded much **less aggressively** to being frustrated by a confederate if they were given a **reasonable explanation** for the frustrator's behaviour.

Environmental Triggers May Be **Necessary** For **Aggressive Behaviour**

1) **Berkowitz (1965)** proposed a **revision** of the frustration-aggression hypothesis, known as the **aggressive cues hypothesis**.

2) He argued that frustration doesn't usually **directly** produce aggression, instead it creates a '**readiness to aggress**'. For aggressive behaviour to occur it must be **triggered** by the presence of **environmental cues**.

Berkowitz and LePage (1967) gave participants **electric shocks** to make them feel angry. Afterwards, levels of aggression were tested with either a **weapon**, **badminton racket** or **no objects** present. They found that people behaved **more aggressively** when the aggressive **cue** of the weapon was present, than in the other two conditions.

Social Learning Theory Says **Experience** Explains Aggressive Behaviour

1) The **social learning theory of human aggression** says that aggressive behaviour is **learned**.

2) People learn aggression by **observing** and **imitating** the behaviour of **aggressive models**.

3) Reinforcement (behaviour being rewarded) affects **how likely** somebody is to imitate an observed behaviour.

4) This can be **positive reinforcement** (something good happening), or **negative reinforcement** (something bad stopping).

5) Reinforcement can also be **direct** (being rewarded yourself), or **vicarious** (observing the model being rewarded).

> Make sure you've learnt the social learning theory stuff that you covered in Year 1 — you need to be able to apply this to aggression. (You also need to be able to evaluate the theory, and Bandura's research.)

6) Bandura's (1961) **Bobo doll study** (you'll have seen this in Year 1), showed that children can learn aggression through imitation. In a similar experiment, **Bandura (1965)** found that **vicarious reinforcement** affected imitation:

Bandura (1965) got children to watch a video of a model **behaving aggressively** towards a Bobo doll. The model was either **rewarded**, **punished**, or **neither** (in the control condition). When the children played with the doll, those in the **reward** and **control condition** behaved **more aggressively** than those in the **punishment** condition.

Social Explanations of Aggression

Deindividuation *Theory Says Being* Anonymous *Encourages Aggression*

Another **social psychological** explanation of aggression suggests we're **disinhibited** when we're an **anonymous** part of a **crowd**. When they're part of the group, people may feel less **personal responsibility** and less fear of **public disapproval** than when they're clearly identifiable as an individual. **Festinger et al (1952)** coined the term **deindividuation** to describe this state of reduced self awareness.

There's some **real-world evidence** for this effect:

1) **Mullen (1986)** analysed newspaper reports of **lynch mob violence** in the US. The **more people** there were in the mob, the **greater** the level of violence.

2) **Mann (1981)** analysed 21 reports of **suicides** and identified ten cases where a crowd had **baited** the person threatening suicide (e.g. shouting 'jump'). Baiting was more likely to happen **at night**, when the crowd was **at a distance** and when the crowd was **large** (more than 300 people).

Research studies have also supported deindividuation:

1) **Zimbardo (1969)** showed that **anonymity** affects behaviour. Participants in his study believed they were administering **shocks** to another participant in a learning experiment. **Individuated** participants wore normal clothes, large name badges and were introduced to each other. **Deindividuated** participants wore coats with hoods, were instructed in groups and weren't referred to by name. The **more anonymous** participants administered more and longer shocks.

2) **Diener et al (1976)** observed 1300 trick-or-treating children in the US. If they were **anonymous** (in costumes, masks or large groups) they were **more likely** to steal money and sweets.

"Hands up if you're deindividuated!"

This evidence supports the idea that deindividuation **increases** aggression. But there are also examples of it having **no effect** or even **reducing** aggression. For example, individuals in crowds at religious festivals often express goodwill to others. It could be that being in a group means that you **conform to group norms**. If group norms are **prosocial** (rather than anti-social), the individual may behave that way too.

Practice Questions

Q1 Describe the results of Berkowitz and LePage's (1967) study.

Q2 What did Bandura's Bobo doll studies show?

Q3 What is deindividuation?

Exam Questions

Q1 Which of these processes is **not** part of the social learning theory of human aggression?
   A Observation   **B** Reinforcement   **C** Deindividuation   **D** Imitation   [1 mark]

Q2 Read the item below and answer the question that follows.

> A media report following the UK riots in 2011 described otherwise law-abiding people who engaged in destructive and criminal behaviour, as having been 'swept away with the crowd'.

Using your knowledge of social explanations of human aggression, outline how being part of a large crowd may have affected the behaviour of the rioters.   [4 marks]

Q3 Describe and evaluate the frustration-aggression hypothesis.   [16 marks]

Aggressive cues — the smash-hit competitive-snooker movie of the year...

As ever, make sure you can explain all these theories, and come up with some strengths and weaknesses of each of them. It's really important that you've got all the social learning theory stuff from Year 1 down too — you need to know all of the grisly details of this for aggression. Once you've got it all you can celebrate with a cup of tea, or some light aerobics.

Aggression in the Real World

These pages are really interesting. Not that the whole book isn't, obviously. Violent media and prison violence always seem to crop up in the news — learn these pages and you can wow everyone with your knowledge of the issues of the moment.

Violence in the Media Has Been Linked To Aggression

1) The two students who carried out the Columbine High School massacre in the US in 1999 were both alleged to be fans of **violent computer games**. Some people have linked this to the killings.

2) It's since been suggested that violent computer games have played a part in causing other recent **American school shootings**.

Not everyone agrees that there is a link — other causes have been suggested too.

3) Seeing characters in computer games being **rewarded** for violent behaviour could encourage aggression in the players themselves through **vicarious reinforcement**.

4) **Correlations** between aggressive behaviour and violent computer games have been shown by some studies, but the relationship isn't necessarily **causal** — it may just be that more aggressive individuals have a **preference** for more violent games — not surprising really...

	Paik and Comstock (1994) — Media violence and aggression
Method:	Paik and Comstock conducted a **meta-analysis** investigating the impact of **media violence** on behaviour. They analysed the results of **217** different studies dating from **1957 to 1990**.
Results:	The results showed that there was an overall **significant correlation** between **watching violent television** and **films** and **violent behaviour**. The correlation for **men** was slightly **stronger** than for women, and those who watched violent cartoons and fantasy programmes also showed more aggressive behaviour than people who watched other types of films and programmes.
Conclusion:	There is a **correlation** between **aggressive behaviour** and watching **violent media images**.
Evaluation:	Although this review was **large** and included many studies, lots of the experiments took place in **laboratories** and may therefore have lacked **ecological validity**. The results also only show a correlation, and not a **causal relationship** — it might just be that people who are more aggressive are also more likely to **choose** more violent and aggressive media.

5) Some studies have found **no link** between media violence and aggression. For example, **Charlton et al (2000)** looked at the **long term effects** of TV being introduced to an island population, and found little change.

Charlton et al (2000) studied children in **St. Helena** (a remote British territory in the South Atlantic), **before** and **after** television was introduced to the island in 1995. They observed children **aged 3-8** in the school playground before television, and children of the same age **5 years** after TV was introduced. The results showed a very slight **decrease in anti-social behaviour** in the **post-television** group.

Anti-social behaviour includes things like shouting at or shoving other people.

Violence in the Media May Cause Desensitisation, Disinhibition and Priming

There are several ideas about **how** seeing **violence in the media** might lead to aggression in **real life**.

Desensitisation

People usually have an **anxious reaction** to violence and aggression — we respond **emotionally** to it. Repeated exposure to violence in the **media** may reduce this response, making people **desensitised** to violence.

Disinhibition

Most of the time people have **inhibitions** about **behaving aggressively** — it's seen as **unacceptable** behaviour. Seeing violence repeatedly in the **media** may mean it begins to seem **acceptable**, making people **disinhibited**.

Cognitive Priming

Cues associated with violence in the **media** (e.g. guns), may **trigger aggression** in us when we see them in real life. The violent material we see in the media is **stored** as a memory, connected to other **violent memories**. We're **primed** to retrieve these memories if we come across anything **associated** with them, which may **prompt aggressive behaviour**.

Aggression in the Real World

Institutional Aggression in Prison Has Two Explanations

Institutional aggression is the term used to describe aggression within an **institutional environment**, like a prison. There are two main approaches to explaining institutional aggression in **prisons** — the **dispositional** and **situational** explanations.

> An institution is an organisation governed by some sort of authority, usually with strict social guidelines. Schools, hospitals, and the military are other examples of institutions.

The **Dispositional** Explanation

Dispositional explanations argue that institutional aggression stems from the characteristics of the **individuals** in the institution (their disposition).

The Importation Model	**Irwin and Cressey (1962)** suggested that the **characteristics** and **social norms** that inmates bring with them when they enter prison are the main factors that lead to institutional aggression. This is called the **importation model** — inmates **import** characteristics from their life outside. E.g. they bring in the norms of criminal gangs, where aggression may be a respected trait.

Harer and Steffensmeier (1996) looked at data from 58 male prisons in the US. They found that levels of **violent behaviour** in prison were significantly higher among **black inmates**, whereas **drug offences** in prison were significantly higher among **white inmates**. Harer and Steffensmeier concluded that this supported the **importation model**, as these results mirror trends in American society outside of prison.

However, this research has been criticised for being **androcentric** (see page 40), as it didn't include female prisons.

The **Situational** Explanation

Situational explanations claim that institutional aggression is caused by the **environment** in the institution.

The Deprivation Model	The **deprivation model** states that the **conditions** in prison (e.g. overcrowding) cause **stress**, which results in aggression. **Sykes (1958)** described the particular deprivations that inmates experience in prison as the '**pains of imprisonment**'. These include loss of autonomy, loss of liberty, loss of security, and so on.

Megargee (1977) studied inmates in an American prison for young offenders over a period of **three years**. He found that **crowding** levels in the prison were significantly correlated with levels of disruptive behaviour.

Research Suggests Both Explanations Are Important

1) Research evidence for the **dispositional** and **situational** explanations of institutional aggression in prisons is often **contradictory** — in practice **both types of factor** probably play a part.

2) **Jiang and Fisher-Giorlando (2002)** looked at disciplinary reports from a prison in the US. They found that the **importation model** was best suited to explaining violence towards **other inmates**, whereas the **deprivation model** best explained violence towards **prison staff**.

Practice Questions

Q1 What is cognitive priming?

Q2 How does Harer and Steffensmeier's (1996) study support the dispositional explanation of aggression in prison?

Exam Questions

Q1	Distinguish between the dispositional and situational explanations for institutional aggression in prisons.	[4 marks]
Q2	Discuss media influences on aggression.	[16 marks]

I blame my aggressive behaviour on playing too much snap as a child...

A few key things you need to learn here — how violence in the media may lead to aggression through desensitisation, disinhibition and cognitive priming, and the dispositional and situational explanations for institutional aggression in prisons.

Defining and Measuring Crime

Now you're onto the really fun stuff. Solving crime and saving the world from convicts, criminals and thieves. But first, it'd be a good idea to learn what crime actually is. Turns out, it's harder to define than you might think.

Crime Involves **Breaking the Law**

Forensic psychology uses psychological principles to try to explain why people might commit crime.

Crime can be described as a behaviour that breaks the **formal laws** defined by a given society. Crimes can range in severity — from **petty theft** to causing **injury**, or even **death**, to another person.

There Can Be **Problems** With **Defining Crime**...

Crime is **Time Relative**

- **Historically**, some behaviours were considered criminal acts, but today they're not even given a second thought. This is because peoples' **attitudes**, **social norms** and **moral values** change over time. In turn, this affects the behaviours people deem acceptable, and laws change.

- For example, **homosexuality** was **illegal** before **1967**, but now laws permitting same-sex marriages have been passed in England, Scotland and Wales.

- **Smoking** in enclosed public places was **legal** in England until **July 2007**. However, we are now more aware of the harmful impact of secondary smoke, so many people's **views** towards smoking in public have **changed**. It is now illegal across the whole of the UK.

Crime is **Culturally Relative**

- **Attitudes** are not always the same across all **cultures**. For instance, some countries have strict religious laws which tell people how they should behave. This means that what is considered **legal** in one culture might be **illegal** in another culture.

- For example, in Saudi Arabia, there is **no minimum legal age** for marriage. But in the UK, it is **illegal** to marry **before the age of 16** (even then, parental consent is needed in England and Wales before the age of 18).

Crime is **Age Relative**

- It's the classic case of a toddler in a supermarket picking up a pack of biscuits (without their parents noticing) and wandering out the shop. But does that make the child a **criminal**? Not really.

- Something is only really considered a crime when it has been done **deliberately** and **with intention**. As the toddler **wouldn't** have understood what they were doing, they're **not a criminal**. But a group of youths **intentionally** shoplifting would be a whole other story.

- In the UK, children **under 10** can't be arrested or charged with a crime because they're not considered fully responsible for their actions.

There are **Different** Ways to **Measure** Crime

Measuring crime can be just as problematic as defining it. Many methods used to measure crime often give a **misleading** idea of how much crime there really is. There are several ways that crime can be **measured**:

Official Statistics

1) Official statistics are created by **official bodies**, such as the **police**, the **criminal justice system** and the **civil service**.

2) They've been used in England and Wales since **1805**, giving a useful overview of how crime trends have **changed** over time.

3) But they're not always that **accurate**. Official statistics only show crimes which have been **reported to** and **recorded by** official bodies. The **dark figure of crime** refers to the number of crimes which go undetected.

4) **Farrington and Dowds (1985)** compared the crime statistics in **Nottingham** and two neighbouring counties. They discovered that the reason crime rates were higher in Nottingham was due to the fact that police recorded all crimes, including petty crimes, whereas other counties didn't.

Defining and Measuring Crime

Offender Surveys

1) Offender surveys ask people to report what crimes **they** have committed **themselves**.

2) They allow people who **wouldn't** normally be **caught** by the police to record their crimes, and they also provide a way of measuring **victimless crimes**.

3) One example of an offender survey is the **Offending, Crime and Justice Survey** — 10 to 25 year olds from England and Wales were asked to admit whether they have ever done things like shoplifting, taken illegal drugs, etc.

4) But, as might be expected, people often **lie about** and **overexaggerate** their behaviour. Their reports might also be **misleading** or interpreted in a **different way**.

5) Offender surveys could be **biased**, as it might be that only certain types of people, committing **certain types** of crime, are likely to disclose information about the crimes they've committed.

Victimless crimes are crimes that don't directly hurt other people. They include things like illegal drug use or underage drinking.

Victim Surveys

1) Victim surveys are collected from the **people** who've had crimes committed against them.

2) The main victim survey in Britain is **The Crime Survey for England and Wales**. It is conducted on a regular basis.

3) The police don't always record crimes, particularly if the crimes aren't deemed 'worthy enough' to write up (as shown by Farrington and Dowds on the previous page). Victim surveys are useful because they can record crimes like these, so they give a **more accurate** representation of the effect of crime.

4) However, victim surveys rely on people remembering what happened — and people's memories can often be **faulty** or **biased**.

5) They also don't consider more 'impersonal crimes', such as **fraud** or **corporate crime**, where an individual isn't singly affected.

Prunella insisted she wasn't a fashion victim. She just liked big hats.

Practice Questions

Q1 Give an example of how defining crime has changed historically.

Q2 When did official criminal statistics start being collected?

Q3 What are offender surveys?

Q4 Name the main victim survey used in England and Wales today.

Q5 Explain why victim surveys might be useful.

Exam Questions

Q1 Which of the following is **not** used to measure crime?

A official statistics   B offender surveys   C geographical profiling   D victim surveys   [1 mark]

Q2 Read the item below, then answer the question that follows.

> Shehan lives in the Maldives, where bigamy (having multiple spouses) isn't considered a crime. He recently moved to the United States where bigamy is illegal.

Outline how Shehan's situation highlights a problem with defining crime.   [2 marks]

Q3 Describe and evaluate ways of measuring crime.   [16 marks]

It'd be criminal not to learn these pages...

See what I did there? Hahaha — sometimes I just crack myself up. Other times, I just think I need to get out more... But, all that aside, here are two lovely pages all about defining and measuring crime. Make sure you learn about the problems that go along with defining and measuring crime too — it's actually really interesting stuff. Really it is.

Offender Profiling

Finding the person who committed a crime is often tricky. Offender profiling can help with this.

The Police Use **Offender Profiling** to Help Them **Identify** Suspects

The aim of profiling is to create an idea of the offender's **likely characteristics**. This helps the police to focus their resources on more likely suspects, and can create new leads within an investigation. There are different styles of approach in offender profiling.

The American 'top-down' approach

The **FBI** began by **interviewing** 36 convicted serial killers and sex murderers to gain an insight into their thinking and behaviour. They were classified into two groups, **organised** and **disorganised**. Organised offenders were intelligent, socially and sexually competent, lived with somebody and planned their attacks. **Disorganised offenders** were less intelligent, socially and sexually incompetent, were loners and were more likely to behave impulsively and not plan the attacks in advance. These groups are used to compare information from **new crime scenes** to make judgements based on past experience. However, based on **self-report interviews** and a **restricted sample**, the categories devised by the FBI lack validity and can't be generalised to the wider population.

The British 'bottom-up' approach

This approach was developed by **David Canter** and uses **investigative psychology** (applying psychological research and theories to criminal investigations) more than the FBI approach. Canter's **geographical profiling** saw the **crime scene** as a source of information — the behaviour of the offender at the crime scene would reveal information about their everyday life and characteristics (see below). Although Canter also analysed behaviour of convicted offenders, this is a much more **bottom-up approach**, as the focus is on the unique circumstances of an individual offender.

Several Factors Are Considered When **Developing a Profile**

Douglas et al (1986) reported that the **FBI** use **four** main stages when building a profile:

1) Assimilating **data** — collecting all the information available about the crime scene and victim.
2) **Classifying** the crime — identifying the **type** of crime committed.
3) **Reconstructing** the crime — this includes the behaviour of both the **offender** and the **victim**.
4) Creating a **profile** — making judgements about possible physical and lifestyle **characteristics** of the offender.

Geographical profiling uses a crime scene to predict the characteristics of a criminal's profile.
Canter (1994) identified **five** main characteristics that should be included in a profile:

1) **Personal** characteristics — e.g. personality traits.
2) **Criminal** history — types of offences they may have committed in the past.
3) Residential **location** — e.g. if a circle is drawn around an offender's crime scenes on a map, the offender is often found to live in the middle. This is known as **circle theory**.
4) **Domestic** and **social** characteristics — e.g. if the person is likely to live alone or have a family.
5) **Occupational** and **educational** history — likely type of employment and level of qualifications.

There Are a Number of **Biases** and **Pitfalls** in Offender Profiling

1) Profiles can only be used for a **limited** range of crimes such as murders or rapes. They've been used to identify stalkers and arsonists but aren't suitable for use in crimes motivated by **material gain** such as robbery and theft.
2) **Douglas et al (1986)** suggest that the aim of offender profiling has been **misrepresented**. Profiling is not intended to identify a specific person, but instead aims to focus the investigation on a particular **type** of person.
3) Research into the effectiveness of offender profiling shows that it is **limited**. **Holmes (1989)** reported that in **192** cases where offender profiling had been used, arrests had been made in **88** cases. However, the profile only contributed to **17%** of these arrests.
4) **Copson (1995)** found that only **14%** of senior police officers felt that profiling had helped them to solve a case.

Offender Profiling

The *Rachel Nickell* Murder Case Was a *Misuse* of Offender Profiling

Rachel was a young woman murdered in front of her two-year-old son during a walk in the park in 1992. An offender profiler called **Paul Britton** developed a profile which was broadcast on TV, and four callers all identified the same person. The man **fitted the profile** although there wasn't any forensic evidence to link him to the crime.

An **undercover** female police officer befriended the suspect (Colin Stagg) and attempted to get him to confess to the crime during their 'relationship'. The suspect **never** admitted to her that he was the killer and denied involvement, but was still arrested and charged. When the case went to court he was **acquitted** and the misuse of the profile and the police tactics were strongly **criticised** by the judge. In 2008, another man, Robert Napper, **pleaded guilty** to Rachel's manslaughter on the grounds of diminished responsibility.

The Case Study of *John Duffy* is a More *Successful Example*

John Duffy is known as the **Railway Rapist** — between 1982 and 1986 he was responsible for 24 sexual assaults and three murders. **Canter** was asked by the police to analyse the details of the crimes to generate a profile, as forensic evidence suggested they were committed by one person (although sometimes with an accomplice).

The profile made Duffy seem a much more **likely suspect** than had previously been thought. The details of the profile Canter had created were very similar to Duffy's actual circumstances and characteristics. Canter suggested that the offender would:

1) **Live close** to the first three crimes — Duffy lived in Kilburn as suggested.

2) Be **aged** in his mid to late 20s — Duffy was in his late 20s.

3) Work in a semi-skilled or skilled **occupation** — Duffy was a carpenter.

4) Be knowledgeable about **railways** — Duffy worked for British Rail.

5) Have a **criminal record** that included violence — Duffy had been interviewed by the police for raping his wife at knifepoint.

6) Be small and feel **physically unattractive** — Duffy was 5' 4" and suffered from acne.

7) **Fantasise** about sex and violence — Duffy had hard-core pornography videos.

8) Be interested in **martial arts** — Duffy was in a martial arts club.

Canter believed that behaviour is generally **consistent**, so analysis of Duffy's behaviour during the crime gave information about his life and general behaviour. Once Duffy was arrested for the crimes it was discovered that he had started to murder his victims because he was once nearly recognised. Canter also discovered that Duffy burned the bodies of his victims to destroy the **forensic evidence** — he had learned about the procedures used by police for collecting evidence when he was arrested for raping his wife.

Practice Questions

Q1 Who developed the bottom-up approach to offender profiling?

Q2 Outline two aspects included in Canter's profiles.

Q3 Describe one problem with offender profiling.

Exam Questions

Q1 Describe **two** different approaches to offender profiling. [8 marks]

Q2 Evaluate the use of offender profiling in criminal investigations. [8 marks]

The offender is likely to be a sweet old lady who likes kittens and scones...

Offender profiling has long been a popular choice for TV dramas, like 'Silent Witness'. Great show, but even before I read these pages I did have a suspicion that perhaps it wasn't realistic for a profiler to conclude from a couple of bloodstains and a shoelace that the killer is a car salesman aged 43 who collects stamps and wears loud ties...

Biological Explanations of Offending Behaviour

As with most topics in Psychology, biology can be used to explain behaviour. But that doesn't mean to say you can nick a chocolate bar from the corner shop, or cheat in your exam, and then blame it on your genes...

Lombroso Linked *Physical Characteristics* to *Crime*

1) **Positivist criminology** says that criminal behaviour results from **physical** or **psychological** features — **no free will** is involved. **Cesare Lombroso (1835-1909)** believed in positivist criminology, though he only focused on **physical** features.

2) During the late-1800s he studied the physical characteristics of criminals (often studying people **after** they had died). He wanted to discover if certain features were **more common** in criminals than non-criminals.

3) Lombroso concluded that criminals were more likely to have **atavistic** (primitive) features than non-criminals. He described the **atavistic form** of a criminal as being characterised by a **strong jaw** and **heavy brow**.

4) Other **features** included drooping eyelids, large ears, lobeless ears, high defined cheekbones, a flat nose, long arms relative to the body, and sloping shoulders.

5) Lombroso thought that criminal behaviour came from **primitive instincts** which had survived the evolutionary process — criminals were a sort of genetic 'throwback' and this could be identified by their **atavistic features**.

6) He later went on to suggest how certain **combinations** of characteristics could describe **different types** of criminals. For example, he claimed **murderers** had **bloodshot eyes** and **curly hair**.

Strengths

- Lombroso highlighted the **role of biology** in criminology.
- However, he also considered that criminal behaviour was likely to come from an **interaction** between **biological**, **psychological** and **social factors** — an idea which has been highly influential in future theories of criminology.

Limitations

- Lombroso didn't use a non-criminal **control group** to see if his atavistic features were unique to criminals.
- Lots of his sample may have had **psychological disorders** or **chromosomal abnormalities** which may have been a factor in their criminal behaviour.

Criminality Could Have a *Genetic* Basis

There is lots of evidence supporting a genetic cause for offending behaviour:

1) **Adoption studies**
   Some adoption studies have shown higher concordance rates of criminal activity between adopted children and their biological parents than with their adoptive parents.

	Mednick et al (1984) — Criminal behaviour in adopted children
Method:	A **concordance analysis** of 14 427 Danish **adoptees** was conducted. Rates of concordance for **criminality** between the adoptees and their **adopted** and **biological parents** were compared.
Results:	**13.5%** of adoptees with parents (adoptive or biological) **without** a criminal conviction had a criminal conviction themselves, compared to **14.7%** of adoptees with at least one criminally convicted **adoptive** parent, **20%** of adoptees with at least one criminally convicted **biological** parent, and **24.5%** of adoptees with at least one convicted adoptive **and** one convicted biological parent.
Conclusion:	A **genetic link** is supported. However, the **concordance rates** are quite **low**, suggesting that there are **other** factors that lead to criminality.
Evaluation:	Adoption studies allow **separation** of the genetic and environmental influences. Just because a person has not been **convicted** of a crime does not necessarily mean that they have never committed one.

2) **Genetic influences on aggression**
   Some psychologists believe that **aggression** can lead to **offending behaviour**. Studies have shown a link between **genes** and levels of **aggression**, particularly through the use of twin studies (see page 47).

3) **An extra Y chromosome**
   Jacobs et al (1965) found a higher percentage of people from a **prison population** had the atypical sex chromosome pattern, **XYY**, compared to a normal population. They believed the addition of the extra Y chromosome led to increased testosterone and increased violence, resulting in offending behaviour. However, further studies have since suggested that those with such a chromosomal abnormality are more likely to be **hyperactive**, **more impulsive** and have a **lower IQ**, which would be more likely to explain their criminality.

Biological Explanations of Offending Behaviour

There are also *Neural Explanations* of *Offending Behaviour*

Raine investigated the link between brain dysfunction and criminality. He believed that there was an identifiable **biological disposition** for criminal behaviour. Raine suggested that a **biological dysfunction** within the **brain** could cause an individual to commit acts of violence.

Raine et al (1997) — A neural explanation of criminality

Method:	Raine used **PET scans** to create 3-D images of the functional processes happening in the brains of 41 murderers (pleading not guilty by reason of insanity) and 41 control participants.
Results:	The murderers showed **reduced glucose metabolism** in the prefrontal cortex, superior parietal gyrus and the corpus callosum, and **asymmetrical activity** in the two hemispheres. In other words some of their brain processes were **dysfunctional**.
Conclusion:	The evidence **supported** a link between brain dysfunction and predisposition to violent acts.
Evaluation:	The researchers used a **control group** who were matched on variables such as age and sex. However, researchers could not **randomly allocate** participants to the 'control' or 'killer' groups, so needed to be cautious when drawing conclusions about **causal relationships**.

There are *Strengths* and *Weaknesses* to the *Biological Explanation*

Strengths

- A number of studies have provided support to suggest there is some **contribution** from biological factors.
- The biological theories can often be tested **scientifically**, making them more reliable — for example, Raine et al's study above.

When her Mum was Marigold's age, she too nicked flowers from the neighbour's garden*.

Weaknesses

- Since **no** study has shown a 100% concordance rate between MZ twins or biological parents and their children for offending behaviour, biology **cannot** be the only influencing factor. The environment **must** play a role.
- **Andrews and Bonta (2006)** stated that the concordance rates for criminality between biological parents and adopted children might not be **directly** due to genetics. Criminality could be a result of **inherited emotional instability** or a **mental illness**, which could **indirectly** result in offending behaviour.
- Some people think that biological explanations are too **reductionist** (page 45) and too **deterministic** (page 44).

Practice Questions

Q1 Give three features of atavistic form, as described by Lombroso.

Q2 Describe the method used by Mednick et al (1984) to investigate offending behaviour in children.

Q3 What did Jacobs et al (1965) believe the addition of an extra Y chromosome could lead to?

Q4 Give two weaknesses of the biological explanation of offending behaviour.

Exam Questions

Q1 Describe the atavistic form as an explanation of offending behaviour.	[4 marks]
Q2 Discuss genetic explanations for offending behaviour.	[16 marks]

I was always taught never to judge a book by its cover...

Lombroso's theory was influential for its time, but treat it with a pinch of salt. You can't go accusing all the strong-jawed, lobeless-eared people you know of being criminals. That's just mean. And probably wrong. So don't do it.

---

* CGP does not condone 'nicking of flowers from the neighbour's garden'.

Psychological Explanations of Offending Behaviour

So the excitement continues. If you've ever wondered why some of us are law-abiding goody two-shoes while others seemingly couldn't give two hoots about the law, then you'll like these next few pages.

Eysenck *Explained* Criminal Behaviour *in Terms of* Personality Types

Hans Eysenck was one of the first psychologists to examine human **personality**. He initially identified **two** main **personality dimensions** (scales) and suggested that everyone fits in somewhere along these dimensions:

1) **Neuroticism-stability** — individuals towards the neurotic end of this dimension show traits such as anxiousness and restlessness. Traits at the other end of the scale include reliability and calmness.

2) **Extraversion-introversion** — individuals towards the extravert end of this dimension tend to be sociable, impulsive and assertive. Those at the other end tend to be quiet, passive and reserved.

Thomas didn't want to come out of his shell. He was a neurotic, introverted soul.

In later research during the 1970s Eysenck added a **third personality dimension**:

3) **Psychoticism** — this scale shows how disposed an individual is to psychotic breakdown. Those who score highly tend to be aggressive, hostile and uncaring.

Psychoticism isn't the same as psychosis.

- Eysenck suggested that individuals have a **genetic predisposition** to a particular personality type, but environmental factors play a role too. This leads to particular behaviours, including **criminal behaviours**.

- Eysenck believed that **psychoticism** was a good **predictor** of criminal behaviour. He also thought **extraversion** was a good indicator of criminal behaviour for **young** people, but **neuroticism** a better indicator for criminal behaviour in **older** people.

- Eysenck's theory has been influential across psychology, especially in how it **combines** biological, psychological and social approaches together. However, his theory of the criminal personality was chiefly developed from studies which involved **self-report measures**, meaning his findings **lack reliability**.

Criminals May Have Different Thinking Patterns

The **cognitive approach** to offending behaviour suggests that **criminal thinking patterns**, **cognitive distortions** and different **levels of moral reasoning** are all important factors in explaining why people may turn to a life of crime. **Yochelson and Samenow (1976)** looked into criminal thinking patterns:

	Yochelson and Samenow (1976) — Criminal thinking patterns
Method:	A **longitudinal study** over 14 years examined **255 male offenders** from a variety of different backgrounds. The researchers compared two groups, roughly the same size. The first group consisted of offenders at a hospital for 'secure treatment' as they had been found not guilty due to mental illness. The second group consisted of offenders from a 'normal' prison population. Each participant underwent a series of **interviews** over several years.
Results:	Although only **30** participants finished the study, **52 thinking patterns** were found to be common across **all** the criminal participants. These included **criminal thinking patterns** (fear and the need for power), **automatic thinking errors** (e.g. lack of trust, lack of empathy, impulsiveness, manipulativeness) and **crime-related thinking errors** (fantasising about criminal behaviours).
Conclusion:	Criminals **share** common **thinking patterns** and **thinking errors**. The researchers acknowledged that even though these characteristics are not unique in criminals, they are thought to be more likely to exist in criminals.
Evaluation:	Since there was **no control group** in the study, the results are less **valid**. There is also evidence of **gender bias** (page 40) since only males were studied, and so the results cannot be generalised. Since the study was **longitudinal**, it would be difficult and expensive to replicate, but it does have an element of **ecological validity**.

Psychological Explanations of Offending Behaviour

Criminals May Show Cognitive Distortions

Cognitive distortions are irrational thought patterns which give people a distorted **view of reality**, so affect how they behave. **Gibbs et al (1995)** outlined several cognitive distortions which they linked to offending behaviour. They include:

1) Being **self-centred**
2) **Minimisation** — minimising the seriousness of their offending behaviour
3) **Blaming** problems on others
4) **Hostile attribution bias** — believing that others are 'out to get them' and have hostile intentions

Liau et al (1998) found cognitive distortions were **higher** in a group of 52 male '**delinquents**' than in a **control group**. However, studies like this don't show that these thought patterns **cause** criminal behaviour, it could be the other way round.

Criminals Could Have a Different Level of Moral Reasoning

1) **Kohlberg** thought that moral reasoning progresses in **stages**. He argued that your **moral understanding increases** as you grow older because at each stage you take more and more of the **social** world into account.

2) He investigated this idea using a series of ten **moral dilemma** stories. An example of this type of dilemma is the **'Heinz dilemma'**. In the story, Heinz chose to break into a shop to steal expensive drugs to cure his dying wife.

3) The participants had to decide whether these actions were **justified**. Kohlberg was interested in the participants' **reasons** for their decisions.

4) **Kohlberg** used a sample of 72 boys ages 10, 13 and 16. He used his findings to come up with **six progressive stages** of moral reasoning, which fall under **three levels**:

Level 1: Preconventional Reasoning

1) An action is morally wrong if the person who commits it is **punished** as a result (most common in children).
2) The right behaviour is the one that is in **your own best interest**.

Level 2: Conventional Reasoning

Most people tend to fall into Level 2.

3) The right behaviour is the one that makes **other people** think positively about you.
4) It is important to **obey laws** and follow **social conventions** because they help **society** to function properly.

Level 3: Postconventional Reasoning

5) The right course of action is the one that promotes the **greatest good** for the **greatest number of people**.
6) Actions are driven by **abstract**, **universal principles** of right and wrong, which **don't** depend on the situation.

Serious offenders have a **moral outlook** that **differs** from that of the law-abiding majority — they **don't** progress through these stages of moral development in the same way as law-abiding people. **Allen et al (2001)** supported this assumption by showing that criminals tend to have a lower **level of moral reasoning** than non-criminals.

Evaluation

Kohlberg's theory can be considered **gender-biased** — most of Kohlberg's work was carried out on US males, so his findings may not apply to other groups. **Gilligan (1982)** claimed that the theory was **androcentric** and focused too much on **male-oriented ideas** about justice rather than also taking into account other moral approaches that might appeal more to women.

Practice Questions

Q1 Describe Yochelson and Samenow's (1976) study into criminal thinking patterns.

Q2 Name two cognitive distortions described by Gibbs et al (1995).

Exam Question

Q1 Describe how Eysenck's theory of the criminal personality can explain offending behaviour. [4 marks]

I bet examiners are lovely people really — but I'm sure they're out to get us...

Not that I'm showing a hostile attribution bias to all the examiners in the world at all. Never... Ahem. Anyway, time to learn the stuff on these pages. It's all about thinking patterns and cognitive distortions — definite bedtime reading.

Psychological Explanations of Offending Behaviour

Just when you thought things were tailing off, it gets even better. There are more psychological explanations of offending behaviour on these two pages. And this time, Freud is back. Oh yeah...

The **Psychodynamic Approach** May Explain **Criminality**

1) **Freud** claimed that the only way to really understand how people behave is to look at their past.
2) He proposed that offending behaviour was therefore linked to **early childhood experiences**.
3) Several of Freud's **psychodynamic theories** can be used to explain offending behaviour:

There's lots more about Freud's ideas on pages 2-5.

1) An Inadequate Superego

Criminality could be due to the **abnormal** development of the **id**, the **ego** and the **superego** which occurs during early childhood. Freud suggested that the **id** provides an **instinctive** drive towards **criminal behaviour**. But the **superego** is there to keep it in line.

Blackburn (1993) proposed that there are three different types of superego which lead to offending behaviour:

- A **weak superego** — often found in those with **no same sex parent**, as they can't internalise that parent's moral code. As such, they would have **fewer inhibitions** towards conducting antisocial behaviour, and would fully respond to their **id** (the 'pleasure principle').

- A **deviant superego** — usually found in those whose **same sex parent** is immoral. So if a girl had a criminal mother, her **superego** might be **less responsive** to crime than someone without a criminal mother.

- A **strong (or over-harsh) superego** — if the person thinks about acting on the id's desires, they'll end up feeling really **guilty** if they have a strong **superego**. The individual is then likely to feel they should '**get punished**' to relieve their guilt, and so engage in crimes in order to get caught. Sounds a bit bonkers really...

2) Defence Mechanisms

Freud outlined different **defence mechanisms** — **displacement**, **repression** and **denial** (see page 3). These could all be used to explain offending behaviour:

- **Englander (2007)** described how **displaced aggression** in offenders might explain their antisocial behaviour. If offenders **cannot control** their aggression (which comes from their **instinctive id**), this aggression may then 'spill out' of their **unconscious**, resulting in violent and offending behaviour.

- Most people can **repress** and **deny** their urges (such as aggression or anger) and keep them at bay. However, the **psychodynamic approach** suggests that a **triggering incident** or **stimulus** might **release** these feelings, resulting in antisocial and offending behaviour.

The **Psychodynamic Approach** to Crime has Several **Weaknesses**

As you've seen, the psychodynamic approach offers a number of explanations for criminality. But in terms of explaining offending behaviour there are a number of **issues**:

- It is difficult to **scientifically** test the theories because the psychodynamic approach considers **unconscious processes** — this makes it **unreliable** and lacking in **validity**.

- Lots of the data in the psychodynamic approach to criminology is from **case studies** and is **qualitative** (page 22), and so it's **hard** to use it to state laws that can be **generalised**.

There's more strengths and weaknesses of the psychodynamic approach on page 5.

Psychological Explanations of Offending Behaviour

Sutherland (1939) Developed the Differential Association Theory

The **differential association theory** is used to explain offending behaviour.
Sutherland believed that criminal behaviour could be **learned** in interactions with other deviant individuals.
People not only learn the **techniques** and **methods** involved in certain crimes, but they also pick up the **motives** and **attitudes** behind the crimes. He argued that:

1) Criminal behaviour is **learnt** — in the same way any other behaviour can be learnt.

2) Criminal behaviour comes from **interacting** and **communicating** with other people.

3) Criminal behaviour is most likely to be learnt whilst among **small groups** of people — this is where people are the most influential.

4) Learning about criminal behaviour involves not only the **techniques** of committing the actual crime, but also the **motivation** and **attitudes** towards crime.

5) The **law** tells a criminal what is **right** and **wrong** — the criminal then decides whether an action or behaviour is **favourable** or **unfavourable**.

6) **Repeated exposure** to criminal behaviour is more likely to result in someone committing a crime themselves — this is especially true if the crime results in a **favourable** outcome.

7) The **frequency**, **duration**, **priority** and **intensity** of interactions between criminals and those learning about criminal behaviour will affect the likelihood of them developing offending behaviour.

8) The general theory of learning by **association** is also applicable to learning about crime.

9) **Anyone** can become a criminal — regardless of **age**, **sex**, **background**, etc.

Sammy's dad was a serial bread thief. Says it all really.

Here, 'priority' means how early in their life the interaction occurred, not how important it was.

This theory explains why individuals imprisoned for a minor offence often **reoffend** when they're released. Spending time with **other criminals** in the institution (who may have committed more serious crimes) makes them likely to learn further criminal behaviours.

The Differential Association Theory Has Strengths and Weaknesses Too

Strengths	Weaknesses
• The differential association theory accounts for **all types** of people — not just juveniles or lower class people who are often described in theories of crime. • His theory was supported by **Short (1955)** who studied 176 school children, using a questionnaire. Short measured self reported **delinquent behaviour** (e.g. drug taking, petty stealing etc.) and **association** with delinquents or criminals, and found a **positive correlation** between the two measures.	• Not everyone is influenced by people around them — this theory doesn't consider **individual differences**. • Problems in defining crime make this theory **hard to test** as it is hard to objectively measure attitudes towards the law and crime.

Practice Questions

Q1 What did Blackburn (1993) propose leads to offending behaviour?

Q2 Give two weaknesses of the psychodynamic approach to criminality.

Exam Questions

Q1 Outline the psychodynamic explanation of offending behaviour. [4 marks]

Q2 Discuss the differential association theory of offending behaviour. [16 marks]

Personally, I find Freud quite offensive...

The psychodynamic theory of forensic psychology isn't the most popular, but you still need to know your stuff. You might not agree with what Freud said, but you have to hand it to him... he certainly made an impact on psychology.

Imprisonment

So, the jury's reached a verdict — they've decided the defendant is guilty and needs a spell in prison.
But there's debate about whether or not this will change the criminal. Cue two handy pages on imprisonment.

There are Several **Aims** of **Custodial Sentencing**

People aren't locked up and thrown in jail 'just because'. Custodial sentencing (sending someone to prison) has a **purpose**. In fact, it has lots of **different** purposes:

1) **Retribution (punishment)** — the offender should rightfully 'pay' for their crime, and deserves the punishment.

2) **Rehabilitation** — reforming and offering offenders the chance to get their lives back on track.

3) **Incapacitation** — protecting the public by removing the offender.

4) **Denunciation** — showing the public that the offender's actions were wrong.

5) **Deterrence** — stopping future crimes by the criminal themself (specific deterrence), or stopping the public committing the same crime by showing them the punishment (general deterrence).

Imprisonment Can Have a **Big Effect** on **Criminals**

There are lots of different psychological effects of custodial sentencing.

Mental Health Problems

It's thought that prisoners may be more susceptible to problems with **depression** and more likely to attempt **suicide** than other people. **Dooley** studied suicides in prisons in England and Wales.

Dooley (1990) — Depression and suicide risk in prison

Method:	The **case notes** of **295** of the 300 suicides that happened in prison between 1972 and 1987 were studied.
Results:	Prisoners serving **life sentences** and those convicted of **violent** or **sexual** offences were most at risk. There was an association between suicide and **guilt** over the offence. There was a history of **psychiatric problems** in about a third of cases and **self-harm** was common.
Conclusion:	**Depressive illness** is likely to be a contributing factor to suicides in prison. Dooley thought that better **communication** between staff and prisoners is needed to reduce suicide rates.
Evaluation:	Prisoners **don't** form a **random sample** of the general population — as a group they differ in terms of ethnicity, age, psychiatric history, socio-economic status, and marital and employment status. This makes it hard to measure exactly how much **more susceptible** to depression and suicide prisoners really are.

Zimbardo's prison study (you came across this in Year 1) also showed the 'prisoners' experiencing high levels of **emotional distress**, further emphasising the **psychological effects** of custodial sentencing.

Although studies have shown prisoners to have depression, it is difficult to determine **cause** and **effect** — prisoners may have had psychological problems, such as depression, **before** they were imprisoned.

Institutionalisation

Being kept in a prison often **strips** offenders of their **autonomy**. Studies such as **Zimbardo's** have shown that prisoners are quick to **conform** to given roles and become dependent on others within their environment.

Reinforces Criminal Behaviour

Putting people who've committed crimes all together in one place might seem like a good idea. But it can become a **breeding ground** for crime. Prisons can **reinforce** the criminal lifestyle and **support criminal behaviour** as a result of inmates teaching each other about crime. This can result in high recidivism rates (see next page).

Psychological effects of imprisonment don't have to be negative — there can be positive effects too. Inmates can experience remorse, benefit from new opportunities and undergo treatment to rehabilitate their lives.

Labelling

When offenders are released from prison, they still hold the **stigma** of having been 'inside'. They may find it **difficult** to get a job or **maintain** their **social network**, which in turn increases the likelihood of recidivism (next page).

Imprisonment

There are **Good** and **Bad** Things About Imprisonment

- There are lots of arguments **for** custodial sentencing — it **can** fulfill its aims whilst having positive psychological effects, such as having a new outlook on life, and giving prisoners the opportunity to **reform** and become better people.

- But some people argue that custodial sentencing **doesn't really work**. It only exists to **please** the public, as a sign of 'justice' being served. Some argue that if it **did** really work as a deterrent, there wouldn't be any criminals today.

Bruce really wasn't a fan of prison — his hat gave him the most awful hat hair.

- Putting money and resources into **prevention** might be more efficient. This could **eliminate** labelling and other detrimental consequences of imprisonment.

- There are many **other types** of custodial sentences — imprisonment doesn't suit all. For example, **community service** might be better for those who have committed small crimes. This would enable **low-risk offenders** to keep their social contacts and jobs — important for when they finish their sentence.

Lots of Criminals **Continue** to Commit Crimes **After** Being in Prison

Recidivism is just a fancy word that means **repeating** an undesirable behaviour after you've been punished for it. In the case of criminals and prison there are many factors which influence this:

1) Length of **time** spent in prison.
2) **Supervision** after conditional release.
3) **Disciplinary** reports.
4) **Education** level.
5) **Seriousness** of crime committed.
6) Prisoner **ethnicity**.
7) Individual **experiences** in prison.

> Conditional release is where a person is released early from prison under specified conditions, e.g. they may be monitored or supervised.

In the UK, rates of adult recidivism have slowly decreased over time. In **2012**, nearly **27%** of criminals re-offended. However, in the same year, there was a reported rise in the proportion of re-offenders who served **less than 12 months** — this was reported as happening in **over 50%** of cases.

> Recidivism costs the economy a great deal — so reducing these rates would benefit everyone.

Studies have also shown a link between **employment** after imprisonment and the likelihood of reoffending. For example, **Gillis et al (1998)** found that offenders who found employment within six months of being released had fewer convictions than offenders who didn't take up employment during this time. **However**, this link doesn't necessarily show **cause and effect**.

Practice Questions

Q1 What is reparation?
Q2 Describe Dooley's (1990) study into suicides in prisons.
Q3 Give two factors which could affect recidivism.

Exam Questions

Q1 Which term is used to describe the repetition of undesirable behaviour after punishment?

    A Incapacitation   **B** Denunciation   **C** Recidivism   **D** Retribution   [1 mark]

Q2 Outline the aims of custodial sentencing.   [6 marks]

What did the policeman say to his stomach...?

Whilst you're pondering the answer to this very important question (hint: it involves a pun on the word 'arrest'), perhaps make sure you've learnt these pages back-to-front, inside-out and upside-down. It's gripping stuff...

Behaviour Modification in Custody

Even though recidivism rates may be dropping in the UK, they're still very much there — criminals are still reoffending. Lots of studies have shown that sending a criminal to prison may not do anything to change their behaviour. But that doesn't stop people trying. These pages will tell you all about the methods used to try to modify criminal behaviour.

The Token Economy Programme is a Behaviourist Treatment

1) The **token economy programme** has been used with various groups, including prison inmates.

2) It's a form of **behaviour modification** based on the behaviourist idea of **operant conditioning**.

3) Operant conditioning deals with the modification of behaviour through **consequences** — rewards which reinforce behaviour, and punishments which discourage the behaviour from happening again.

4) The token economy programme reinforces good behaviour by rewarding subjects with '**tokens**' for meeting their behavioural '**goals**'.

5) Tokens are saved up and can be **spent** to gain 'treats' or 'rewards'.

Token economy programmes must be **adhered to** in order for them to work. No other rewards can be given to the inmates or the token system will become pointless. Also, several things need to be established in order for the system to be set up:

> 1) The behaviour that is desired from the inmates must be clearly **defined**.
> 2) A **variety** of rewards must be given to encourage participation.
> 3) The **reasons** for token allocation must be clear.
> 4) What a token is **worth** must be clearly established, e.g. how many tokens equal a chocolate bar, etc.
> 5) The **rate** of earning tokens must also be established, i.e. how many a particular behaviour will earn.

Token Economy Programmes have Strengths and Weaknesses

There is evidence that token economies can **improve inmates behaviour** while they're in prison. For example:

> **Milan and McKee (1976)** studied the effect of using a token economy in a cellblock of an American male prison. They compared the inmates behaviour between several conditions, including **normal prison methods**, a system of **behaviour monitoring and encouragement** without issuing tokens, and a full **token economy**. They found that the inmates' performance for the **monitored behaviours** (e.g. getting up on time, keeping a tidy cell) was **best** when the full **token economy** was in place.

However, the positive effect of token economies **may not last** once people leave the programme.

> **Kirigin et al (1982)** studied the effectiveness of a programme for 'delinquent' youths, which included a **token economy**. They found that **rates of criminality** and of behaviour like truancy were **reduced during the programme**, but returned to the **same rate** as the control group **after the programme**.

Token economies can be considered **unethical** — it can be argued that to work properly they need to involve withholding access to basic things like food and drink, which should be a **right**, not a **privilege** that is earned.

Anger Management is a Therapeutic Programme

1) **Anger management** is a **therapeutic programme** often used with convicted violent criminals.

2) This approach assumes that violent behaviour is caused by **anger** and **frustration** — it's hoped that if individuals can learn to **control** this anger then their violent behaviour patterns will decrease.

3) Anger management is based on **cognitive behavioural techniques** and a specific programme has been designed for use in penal institutions.

4) The main aims of this treatment are to **reduce** the amount of **violence** within the prison and to improve individuals' **self-awareness** and **control**. It's hoped that it will still make a difference **after** release.

5) Courses usually involve a **two-hour session** each week for **eight weeks**. Participants are encouraged to **monitor** their own behaviour patterns and emotions so that they become increasingly aware of their own emotional changes. It's thought that this will help them to control their own emotions.

Behaviour Modification in Custody

Anger Management Isn't Effective for Everyone

Studies looking at how **effective** anger management is at reducing inmates anger have had mixed results. This may be because it's **only helpful for certain offenders** — not all crimes are committed through anger. **Howells et al (2005)** found in a study of Australian offenders that a short course of anger management **did not have a significant effect** on self reported anger. However, some studies have found that it can be effective:

	Ireland (2000) — The effectiveness of anger management
Method:	Aggression levels of **50 inmates** in a young offenders' institution were measured two weeks **before** an anger management treatment programme was started. A **record** of each prisoner's aggressive **behaviour** over one week was kept, and they each completed a **questionnaire** and had a **cognitive-style interview**. A treatment programme of twelve one hour sessions over three days was started, and eight weeks later the measurements were **repeated**.
Results:	There was an **improvement** in **92%** of participants. **8%** of prisoners were **worse** after the treatment.
Conclusion:	The anger management programme was **useful** for treating aggressive behaviour in the short term.
Evaluation:	It will have been difficult to **control other variables** that may have had an effect on inmates' anger, such as news from friends and family, interaction between inmates and relationships with staff. Also, all the participants in this study were young offenders in an institution, so the results can't be **generalised** to other groups, e.g. offenders in prison, released offenders, etc.

Restorative Justice is About Criminals Making Amends

Traditional justice is all about being **punished** for committing crimes. The **restorative justice programme**, on the other hand, focuses on criminals **making amends** directly to the people they've harmed with their behaviour. This helps the criminal to **take responsibility** for their actions, and makes them aware of the **real damage** they've caused.

1) It can be used for various offences from antisocial behaviour (e.g. **vandalism**) to serious offences like **assault**.
2) The victim must **volunteer** to use the approach and the offender must have **admitted responsibility**.
3) The process may involve the victim and offender **meeting** face-to-face or communicating by **letter**.
4) It can also involve offenders working to **undo** the damage they have caused, e.g. by removing graffiti.

A study by the Smith Institute (**Smith Report 2007**) found that the restorative justice programme has many advantages:

1) It **reduced post-traumatic stress** in the victims, and they were **less likely** to want **violent revenge**.
2) Both criminals and victims were **more satisfied** with this approach than with traditional justice solutions.
3) It decreased the **costs** involved.

One of the main **problems** with the restorative justice programme is that people are **reluctant** to use it. A report by The Ministry of Justice in 2012 also highlighted the **lack of awareness** by the public and their **confusion** over what restorative justice really means.

Practice Questions

Q1 What is a token economy programme?
Q2 Give a weakness of token economy programmes.

Exam Questions

Q1 Briefly outline how restorative justice programmes work. [4 marks]

Q2 Discuss how anger management can be used to deal with offending behaviour. [16 marks]

Kev woz ere — restorative justice sucks...

You've probably just read the stuff on token economy programmes and realised they ring a bell. That's because they crop up in other areas of Psychology too. Take a look on page 88 where you can read about them again. Hoorah.

Addictive Behaviour — Smoking

Loads of people smoke, even though it causes all sorts of illnesses. A big part of this is that it's addictive — once people start smoking, they can find it very difficult to stop. As usual, psychology has come up with reasons for this.

Addictions Can Be **Physical** or **Psychological**

1) **Physical dependence** is where your body becomes dependent on a drug (e.g. the **nicotine** in cigarettes). You get **withdrawal symptoms** (see below) if you don't take the drug. This is your body's way of telling you that you need more of the drug to feel 'normal' again.

2) **Psychological dependence** is more of a **mental state** than a physical need. For example, you believe that you need the drug to stay relaxed — and are drawn back time and time again to take it.

Addictions Involve **Tolerance** and **Withdrawal Symptoms**

Addictions, including addictions to drugs such as nicotine in cigarettes, involve **tolerance** and **withdrawal symptoms**.

Tolerance

Tolerance happens when the body becomes **used to** a substance — taking the same amount of a drug no longer has the **same effect**. You need to take **larger quantities** to feel the same effect.

Withdrawal Symptoms

Withdrawal symptoms are uncomfortable **symptoms** that occur when a person **stops taking** the substance they're addicted to, or **reduces** the amount they take. These are removed by taking more of the drug again.

Many People Are **Addicted** to Smoking

The chemicals in cigarettes can cause diseases such as **cancer**, **emphysema** and **bronchitis**. Despite this, many people smoke and some continue to smoke after being diagnosed with one of these conditions — this is because smoking is **addictive**. Even though many smokers want to quit, the **success rate** of those who attempt it is **very low**.

As with most things in psychology, addiction to smoking can be explained in more than one way.

Smoking Can Be Explained in Terms of **Brain Neurochemistry**

1) There are many chemicals in cigarettes but it's the **nicotine** that causes **addiction**.

2) Nicotine stimulates the release of **dopamine**, increasing the level of dopamine in the brain and stimulating dopamine receptors on neurons. This provides feelings of **pleasure** and **relaxation**.

3) Once the dopamine has been removed from the synapses (reuptake), this feeling **disappears**. In order to regain it, the person wants to take **more** of the substance.

4) If nicotine's taken **regularly** the body **expects it** and **reduces** the amount of dopamine that's released naturally.

5) In order to maintain **normal dopamine levels** and the effect that they have on the body, nicotine needs to be taken regularly. This **reinforces smoking behaviour**, leading to more frequent smoking and **addiction**.

6) **Quitting** smoking is very difficult as the body becomes used to nicotine and **relies** on it to stimulate dopamine release. Quitting deprives the body of nicotine, leading to **low dopamine levels** until the body readjusts.

7) This can lead to **withdrawal syndrome**, which may result in **symptoms** such as anxiety, sleep disturbance and nausea.

	Olds and Milner (1954) — The effect of dopamine in rats
Method 1:	Rats had an electrode connected to the **hypothalamus** in their brain. When the rats pressed a **lever**, the electrode stimulated the hypothalamus, leading to the release of **dopamine**.
Results 1:	Rats voluntarily **chose** to press the lever.
Method 2:	In a second experiment, the rats had to walk over an area with a **painful electric current** running through it in order to get to the lever.
Results 2:	Rats **chose** to walk over the area which would shock them in order to press the lever.
Conclusion:	As rats pressed the lever voluntarily, even if it meant being shocked, it suggests the feeling associated with the release of dopamine was **rewarding** and the stimulus that caused it was **addictive**.
Evaluation:	Although it was a laboratory study and therefore highly **controlled**, the experiment was carried out on **rats** and so the results can't be **generalised** to humans. The procedure also has **ethical issues**.

Addictive Behaviour — Smoking

The *Brain Neurochemistry Explanation* has *Strengths* and *Weaknesses*

Strengths

1) Research, such as that by **Olds and Milner (1954)**, has provided **support** for the idea that **dopamine** is involved in addiction.

2) Studies into **biochemical factors** involve **laboratory experiments** where the **variables** are strictly **controlled**. This means that it should be possible to establish **cause and effect**, because it's less likely that the results were caused by an **extraneous variable**.

3) **Zhang et al (2012)** also provided support that dopamine is involved in smoking addiction, finding that levels become **abnormal** if an addict gives up smoking. They studied mice which had been given nicotine for several weeks, and found that when it was suddenly **stopped**, production of dopamine became **lower** than normal.

Brain neurochemistry is a biochemical explanation.

Weaknesses

1) Explaining substance misuse in terms of neurotransmitter levels is **reductionist** (see page 45) because it **ignores psychological factors**.

2) Focussing on brain neurochemistry ignores the impact of **genetics** — it could be that **inherited tendencies** influence substance misuse. For example, **Doweiko (2002)** looked at **adoption records** for over 3000 people and found that **children** of **alcoholics** were much **more likely** to grow up to be alcoholics themselves. Being raised by **adoptive** parents who **weren't alcoholics** seemed to have **little effect**. This suggests that there's a **genetic influence** in **addiction**.

3) There are problems with **generalising** results from **animal** research to **humans**.

Smoking Can Be Explained Using *Learning Theory*

Learning through observation is explained by social learning theory (you met this in Year 1).

1) New behaviour (in this case smoking) can be learned through **observation** or **modelling**. Whether the behaviour is imitated depends on the perceived **consequences**.

2) Through **operant conditioning**, if smoking is **positively reinforced**, e.g. by **benefits** such as fitting in with peers, it's likely to be **copied**. Seeing **role models** (e.g. parents or celebrities) smoking also encourages people to smoke.

3) Once someone has started smoking they will experience withdrawal symptoms if they stop. These encourage people to start smoking again (to remove the symptoms). This is known as **negative reinforcement**. Drug users may also want to **avoid** feelings of stress or boredom, or negative **social** factors like being the 'odd one out'.

4) Often, smoking becomes **associated** with other activities and objects, which makes it difficult not to smoke in certain **environments**. This is known as **cue reactivity**, and can be explained by **classical conditioning**.

5) For example, repeatedly smoking in the same environment could lead to **associations** forming between smoking and **other stimuli** in the environment, such as alcohol, other smokers or cigarette lighters. When these stimuli are present, the body **expects** to receive nicotine, and will **compensate** in advance for certain effects of the drug — the person will then develop a **craving** to smoke.

Studies have provided **support** for the **learning theory** approach to addiction. For example:

	Akers and Lee (1996) — The effects of social learning over time
Method:	A five year **longitudinal study** of 454 secondary school students was conducted using **self-report questionnaire surveys**. These measured how frequently the students smoked and 'social learning variables'. These were things like whether friends smoked, how often friends smoked, and perceived attitudes of friends and parents towards smoking.
Results:	Significant **positive correlations** were found between the social learning variables and smoking.
Conclusion:	Social learning can partly account for whether smoking begins in adolescence.
Evaluation:	Methods relying on self report may be **unreliable**, and correlation doesn't prove that social learning causes smoking to begin. Also, the effect of social learning wasn't analysed to show the relative influence of different **variables**, e.g. gender or parental vs. peer influence.

Addictive Behaviour — Smoking

Using **Learning Theory** to Explain Smoking has **Strengths** and **Weaknesses**

Strengths

1) Studies of learning theory usually use **human participants**, so they **avoid** the problems of generalising from **animal** experiments encountered in much biochemical research.

2) The learning approach can be used to explain physical addiction as well as **psychological addiction** to substances that **don't** cause unpleasant physical withdrawal symptoms, e.g. cannabis.

3) **Moolchan et al (2000)** found that **75%** of **teenage smokers** have at least one **parent** who **smokes**. They also feel that smoking helps them to **fit in** with their **peers**. These findings support **social learning theory**, as the subjects were **imitating** their parents. They also support the **operant conditioning** explanation — the **social approval** that subjects got from their friends for smoking acted as **positive reinforcement**.

4) A **meta-analysis** of **fMRI** (see page 14) studies by **Engelmann et al (2012)** provided support for the idea of **cue reactivity**. They looked at studies that had compared fMRIs of smokers shown **smoking-related cues** compared to **neutral cues**, and found that the smoking-related cues caused a **larger neural response**.

David was going to have to find a new hobby. Seeing the cue would be too much for his chocolate addiction.

Weaknesses

1) The learning approach is too **nomothetic** because it assumes that everyone can become **addicted** in the **same way**. It **ignores individual differences**, and doesn't place enough importance on other explanations such as **biochemical** or **genetic** factors.

2) The learning approach doesn't explain how **free will** (see page 44) plays a part in behaviour such as smoking. It doesn't take into account the idea that people can make their **own decisions** about what they do or don't do, e.g. whether they smoke or not, based on what they know about the dangers.

It's likely that a **combination** of **biological** and **psychological** factors contribute to addiction to smoking. For example, it might be that **brain neurochemistry** plays a big part, but that it also depends on the **environmental variables** (e.g. exposure to role models) that people come into contact with.

Practice Questions

Q1 Distinguish between physiological and psychological dependence on smoking.

Q2 What is tolerance?

Q3 Outline research that suggests the release of dopamine is rewarding and addictive.

Q4 Describe the study by Akers and Lee (1996).

Q5 Describe the findings of Moolchan et al's (2000) study on teenage smoking.

Exam Questions

Q1 Outline how nicotine addiction can be explained in terms of brain neurochemistry. [4 marks]

Q2 Discuss how learning theory can be applied to smoking behaviour. [16 marks]

My tolerance for this topic is rapidly reducing...

So there you have it. I reckon the neurochemical explanation could also be used to explain my chocolate spread addiction. I can't get through the day without it, and I think I'd happily take a quick electric shock to get my hands on some. Anyway, enough about me — you need to make sure you get to grips with everything on these pages.

Addictive Behaviour — Gambling

Now that you know all about addiction to smoking, it's time to learn about a completely different type of addiction — addiction to gambling. It seems that some people can't help going back again and again for that elusive win.

Gambling Addictions Can be Explained by *Cognitive Biases*

1) Cognitive biases are **mental errors** or **distortions of thinking** that lead to **perspectives** and **judgements** that can be very different to reality.

2) These faulty judgements can come about because we often subconsciously **simplify things** and use **rules of thumb** when processing information and making decisions.

3) Cognitive biases can be like **optical illusions**. Even when you're aware of the mistaken thinking, it still seems right. Because of this, they can be pretty difficult to overcome.

4) Cognitive biases appear in **gambling**. For example, people often believe that the **probability** of a future event, such as tossing a coin, is dependent on **past events** (see representative bias below).

5) **Wagenaar** (1988) identified 16 rules that gamblers commonly use when making decisions. These include:

- **The illusion of control** — gamblers think of gambling as **skill-based**, and believe that they have some control over the outcome. This creates superficially high expectations when, in reality, the outcomes are often determined by chance alone.

- **Representative bias** — gamblers believe that **random events** should **look random**, e.g. 'tails' seems increasingly likely the longer a run of consecutive 'heads' lasts.

- **Gambler's fallacy** — many gamblers believe that the longer a losing streak lasts, the more likely a win will follow.

- **Illusory correlations** — gamblers have **superstitions** which they believe help them succeed, e.g. blowing the dice for a 6.

- **Fixation on the absolute frequency of successes** — gamblers can **recall many past wins**, just because they gamble so much. This creates a false image of how often they win.

- **Sunk cost bias** — gamblers put a lot of money into gambling and so there's the belief that they'll eventually get a return. They don't like to stop gambling just in case they lose out on the win.

There's *Evidence* for *Cognitive Bias*

Griffiths (1994) — Cognitive bias using fruit machines

Method: 30 participants who only **occasionally** used a fruit machine volunteered to take part in a **field study** with 30 **regular gamblers**. Each participant was given £3, which gave 30 gambles on the fruit machine. Participants were asked to try to stay on the machine for at least 60 gambles. If they reached 60, they were given the choice of keeping any winnings or carrying on gambling. Participants were asked to **think aloud**, which required them to say their thoughts out loud during the task. The total number of gambles each participant made was recorded, along with the amount of winnings and the outcome of every gamble.

Results: Regular gamblers were more likely to reach 60 gambles than non-regular gamblers. However, they were also much more likely to play until they had **lost everything**. Some regular gamblers **objected** to gambling on the fruit machine chosen for the study. Regular gamblers also made **more irrational verbalisations** than non-regular gamblers, such as personifying and talking to the machine whilst gambling (e.g. "the machine likes me"). They also tended to refer to losses as '**near misses**' or '**near wins**'. In a later interview, the regular gamblers saw themselves as more **skilful** than occasional gamblers.

Conclusion: There is evidence for the existence of **cognitive biases** in gambling. For example, the fact that some gamblers opposed to using the fruit machine selected for the study indicates that an **illusion of control** exists, where they believe that if they are familiar with a machine they will win more. Also, the fact that many regular gamblers **talked to the machine** shows that their behaviour was not in line with **reality**.

Evaluation: The experiment took place in a natural setting, increasing its **ecological validity**. However, this also means that the results could have been affected by **extraneous variables**. Only one of the regular gamblers was **female**, so the results may not have been **representative** of the whole population. Also, thinking aloud might have an effect on the **cognitive processes** taking place, making the study **invalid**.

Addictive Behaviour — Gambling

The Cognitive Theory of Gambling has Strengths and Weaknesses

Strengths

1) Studies like Griffiths (1994) have shown that there is a **difference** between the **cognitive processing** in occasional gamblers and in regular gamblers.

2) Other studies have supported the idea of cognitive biases. For example, in a study by **Henslin (1967)**, it was found that gamblers playing craps (a dice game) in a casino were likely to adjust how they rolled the dice depending on what they wanted to score. If they needed a **higher number**, they tended to throw the dice **harder**.

3) **Strickland et al (1966)** also found evidence of cognitive biases in gambling. They showed that people would make **higher bets** and were **more confident** that they'd win if they were able to throw the dice **themselves** rather than having someone else throw for them.

"Is there one there that you're happy with, sir?"

Weaknesses

1) **Not everyone** develops cognitive biases which lead them to become addicted to gambling. So the cognitive explanation can't be the **only** explanation as it doesn't take **individual differences** into account. There may be other reasons why some people are more likely to become addicted to gambling than others, e.g. genetic explanations.

2) It is difficult to separate **cause and effect** — it might be that the cognitive biases don't cause the addiction, but rather that they are a **result** of the addiction.

3) The approach can help to explain gambling addictions, but it can't be **generalised** to **other types** of addictions, such as smoking or drug addictions, as they seem less linked to faulty processing mechanisms.

Learning Theory Can be Applied to Gambling Addiction

You covered classical and operant conditioning in Year 1 — make sure you're clear on how they work.

Both classical and operant conditioning can be used to explain gambling addiction:

Classical Conditioning

1) Classical conditioning explains gambling addiction in terms of the person becoming **conditioned** to the **excitement** and **arousal** they feel when they gamble.

2) The **unconditioned stimulus** in this situation is the **gambling win**, which produces **excitement** and increases **heart rate**, which is the **unconditioned response**. If wins and excitement repeatedly happen together in a typical **gambling environment**, other stimuli associated with gambling (e.g. packs of cards, dice) become the conditioned stimulus and will also cause excitement, the **conditioned response**.

3) This feeling of excitement could then be **temptation** to have a go at gambling.

Operant Conditioning

1) Gambling could also be explained by operant conditioning in terms of **reinforcement**.

2) However, unlike some operant conditioning situations, when someone gambles, they are not rewarded at every go — a lot of the time, they **lose**. So, only **partial reinforcement** is present.

3) One type of partial reinforcement which is important in the explanation of gambling is **variable reinforcement**. Gambling wins **don't** follow a **pattern**, and so the pattern of **reward** and **reinforcement** is also **irregular** — it **varies**.

4) Research has shown that variable reinforcement is enough to maintain a **gambling addiction**. Even if you don't know when you're going to win, you **keep trying**, because it could be on the next go and you don't want to miss out.

Addictive Behaviour — Gambling

A *Big Win* Must Come *First* Though

1) Not everyone who gambles develops an addiction.

2) **Skinner (1953)** believed that this was down to whether they'd had a **big win** early on.

3) His reasoning was that people who have had a big win will have been **positively reinforced**, and will be more likely to **continue their behaviour** to try to achieve the same again.

4) **Custer (1982)** supported Skinner's (1953) ideas that reinforcement could come about as a result of a big win.

Social Learning Theory Can Explain Why People *Start Gambling*

1) **Bandura's (1977)** social learning theory can be used as an explanation for how people become **involved** in gambling in the first place. (You covered social learning theory in Year 1).

2) People might initially start gambling after **watching** someone make a win and seeing the positives that come from it — in other words, they learn to start gambling through **vicarious reinforcement**.

3) If they themselves go on to make a win, **classical** and **operant conditioning** (see previous page) could then explain why they **continue** to gamble and become addicted.

The Learning Theory Approach to Gambling has *Strengths* and *Weaknesses*

Strengths

1) Learning theory can explain why people continue to gamble even when they lose, by showing that reinforcement can be just as effective even if it is **irregular**.

2) **Meyer et al (2004)** found that **heart rate** and other signs of excitement **increased** when gamblers began playing a betting game, and that problem gamblers had significantly higher heart rates than non-problem gamblers. This provides support for the suggestion that **excitement** acts as an **conditioned response** to gambling.

Weaknesses

1) Learning theory can't explain why only a **small number** of people who experience a win at gambling become addicted to gambling. This means that there must be **other factors** involved too. For example, genetic factors may play a part.

2) Skinner's ideas of conditioning and reinforcement were based on research using **pigeons** and **rats**. This makes it hard to **generalise** the theories to **humans**.

3) Learning theory can't explain the **cognitive biases** that some people who are addicted to gambling hold.

Practice Questions

Q1 Name three cognitive biases.
Q2 Outline the three cognitive biases that you've named.
Q3 What type of study did Griffith's (1994) carry out?
Q4 How can classical conditioning be used to explain addiction to gambling?

Exam Questions

Q1	What is a cognitive bias in relation to gambling?	[2 marks]
Q2	Outline one limitation of using cognitive theory to explain gambling addiction.	[2 marks]
Q3	Briefly explain how learning theory can be applied to gambling addiction.	[4 marks]

To order chocolate cake or apple crumble — it's a gamble...

I need to put in an order for tonight's birthday meal. Whichever one I order, I'll want the other one when it's put down in front of me. Anyway, I suppose that's not your concern. Make sure you can explain gambling using both cognitive theory and learning theory, and make sure you can evaluate them both. Then go and eat chocolate cake. No, crumble.

Risk Factors in Addiction

Not everybody becomes an addict. Behaviours such as drinking and gambling remain controllable pastimes for many people, so there must be individual differences at work. And, surprise surprise, you need to know what they are.

Stress Could be a Factor in the Development of Addiction

1) **Sinha (2007)** used **brain imaging** to investigate the relationship between **stress** and **drug addiction**. She found that the **same part of the brain** was activated during stress as during drug craving.

2) Sinha suggests that stress makes people more **vulnerable** to reacting to **cues** associated with drugs. This could make them **more likely** to develop an addiction.

3) This research shows an **association** between stress and addiction — but it **doesn't explain** it. Drug use might cause altered brain function, or altered brain function might encourage drug use — or there may be **another cause**, and drug use and altered brain function are both results of this.

I'm stressed just looking at them — pass the chocolate.

4) **Operant conditioning** could explain why stress might make people more vulnerable to addiction if the pleasurable effects of the substance **reduce the symptoms** of stress. For example, alcohol is a **depressant** so it can make a stressed person feel **more relaxed**. This acts as **positive reinforcement** and so they're more likely to **repeat** the drinking behaviour.

Behaviour of Peers is a Factor that Seem to be Linked to Addiction

1) **Martino et al (2006)** carried out a **longitudinal study** to look at the social factors that affect the **drinking habits** of adolescents. They concluded that the norms for drinking behaviour are learned through **social observations** and **interactions**. The **perceived approval** or **use** of alcohol by **parents**, other important adults and **peers increased the likelihood** of future decisions to drink and get drunk.

2) Research has shown that although being **socially withdrawn** can be negative for other reasons, such as loneliness, it actually **protects** young people from the **influence** of their **peers** in relation to addiction:

> - **Fergusson and Horwood (1999)** found that children who were **socially isolated** from their peer group at the age of **10** because of **social anxiety** were **less likely** to use drugs or drink alcohol when they were **15**.
> - **Shedler and Block (1990)** found that **18-year-olds** who hadn't tried drugs were more likely to be **socially isolated**, **over-controlled** by others and **anxious**.

Younger People are More Affected by Peer Pressure

Sumter et al (2009) found that a person's **age** affects their ability to **resist peer pressure**.

	Sumter et al (2009) — Age differences in resisting peer pressure
Method:	**464 children and adolescents** were given a questionnaire that assessed their ability to resist **pressure** from their **peer group**. The questionnaire was written in a **style** suitable for all ages and used hypothetical **everyday situations**.
Results:	The participants' answers showed that they were **more vulnerable** to being influenced by their friends when they were **younger**. The participants became **more resistant** as they got **older**.
Conclusion:	As adolescents become **more mature** they are **less influenced** by others. This could explain why early experiences with substances have **long-term effects**.
Evaluation:	This was a **cross-sectional study** (one which tested different people of different ages) so individual differences could have affected the results. Carrying out longitudinal research avoids this design flaw, but it takes longer to collect the data. Peer pressure can be both **positive** or **negative** when it comes to abusing substances. You're less likely to do it if your friends aren't — but more likely if they are.

Risk Factors in Addiction

People Can be *Influenced* By Their *Family*

Becoming addicted to something can be down to your **family environment**:

- **Adesso (1985)** thought that children develop **expectancies** about the **effects** of **alcohol** through **observing** friends, family and role models. This supports **social learning theory** — it suggests that people learn how to behave when they're **drunk** by imitating others.
- **Christiansen et al (1982)** found that these expectancies are **modified** as an individual's **personal experience** with alcohol **progresses** — their **generalised** expectancies become more **specific**.

  - **Baer et al (1987)** found that adolescents were **more likely** to use **alcohol** if they experienced **family conflict** or **stressful life events**. This suggests that they were using alcohol as a way of **avoiding negative things** — **negative reinforcement**. Learning this behaviour at a **young age** means it's likely to **continue** into **adulthood**.
  - However, because this was a **correlational study** it's difficult to establish **cause and effect**. It could be that people are **more likely** to experience **family conflict** because they **drink alcohol**.

Personality Can Affect *Addictive Behaviour*

Personality Dimensions

You can read more about Eysenck's personality dimensions on page 132.

1) **Eysenck and Eysenck (1976)** outlined three main personality dimensions:

   - **P** for **psychoticism**, which includes being egocentric, aggressive and impulsive.
   - **E** for **extroversion**, which includes being outgoing, happy and sociable.
   - **N** for **neuroticism**, which includes being anxious, moody and irritable.

   Eysenck suggested that some personality characteristics make a person **more prone** to addiction.

2) **Francis (1996)** found that people with nicotine, heroin and alcohol addictions scored **more highly** on N and P scales on psychometric tests compared to the E scales.

3) The exact relationship between addiction and personality is **unclear**. Being irritable and impulsive could mean you are **more likely to use** substances such as alcohol or drugs. Or it could be that these personality characteristics make you **less able to control** your use of the substances.

4) Alternatively, it could be that **having an addiction** leads a person to be moody and impulsive, and makes them less likely to be happy and outgoing.

Self-Efficacy

1) **Bandura (1977)** came up with an alternative theory based on **personality** for what makes people prone to addiction.

2) He proposed that **self-efficacy** is a big indicator of whether or not someone will **change their behaviour**, for example, whether or not they'll succeed in giving up smoking.

3) Self-efficacy is how **strongly** someone believes that they are **capable** of doing something. So, if someone has **high self-efficacy**, they're more likely to **succeed** in changing their behaviour, and vice versa.

4) **DiClemente (1981)** carried out a study which found support for this idea.

5) Self-efficacy was measured in participants who had recently given up smoking. They were then followed up five months later to see if they'd managed to **abstain** from smoking.

6) It was found that those who had managed not to smoke had **significantly higher** self-efficacy than those who had returned to smoking.

Risk Factors in Addiction

People Might Be at **Higher Risk** of **Addiction** Due to Their **Genes**

There's a **genetic explanation** for addiction — it's been suggested that some addictions are **inherited**.

1) A review of studies by Sayette and Hufford (1997) concluded that **identical (MZ) twins** showed a **higher rate of concordance** for **alcoholism** than **non-identical (DZ) twins**, suggesting that alcoholism is controlled to **some extent** by **genes**.

2) This can explain why, despite the fact that many people drink alcohol on a regular basis, only a **small proportion** develop an **addiction** to it.

3) However, there must be an **environmental aspect** to alcoholism as the MZ twins didn't show 100% concordance.

4) It's also not clear whether the result is just **specific to alcoholism**, or can be generalised to addiction as a whole.

1) **Goodwin et al (1973)** found that adopted males whose biological parents had an **alcohol addiction**, were **four times** more likely to become alcoholics themselves than adopted males whose biological parents didn't have alcohol addictions.

2) This implies that there is a **genetic factor** in alcohol addiction.

1) **Slutske (2010)** studied whether **gambling addiction** has a genetic basis.

2) In a study of approximately **5000 participants**, she looked at **concordance rates** in **MZ** and **DZ** twins.

3) The results showed that concordance rates in **MZ** twins were **twice as high** as the concordance rates in **DZ** twins.

4) Slutske concluded that although there is a clear **genetic component**, there must be **other factors** at work. She believed that carrying certain genes makes people **vulnerable** to gambling addiction, but that whether or not this happens also depends on other social factors such as the presence of a **role model** who gambles.

The true cost of his addiction only hit Andy when he was asked to settle his tab.

Practice Questions

Q1 What technique did Sinha (2007) use when investigating the relationship between stress and addiction?

Q2 Identify the relationship that has been established between age and resistance to peer influence.

Q3 Identify the factors associated with drinking alcohol in the Baer et al (1987) study.

Q4 Give the personality characteristics outlined by Eysenck and Eysenck (1976) that P, E and N stand for.

Q5 What were the results of Slutske's (2010) study?

Exam Questions

Q1 Read the item and then answer the question below.

> Mark has moved to a new school and is worried about making new friends. He tries to make friends with a group of students, many of whom smoke. He is keen for them to like him so that he can settle in quickly. Mark is soon a regular smoker.

Using your knowledge of risk factors in addiction, explain why Mark becomes addicted to smoking. [4 marks]

Q2 Discuss risk factors associated with the development of addiction. [16 marks]

I don't stand a chance...

These psychologists are coming up with risk factors here, there and everywhere. How am I meant to avoid become addicted to everything I see? Come to think of it, maybe I haven't... I can't do without my morning cuppa, and then there's the afternoon biscuit craving, and the bedtime hot chocolate. Oh, moody and impulsive, you say...?

Reducing Addictive Behaviour

Because there are lots of different explanations for addictive behaviour, it means that many different ways to combat addictions have been developed. There's a lot to cover here, so take it slow and it'll all be alright on the exam day.

Addictions Can be **Reduced** Using **Drug Therapy**

1) The biological approach to reducing drug and alcohol addictions involves a **gradual detox**, where the **quantity** of the substance used is **reduced over time**. **Medication** may be prescribed to stop addictive behaviour. However, any medication prescribed has to be carefully controlled so it doesn't become an addiction itself.

2) Drug therapy can involve using **agonists** to help addicts cope with withdrawal symptoms when they stop abusing certain substances.

> *Agonists are a type of drug that trigger a response by binding to receptors on cells. Some agonists can replace and replicate the effects of addictive drugs, but with much less harmful side effects.*

For example, **methadone** is used as a biological intervention to help heroin addicts become 'clean'. This drug works by stimulating the opiate receptors, which slows down the nervous system, creating similar effects to heroin but in a **less dangerous** way. Research has found methadone to be an effective way of allowing addicts to **wean** themselves off heroin. For example, **Newman and Whitehill (1979)** found methadone to be significantly more successful than a placebo drug when used by a group of heroin addicts.

3) **Antagonists** are also used in drug therapy to reduce addictive behaviours. They stop the addictive substance from creating pleasurable feelings after someone has taken it, preventing reinforcement.

> *Antagonists reduce the effect of addictive drugs and substances by blocking receptors.*

For example, **naltrexone** is a drug which **stops pathways** in the brain from transmitting feelings of **pleasure**. It's commonly used to treat heroin and alcohol addiction by ensuring that neither drug produces positive side effects for the user. This means there's no longer an association between pleasure and the drug, so **no reinforcement** or conditioning can take place.

4) However, one **problem** with drug therapy is that there's the risk that the medications can cause **side-effects**.

5) Drug therapy is often only **effective** as long as the drugs are taken — people may **relapse** if they stop treatment.

Behavioural Interventions Can Reduce Addictive Behaviour

1) One type of behavioural intervention is called **aversion therapy**.

2) This is where addictions are broken by forming **negative associations** with the addictive behaviour.

3) For example, Antabuse® is prescribed to alcoholics. It causes nausea if it's combined with alcohol, discouraging alcoholics from drinking. The addict will form an **association** between **drinking** and **nausea** — this will continue even when they stop taking Antabuse®.

Meyer and Chesser (1970) carried out a **repeated measures experiment**. A group of alcoholics who were prescribed Antabuse® were compared to a **control group**. Around **50%** of those taking Antabuse® stayed **teetotal** for at least a year — significantly more than in the control group. From this study they concluded that an **unpleasant response** can be **conditioned** to an **addictive behaviour**.

4) Aversion therapy can also take the form of **covert sensitisation**. This is where the person forms negative associations with the addictive behaviour using just their **imagination**, rather than actually experiencing negative consequences.

5) For example, for someone with an alcohol addiction, the aim would be to associate thoughts of drinking with negative consequences. This would be done by them imagining a **horrible experience** in great detail, such as being ill, at the same time as having **cravings** for alcohol.

Kraft and Kraft (2005) studied the effectiveness of **covert sensitisation** using six participants with different addictions — alcohol, nail biting, cigarettes, cannabis, overeating and chocolate. They found that the technique was **effective** for **all** of the addictions, and was successful after only **2-4 sessions**. However, the very small **sample size** means that the results can't reliably be generalised to the population.

6) One problem with aversion therapy is that it has **ethical issues** surrounding the use of the aversive stimuli.

7) Aversion therapy can take a **long time**, and in the case of Antabuse® it relies on people continuing to take the drug for long enough to form the negative association — addicts may just **stop taking it** so that they can drink again.

SECTION THIRTEEN — ADDICTION

Reducing Addictive Behaviour

Cognitive Behaviour Therapy Can Also Reduce Addictive Behaviour

1) **Cognitive behaviour therapy (CBT)** aims to change the way an addict **behaves** by changing their **thought processes**. It identifies the thoughts that cause the behaviour, e.g. 'I can't cope without cigarettes', and then changes this thought process. This is known as **cognitive restructuring**.

2) Cognitive behaviour therapy has had some **success**, e.g. it has enhanced the effectiveness of nicotine replacement treatment for quitting smoking.

3) **Carroll et al (1994)** conducted a study which showed CBT to be **effective**. They compared two different intervention practices using two groups of cocaine users. Group One were given a series of **CBT sessions** whilst Group Two received an alternative form of **non-specific psychotherapy**.

4) Both therapies **reduced** the depressive symptoms of all participants, but **CBT** was **more effective** in stopping the addictive behaviour, and was more **successful** in a **follow-up** one year later.

5) Although there is support for CBT, such as the study above, it has some **weaknesses**:

> - CBT can take a **long time**, so the person needs to be willing to **invest time** in the process.
> - It can be **difficult** for a person to change their thought processes, so they need to be **committed** and **motivated** to complete the therapy.
> - CBT requires a lot of **focus**, **attention**, and **thinking**. People struggling with **substance addiction** may have trouble achieving this without receiving other treatment or help first.

Theories of Behaviour Change Can Be Applied to Addiction

These theories are used to find ways to support people to **change their behaviour**.

The Theory of Planned Behaviour

1) **Fishbein and Ajzen (1975)** initially developed the **theory of reasoned action (TRA)** model of behaviour.

2) It states that an individual's behaviour, e.g. whether they will give up alcohol, can be **predicted** by their **intention** to perform it. Intention is determined by two factors:

> - The person's **attitude to the behaviour** — this is shaped by their **beliefs** about the **outcome** of the behaviour, e.g. 'I'll save money', and their **judgement** of whether the outcome is **positive or negative**, **likely or unlikely**.
> - **Subjective norms** — this describes their **expectations** of the **social consequences** of the behaviour, e.g. 'My friends will think I'm boring', and their **motivation** to **follow these norms**, e.g. 'I want to be popular'.

3) Sheppard et al (1988) carried out a meta-analysis and found that the TRA had a **strong predictive use** — it was pretty good at predicting intentions and behaviour. It's also a useful model for knowing how to **alter** an individual's intentions and behaviour. However, it's been criticised for **neglecting factors** such as **habits** and **emotional aspects**, which are also important when intentions are being formed.

4) **Ajzen (1991)** then added a third factor to the TRA — a person's **perceived behavioural control**, e.g. 'I don't have the will power to give up alcohol'. This factor **increases** the model's **predictive power**.

5) This theory is known as the **theory of planned behaviour (TPB)**. It suggests behaviour is influenced in two ways:

> - **Indirectly** — if a person believes that the behaviour is **too difficult** they don't form the initial intention to carry out the behaviour.
> - **Directly** — if the **perception** of their own level of control is **accurate**, e.g. they don't have sufficient willpower, they won't succeed.

6) In contrast to the TRA, the TPB takes into account the fact that people **don't always have complete control** over their behaviour, as there may be obstacles that stand in their way.

7) Norman et al's (1998) study found that **perceived behavioural control** was a strong predictor of binge-drinking. The TPB could therefore be used to develop **intervention strategies** and **prevention programmes**. For example, programmes that involve **convincing** an individual that they **are in control** of their drinking behaviour.

8) Both models ignore the fact that there may be **discrepancies** between **attitude** and **behaviour** and that a person's behaviour is not always a reflection of their **intentions**. People's actions aren't always rational and based on deliberate decision making processes. This is especially true for **addictive behaviour**, which is often **irrational**.

Reducing Addictive Behaviour

Prochaska's Six-Stage Model

1) **Prochaska and DiClemente (1983)** came up with a model of **behaviour change**.

2) The model has **six stages**. At each stage, the person is given **encouragement**, but it's ultimately down to them to work through the stage and decide for themselves when it is time to **progress** to the next.

Stage	Characteristics	Support Given to the Person
Precontemplation	The person with the addiction **isn't ready** to change. They don't see their behaviour as a problem, and are good at **rationalising** this to themselves.	People show **concern** about the person's behaviour and try to **discuss** the problem.
Contemplation	The person is starting to **consider** that they have an addiction and that it is a problem. They're not yet committed to making any changes though.	The person is encouraged to **weigh up** the pros and cons of their **addiction**, and the pros and cons of **change**.
Preparation	The person has **accepted** that their addiction is a problem and they're **ready** to change. They begin to make **commitments** and to put **goals** in place.	The person is **encouraged** to take their **first steps** to make **changes**.
Action	The person is **actively** working towards changing their behaviour. They've made changes to their **lifestyle** and they're following a **plan**.	The person is given **help** in the changes they're making and is given **social support**.
Maintenance	The person is **focused** on sticking to the lifestyle changes they've made and **avoiding** a return to the addictive behaviour.	The person gets **continued support** to prevent relapse.
Relapse	This is where the person **goes back** to the addictive behaviour after having successfully been free of the behaviour for a while.	The person is shown to treat the relapse as a **learning opportunity** — for example, they can evaluate why it happened, and how they can avoid it happening again.

3) The model has been successfully applied to **addictive behaviours** such as smoking, drinking and drug-taking.

Practice Questions

Q1 Outline one drug therapy used in the treatment of addiction.

Q2 Describe the main findings of the study by Meyer and Chesser (1970).

Q3 What is 'precontemplation' in Prochaska's model?

Exam Questions

Q1 Which of these isn't a stage in Prochaska's six-stage model of behaviour change?
   A control   B contemplation   C maintenance   D preparation   [1 mark]

Q2 Briefly outline how cognitive behaviour therapy is used to reduce addiction.   [2 marks]

Q3 Outline the application of the theory of planned behaviour to addictive behaviour.   [6 marks]

I need an intervention to sort out my TRA — tremendous revision anger...

Phew, that's a whopping amount of information on reducing addictive behaviour. You're just going to have to take it bit by bit, until you know it all. Don't move on until you've got it firmly wedged in your brain. Sorry, there's simply nothing else for it. Still, this is the last page of the very last section you need to learn, so it's not worth giving up now...

Summary of the Exams

Here's what you can expect to see in your three A-Level Psychology exams.

The Exam Papers are **Broken Down** into Sections

A-Level exams are linear, so that means you'll do all the exams at the end of the course.

Paper 1 — *Introductory Topics in Psychology*

Paper 1 is broken down into **four** sections, like this:

These are topics that you should have covered in Year 1.

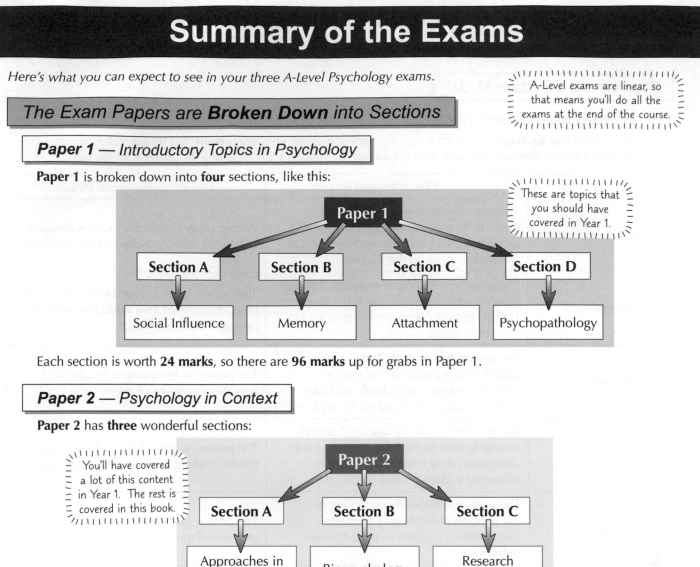

| Paper 1 |
| Section A | Section B | Section C | Section D |
| Social Influence | Memory | Attachment | Psychopathology |

Each section is worth **24 marks**, so there are **96 marks** up for grabs in Paper 1.

Paper 2 — *Psychology in Context*

Paper 2 has **three** wonderful sections:

You'll have covered a lot of this content in Year 1. The rest is covered in this book.

| Paper 2 |
| Section A | Section B | Section C |
| Approaches in Psychology | Biopsychology | Research Methods |

Sections A and B are worth **24 marks** each and Section C is worth **48 marks** — so there are **96 marks** in Paper 2.

Paper 3 — *Issues and Options in Psychology*

Paper 3 has **four** sections. In **Section A**, you'll be asked questions on **one compulsory** topic. In **Sections B**, **C** and **D** you get to **choose** which topic you answer questions on from a choice of three.

Everything you need to know for this paper is covered in this book.

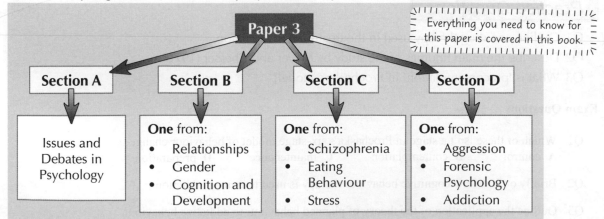

| Paper 3 |
| Section A | Section B | Section C | Section D |
| Issues and Debates in Psychology | **One** from:
• Relationships
• Gender
• Cognition and Development | **One** from:
• Schizophrenia
• Eating Behaviour
• Stress | **One** from:
• Aggression
• Forensic Psychology
• Addiction |

Each section is worth **24 marks**, so there are **96 marks** up for grabs in Paper 3.

Each paper is worth **one third** of your total A-Level Psychology grade. You'll get **2 hours** for each paper. In each section there'll be **multiple choice questions**, **short answer questions** and at least one **extended writing question**.

Assessment Objectives

You can get loads of clues about your answers from the exam paper.

You Need to Meet Certain **Assessment Objectives**

There are three **assessment objectives** — **AO1**, **AO2** and **AO3**.

AO1 is about the facts and theories

Questions containing **AO1** marks cover your **knowledge and understanding of science**, its **processes**, **techniques** and **procedures**. You get marks by **recalling** and **describing** psychological knowledge, such as theories, studies and methods. What you don't need to do is evaluate the theory (unless the question tells you to) — that'd just be a **waste of time** that you could use elsewhere, and you **won't get any extra marks**.

AO2 gets you to apply your knowledge

Questions containing **AO2** marks are slightly different in that they get you to **apply your knowledge and understanding of science**, its **processes**, **techniques** and **procedures**. Rather than just recalling stuff, e.g. listing relevant experiments, you've got to **apply your knowledge** to the different situations or contexts.

You might have to apply your knowledge:

- to a **made-up example** given in the question — e.g. you might be given some information about a person suffering from depression and have to outline behavioural, cognitive or emotional characteristics from the description.

- to a **practical** situation — e.g. you might be given the results of a study about how different reinforcements lead to different behaviours and be asked to explain how these results show evidence for conditioning. So you'd need to apply your knowledge of conditioning to the information given.

- in a situation with **qualitative data** (see page 22).

- in a situation with **quantitative data** (see page 22).

AO3 is about analysing, interpreting and evaluating

In questions containing **AO3** marks you could be given scientific information, ideas or evidence and be asked to **analyse**, **interpret** and **evaluate** them. You might need to **evaluate** a study or theory, or **draw conclusions** from the results of an experiment. You could even be asked to give **suggestions** on how to make a study **better**. You'll also need to be able to **design** psychological **procedures**.

Watch out — a question could contain more than one assessment objective. You need to read the question carefully and work out what you're being asked to do. See the next page for more on this.

Each Paper Has a **Different Weighting** of Assessment Objectives

There aren't a set number of **AO1**, **AO2** and **AO3** marks in each paper.
In **Paper 1**, there are slightly **more AO1 and AO3** marks than **AO2** marks.
In **Paper 2**, there are **more AO2** marks than **AO1** or **AO3** marks.
And in **Paper 3**, there are **more AO3** marks than **AO1** or **AO2** marks.

		Assessment Objective		
		AO1	AO2	AO3
Weighting (%)	Paper 1	11–14	6–9	12–14
	Paper 2	7–10	16–19	7–9
	Paper 3	9–12	5–8	15–17

At least **10%** of your grade will come from questions involving some **maths**. It won't be super hard maths, so don't panic, but it will cover maths you've learnt at GCSE. As long as you're comfortable with **basic arithmetic**, **handling data**, **algebra** and **graphs**, then you'll be fine. (And don't worry — you can take your calculator into the exams.)
25–30% of your grade will come from questions on **research methods**. These questions won't just appear in **Paper 2** — they could crop up **anywhere** (see page 158), so make sure you know your stuff really well.

DO WELL IN YOUR EXAMS

Assessment Objectives

The **Wording** of the Question Can Tell You What to Do

Exam questions contain **content words** and **command words**. The content words give away what the **topic** of the question is. A command word gives you an **instruction** of exactly what you need to do to answer the question. It's really **vital** that you know what they mean so that you can write the **correct** things in your answer. For example, if the question simply asks you to '**describe**' or '**outline**' something, you don't need to go into evaluating or explaining stuff.

Command words that you might find in the exam include:

Command word	What it means
Give/Write	Give a brief answer from memory or from the information in the question.
Name	Use a technical term to identify something.
Identify/State	Give a brief one or two word answer, or a short sentence.
Draw	Illustrate your answer with a diagram.
Label	Name parts of a diagram.
Calculate	Use maths to work out the value of something.
Analyse	Break down into characteristics and features.
Comment	Give a backed-up opinion.
Describe	Give details of something — it might be a theory, concept, process or study.
Outline	This requires less detail than 'describe' — it's more of a brief summary of something. Just give details of the main or important features. You don't need to go into too much depth.
Choose/Select/ Which is/What is	Pick from a range of answer options.
Explain	If a question asks you to explain, you need to give reasons for it and say why it is the case.
Discuss	This is a bit like a debate. Give evidence and examples for what you're saying, and support your points with explanations. These questions tend to be worth quite a lot of marks.
Evaluate	Weigh up the advantages and disadvantages, positives and negatives, or strengths and weaknesses. Keep your answer balanced — don't just concentrate on one side.
Compare	Outline the similarities and differences between two things.
Distinguish	Explain the differences between two or more things.
Complete	Finish the question by filling in the missing information.
Suggest	Present a solution or better way of doing something.
Design	Give details of how to carry out something, e.g. a study.
Justify	Give reasons for your answer, providing evidence to back up your ideas.
Consider	This is quite similar to 'evaluate' — your answer will involve weighing up the point that you've been asked to consider. Again, keep your comments balanced.

Command words can sometimes be **combined** together in a question.
For example, examiners will often ask you to 'outline **and** evaluate' or 'describe **and** explain' something.
Don't let this put you off — just break the question down into bits.
Start your answer with the **outline** or **describe** bit, and then **move on** to your **evaluation** or your **explanation**.

DO WELL IN YOUR EXAMS

What You Need to Write

The **Number of Marks** Tells You **How Much to Write**...

1) The number of marks that a question is worth gives you a pretty good clue of **how much to write**.

2) You get **one mark per correct point** made, so if a question is worth four marks, make sure you write four decent points.

3) There's no point writing a massive answer for a question that's only worth a few marks — it's just a **waste of your time**.

4) For the longer extended writing questions, make sure that you've written **enough** to cover the right number of marks, but don't just waffle.

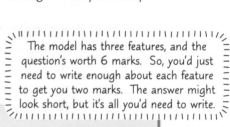

Martha suddenly realised that the question was worth 8 marks, not 88.

...But You Can't Just Write About **Anything**

1) It's important to remember that it's not just a case of blindly scribbling down **everything** you can think of that's related to the subject. Doing this just **wastes time**, and it doesn't exactly impress the examiner.

2) You only get marks for stuff that's **relevant** and **answers the question**.

3) So, make sure you read over the question a couple of times before you start writing so that you really understand what it's asking.

An **Example Answer** to Show You What to Aim for...

This is the sort of answer that would get you full marks.

> The model has three features, and the question's worth 6 marks. So, you'd just need to write enough about each feature to get you two marks. The answer might look short, but it's all you'd need to write.

1 Outline the features of the multi-store model of memory. [6 marks]

The multi-store model proposes that memory is made up of three stores. These are the sensory register, the short-term store and the long-term store. Sensory memory holds the information that is constantly being taken in from the environment, such as visual and auditory information. If you don't pay attention to this information, it will be lost from the sensory register. However, if you do pay attention to it, it will pass into short-term memory. Short-term memory has a limited and temporary capacity, but if the information in it is rehearsed, it will be transferred into long-term memory, which theoretically has an unlimited capacity and duration.

Make sure the information in your answer is relevant, and keep it concise.

Don't open with a general or meaningless sentence — get straight into gaining marks.

Stop writing once you've answered the question — don't add irrelevant detail to fill up the space.

...And an **Alternate Answer** to Show You What **Not** to Write...

I repeat... What **NOT** to write...

1 Outline the features of the multi-store model of memory. [6 marks]

Atkinson and Shiffrin proposed the multi-store model. They thought that memory is made up of three stores — a sensory register, a short-term store and a long-term store. The sensory register holds information from the environment. If you don't listen to this information, it gets lost. If you do listen to it, it will pass into short-term memory. It's then turned into long-term memory.

The primacy effect supports this model. You can remember the first few items on a list well. They have been better rehearsed and have moved to long-term memory. Also, if rehearsal is prevented, memory gets worse.

This first sentence is a bit irrelevant — it won't get you any marks.

You'd only need to give this detail if the question had asked you to evaluate the model — writing it is just a waste of time.

This could do with more detail to explain that STM only has a limited capacity, and rehearsal is needed to move information to LTM.

The second answer lacks the **detail** of the first — it only sketches over the features of the model. It wouldn't earn all the possible marks. Also, there's quite a bit of **irrelevant information** that wouldn't get you any marks.

Worked Exam

Over the next six pages we've given you some examples of the different styles of exam questions that you might come across. You'll get a mix of multiple choice questions, short answer questions and extended writing questions — so make sure you're familiar with them all.

Some Questions Will be Multiple Choice Questions

These questions give you some **answer options** and you just need to pick the right one.

2 Answer the questions on learning approaches below.

2.1 Complete the following sentence about Pavlov's research. Tick **one** box only.

Pavlov's experiments provided evidence for:

A Operant conditioning ☐

B Classical conditioning ☑

C The cognitive approach ☐

D The biological approach ☐ [1 mark]

> Read through all of the options before you choose your answer.

2.2 Which of the following is **not** used in operant conditioning? Tick **one** box only.

A Positive reinforcement ☐

B Negative reinforcement ☐

C Rewards ☐

D Imitation ☑ [1 mark]

> Watch out — the question might ask you to find the wrong answer.

You could even be asked to select **two** answer options.

3 Which **two** of the following occur as a result of the activation of the sympathetic nervous system? Tick **two** boxes only.

A Muscle tension ☑

B Decrease in perspiration ☐

C Increase in pupil size ☑

D Increase in salivation ☐ [2 marks]

> Make sure you read the question carefully. You wouldn't want to get the parasympathetic nervous system mixed up with the sympathetic nervous system.

> You'd get two marks for this question — one mark for each correct answer.

In Some Questions You Might Need to Complete or Label a Diagram

4 Complete the diagram of the working memory model by filling in the boxes.

[2 marks]

> The question gives you some extra help by telling you what memory model you're looking at — make sure you read the question carefully or you'll miss clues like this.

> The questions on this page are all straightforward AO1 marks, so make sure you know your facts.

DO WELL IN YOUR EXAMS

Worked Exam

You'll be Given Questions Where You Have to **Apply** Your **Knowledge**

For example, you could be given a **scenario**, and be asked to use your **knowledge** of psychology to explain it.

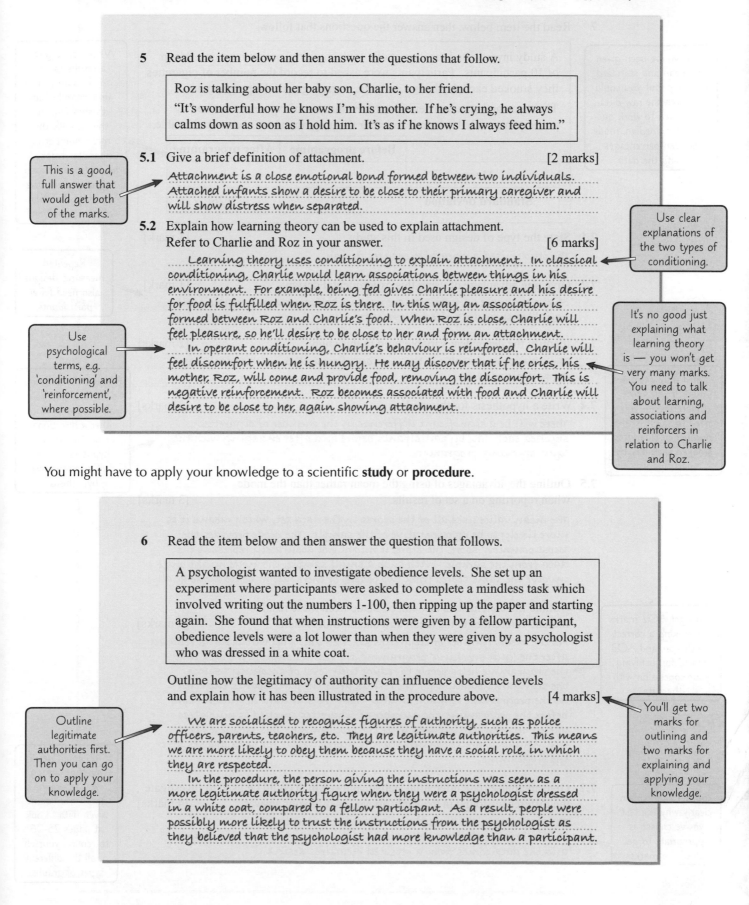

5 Read the item below and then answer the questions that follow.

> Roz is talking about her baby son, Charlie, to her friend.
>
> "It's wonderful how he knows I'm his mother. If he's crying, he always calms down as soon as I hold him. It's as if he knows I always feed him."

5.1 Give a brief definition of attachment. [2 marks]

Attachment is a close emotional bond formed between two individuals. Attached infants show a desire to be close to their primary caregiver and will show distress when separated.

This is a good, full answer that would get both of the marks.

5.2 Explain how learning theory can be used to explain attachment. Refer to Charlie and Roz in your answer. [6 marks]

Learning theory uses conditioning to explain attachment. In classical conditioning, Charlie would learn associations between things in his environment. For example, being fed gives Charlie pleasure and his desire for food is fulfilled when Roz is there. In this way, an association is formed between Roz and Charlie's food. When Roz is close, Charlie will feel pleasure, so he'll desire to be close to her and form an attachment.

In operant conditioning, Charlie's behaviour is reinforced. Charlie will feel discomfort when he is hungry. He may discover that if he cries, his mother, Roz, will come and provide food, removing the discomfort. This is negative reinforcement. Roz becomes associated with food and Charlie will desire to be close to her, again showing attachment.

Use clear explanations of the two types of conditioning.

It's no good just explaining what learning theory is — you won't get very many marks. You need to talk about learning, associations and reinforcers in relation to Charlie and Roz.

Use psychological terms, e.g. 'conditioning' and 'reinforcement', where possible.

You might have to apply your knowledge to a scientific **study** or **procedure**.

6 Read the item below and then answer the question that follows.

> A psychologist wanted to investigate obedience levels. She set up an experiment where participants were asked to complete a mindless task which involved writing out the numbers 1-100, then ripping up the paper and starting again. She found that when instructions were given by a fellow participant, obedience levels were a lot lower than when they were given by a psychologist who was dressed in a white coat.

Outline how the legitimacy of authority can influence obedience levels and explain how it has been illustrated in the procedure above. [4 marks]

We are socialised to recognise figures of authority, such as police officers, parents, teachers, etc. They are legitimate authorities. This means we are more likely to obey them because they have a social role, in which they are respected.

In the procedure, the person giving the instructions was seen as a more legitimate authority figure when they were a psychologist dressed in a white coat, compared to a fellow participant. As a result, people were possibly more likely to trust the instructions from the psychologist as they believed that the psychologist had more knowledge than a participant.

Outline legitimate authorities first. Then you can go on to apply your knowledge.

You'll get two marks for outlining and two marks for explaining and applying your knowledge.

Worked Exam

Remember, Research Method Questions Could Appear Anywhere...

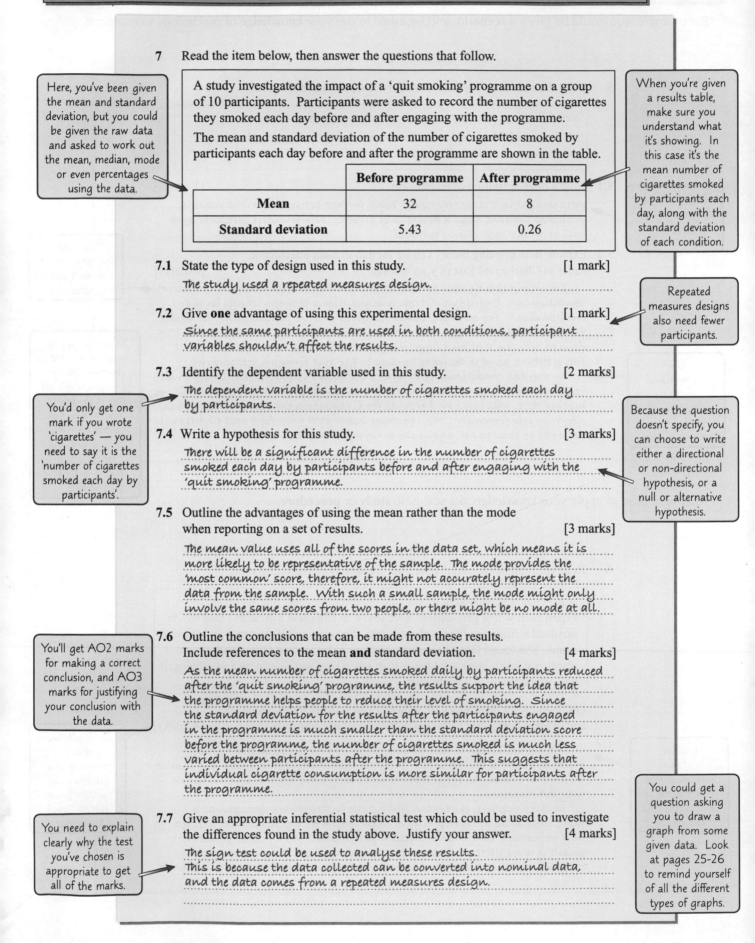

7   Read the item below, then answer the questions that follow.

> A study investigated the impact of a 'quit smoking' programme on a group of 10 participants. Participants were asked to record the number of cigarettes they smoked each day before and after engaging with the programme.
>
> The mean and standard deviation of the number of cigarettes smoked by participants each day before and after the programme are shown in the table.
>
> | | Before programme | After programme |
> | --- | --- | --- |
> | **Mean** | 32 | 8 |
> | **Standard deviation** | 5.43 | 0.26 |

Here, you've been given the mean and standard deviation, but you could be given the raw data and asked to work out the mean, median, mode or even percentages using the data.

When you're given a results table, make sure you understand what it's showing. In this case it's the mean number of cigarettes smoked by participants each day, along with the standard deviation of each condition.

7.1   State the type of design used in this study.   [1 mark]

The study used a repeated measures design.

7.2   Give **one** advantage of using this experimental design.   [1 mark]

Since the same participants are used in both conditions, participant variables shouldn't affect the results.

Repeated measures designs also need fewer participants.

7.3   Identify the dependent variable used in this study.   [2 marks]

The dependent variable is the number of cigarettes smoked each day by participants.

You'd only get one mark if you wrote 'cigarettes' — you need to say it is the 'number of cigarettes smoked each day by participants'.

7.4   Write a hypothesis for this study.   [3 marks]

There will be a significant difference in the number of cigarettes smoked each day by participants before and after engaging with the 'quit smoking' programme.

Because the question doesn't specify, you can choose to write either a directional or non-directional hypothesis, or a null or alternative hypothesis.

7.5   Outline the advantages of using the mean rather than the mode when reporting on a set of results.   [3 marks]

The mean value uses all of the scores in the data set, which means it is more likely to be representative of the sample. The mode provides the 'most common' score, therefore, it might not accurately represent the data from the sample. With such a small sample, the mode might only involve the same scores from two people, or there might be no mode at all.

7.6   Outline the conclusions that can be made from these results. Include references to the mean **and** standard deviation.   [4 marks]

As the mean number of cigarettes smoked daily by participants reduced after the 'quit smoking' programme, the results support the idea that the programme helps people to reduce their level of smoking. Since the standard deviation for the results after the participants engaged in the programme is much smaller than the standard deviation score before the programme, the number of cigarettes smoked is much less varied between participants after the programme. This suggests that individual cigarette consumption is more similar for participants after the programme.

You'll get AO2 marks for making a correct conclusion, and AO3 marks for justifying your conclusion with the data.

7.7   Give an appropriate inferential statistical test which could be used to investigate the differences found in the study above. Justify your answer.   [4 marks]

The sign test could be used to analyse these results. This is because the data collected can be converted into nominal data, and the data comes from a repeated measures design.

You need to explain clearly why the test you've chosen is appropriate to get all of the marks.

You could get a question asking you to draw a graph from some given data. Look at pages 25-26 to remind yourself of all the different types of graphs.

Worked Exam

You Could be Asked to **Design** Your Own Study

It's time to pretend you're an actual psychologist and **design your own** study. The examiners will give you a helping hand in how to structure your answer — so make sure you address **all** the bullet points:

> This question is really open-ended, and gives you the chance to be creative. But keep it simple, and make sure you explain it well — you'll be more likely to get the marks that way.

8 Design a laboratory experiment to investigate the relationship between eating breakfast and memory performance within Sixth Form students.

In your answer, you will need to include:

- details of how the sample will be selected,
- a description of the task involved,
- a description of how the data will be recorded and analysed,
- any ethical issues which may arise.

[12 marks]

> This question just contains AO2 marks. You can get 3 marks for each of these bullet points.

This laboratory experiment will investigate the effect of eating breakfast on memory in Sixth Form students. The alternative hypothesis is that there is a relationship between eating breakfast and memory performance, and the null hypothesis is that there is no relationship between the two. This study will use an independent groups design, where each participant only takes part in one condition.

The independent variable is whether the participants eat breakfast or not, and the dependent variable is the number of words each participant gets correct on a memory task.

A systematic sample will be used to select participants. Within a Sixth Form, every 5th person on the register will be asked to participate in the study. This will continue until there are 20 males and 20 females.

Participants will be asked not to have any breakfast at home before coming to school the following day. When they arrive at school, half of the sample (10 males and 10 females) will be given a standardised breakfast, and the remaining participants won't be given anything to eat. All participants will then be asked to learn the same list of twenty random words. Two hours later, following normal lessons, all participants will be asked to recall all the words they can remember from the list.

The number of words each participant remembers will be recorded in a table. The mean number of words recalled by those who ate breakfast and those who didn't will be calculated and displayed in a bar chart to show the differences between the two groups. Since this is an independent groups design using ordinal data, a Mann-Whitney test will be used to analyse the data, and to determine if the null hypothesis can be rejected.

To make sure the study is ethical, all participants will have to give their consent to participate at the start of the study. They won't be told that this is a study investigating memory, so there is an element of deception involved. But, all participants will be given enough general detail, and will be fully debriefed at the end of the study. Finally, all participants will have the right to withdraw from the study at any time, and all results shall remain confidential.

> Here you need to explain what type of experimental design you're going to use. It could be an independent groups design, repeated measures design or a matched pairs design.

> Try to describe your study in as much detail as possible — your study should be able to be replicated accurately.

> The data is ordinal because you don't know if all the words are equally hard to remember. If you can remember the table on page 37, it'll make it easier to decide which inferential statistical test you could use to analyse the results.

> Ethics are really important. Luckily, the things you need to remember are similar for most studies — all participants have to give consent, cannot be harmed, have the right to withdraw at anytime and should be debriefed at the end of the study.

Keep an Eye on the **Time**

- Time management is one of the most important exam skills to have.

- How **long** you spend on each question is really important in an exam — it could make all the difference to your grade.

- It doesn't matter if you **leave** some questions out to begin with.

- For example, if you're stuck on a question that's worth only a **few marks**, don't spend ages trying to answer it — you can always come back to it if you have time.

Tasha really wanted to answer her exam but it hadn't started ringing yet.

Worked Exam

Take a look at this **describe** and **evaluate** question...

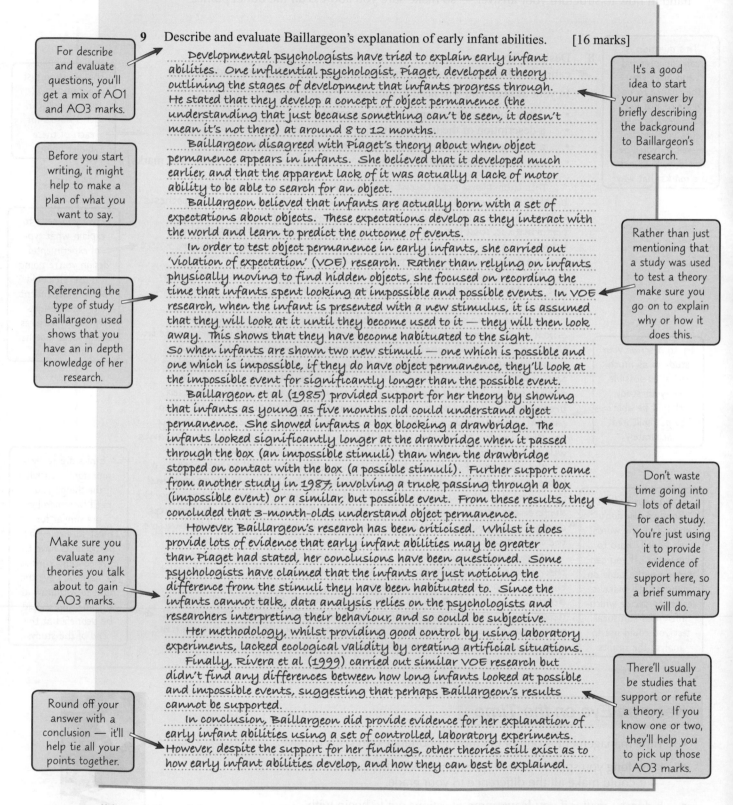

9 Describe and evaluate Baillargeon's explanation of early infant abilities. [16 marks]

> For describe and evaluate questions, you'll get a mix of AO1 and AO3 marks.

> Before you start writing, it might help to make a plan of what you want to say.

> Referencing the type of study Baillargeon used shows that you have an in depth knowledge of her research.

> Make sure you evaluate any theories you talk about to gain AO3 marks.

> Round off your answer with a conclusion — it'll help tie all your points together.

> It's a good idea to start your answer by briefly describing the background to Baillargeon's research.

> Rather than just mentioning that a study was used to test a theory make sure you go on to explain why or how it does this.

> Don't waste time going into lots of detail for each study. You're just using it to provide evidence of support here, so a brief summary will do.

> There'll usually be studies that support or refute a theory. If you know one or two, they'll help you to pick up those AO3 marks.

Developmental psychologists have tried to explain early infant abilities. One influential psychologist, Piaget, developed a theory outlining the stages of development that infants progress through. He stated that they develop a concept of object permanence (the understanding that just because something can't be seen, it doesn't mean it's not there) at around 8 to 12 months.

Baillargeon disagreed with Piaget's theory about when object permanence appears in infants. She believed that it developed much earlier, and that the apparent lack of it was actually a lack of motor ability to be able to search for an object.

Baillargeon believed that infants are actually born with a set of expectations about objects. These expectations develop as they interact with the world and learn to predict the outcome of events.

In order to test object permanence in early infants, she carried out 'violation of expectation' (VOE) research. Rather than relying on infants physically moving to find hidden objects, she focused on recording the time that infants spent looking at impossible and possible events. In VOE research, when the infant is presented with a new stimulus, it is assumed that they will look at it until they become used to it — they will then look away. This shows that they have become habituated to the sight. So when infants are shown two new stimuli — one which is possible and one which is impossible, if they do have object permanence, they'll look at the impossible event for significantly longer than the possible event.

Baillargeon et al (1985) provided support for her theory by showing that infants as young as five months old could understand object permanence. She showed infants a box blocking a drawbridge. The infants looked significantly longer at the drawbridge when it passed through the box (an impossible stimuli) than when the drawbridge stopped on contact with the box (a possible stimuli). Further support came from another study in 1987, involving a truck passing through a box (impossible event) or a similar, but possible event. From these results, they concluded that 3-month-olds understand object permanence.

However, Baillargeon's research has been criticised. Whilst it does provide lots of evidence that early infant abilities may be greater than Piaget had stated, her conclusions have been questioned. Some psychologists have claimed that the infants are just noticing the difference from the stimuli they have been habituated to. Since the infants cannot talk, data analysis relies on the psychologists and researchers interpreting their behaviour, and so could be subjective.

Her methodology, whilst providing good control by using laboratory experiments, lacked ecological validity by creating artificial situations.

Finally, Rivera et al (1999) carried out similar VOE research but didn't find any differences between how long infants looked at possible and impossible events, suggesting that perhaps Baillargeon's results cannot be supported.

In conclusion, Baillargeon did provide evidence for her explanation of early infant abilities using a set of controlled, laboratory experiments. However, despite the support for her findings, other theories still exist as to how early infant abilities develop, and how they can best be explained.

1) You'll have gathered that to write a good answer, you need to show **detailed** and **accurate** knowledge.

2) Basically, you need to show the examiner that you **understand** stuff really well.

3) Picking out studies and theories to **support** your answers is great — but keep it all **relevant** to the question.

Worked Exam

Discuss Questions Allow You to Write in *Detail*

In **discuss** questions you get to show the examiner how much you know about a topic.

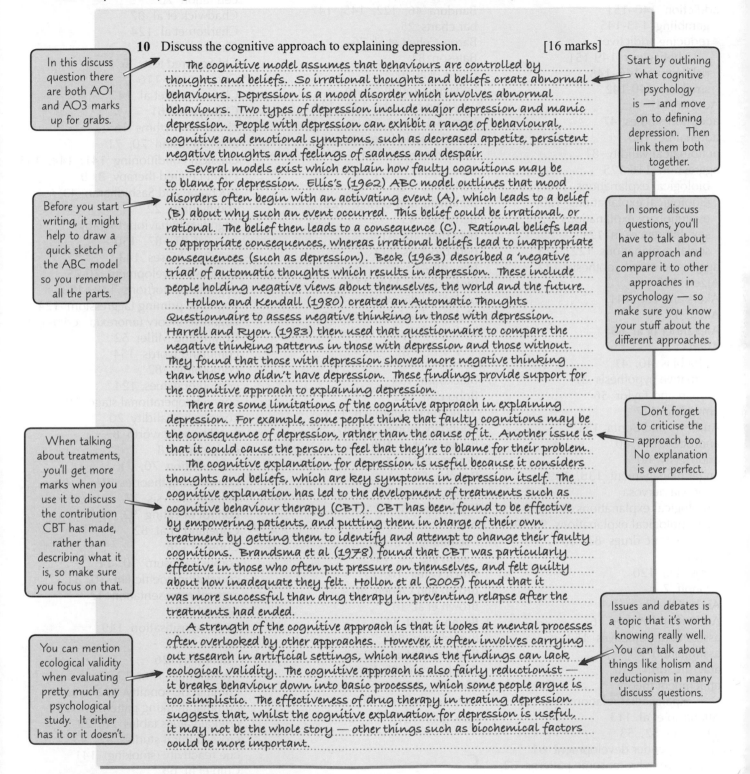

10 Discuss the cognitive approach to explaining depression. **[16 marks]**

In this discuss question there are both AO1 and AO3 marks up for grabs.

The cognitive model assumes that behaviours are controlled by thoughts and beliefs. So irrational thoughts and beliefs create abnormal behaviours. Depression is a mood disorder which involves abnormal behaviours. Two types of depression include major depression and manic depression. People with depression can exhibit a range of behavioural, cognitive and emotional symptoms, such as decreased appetite, persistent negative thoughts and feelings of sadness and despair.

Start by outlining what cognitive psychology is — and move on to defining depression. Then link them both together.

Several models exist which explain how faulty cognitions may be to blame for depression. Ellis's (1962) ABC model outlines that mood disorders often begin with an activating event (A), which leads to a belief (B) about why such an event occurred. This belief could be irrational, or rational. The belief then leads to a consequence (C). Rational beliefs lead to appropriate consequences, whereas irrational beliefs lead to inappropriate consequences (such as depression). Beck (1963) described a 'negative triad' of automatic thoughts which results in depression. These include people holding negative views about themselves, the world and the future.

Before you start writing, it might help to draw a quick sketch of the ABC model so you remember all the parts.

In some discuss questions, you'll have to talk about an approach and compare it to other approaches in psychology — so make sure you know your stuff about the different approaches.

Hollon and Kendall (1980) created an Automatic Thoughts Questionnaire to assess negative thinking in those with depression. Harrell and Ryon (1983) then used that questionnaire to compare the negative thinking patterns in those with depression and those without. They found that those with depression showed more negative thinking than those who didn't have depression. These findings provide support for the cognitive approach to explaining depression.

There are some limitations of the cognitive approach in explaining depression. For example, some people think that faulty cognitions may be the consequence of depression, rather than the cause of it. Another issue is that it could cause the person to feel that they're to blame for their problem.

Don't forget to criticise the approach too. No explanation is ever perfect.

When talking about treatments, you'll get more marks when you use it to discuss the contribution CBT has made, rather than describing what it is, so make sure you focus on that.

The cognitive explanation for depression is useful because it considers thoughts and beliefs, which are key symptoms in depression itself. The cognitive explanation has led to the development of treatments such as cognitive behaviour therapy (CBT). CBT has been found to be effective by empowering patients, and putting them in charge of their own treatment by getting them to identify and attempt to change their faulty cognitions. Brandsma et al (1978) found that CBT was particularly effective in those who often put pressure on themselves, and felt guilty about how inadequate they felt. Hollon et al (2005) found that it was more successful than drug therapy in preventing relapse after the treatments had ended.

You can mention ecological validity when evaluating pretty much any psychological study. It either has it or it doesn't.

A strength of the cognitive approach is that it looks at mental processes often overlooked by other approaches. However, it often involves carrying out research in artificial settings, which means the findings can lack ecological validity. The cognitive approach is also fairly reductionist — it breaks behaviour down into basic processes, which some people argue is too simplistic. The effectiveness of drug therapy in treating depression suggests that, whilst the cognitive explanation for depression is useful, it may not be the whole story — other things such as biochemical factors could be more important.

Issues and debates is a topic that it's worth knowing really well. You can talk about things like holism and reductionism in many 'discuss' questions.

Make a Plan Before You Start Your Answer

- The **quality** of your writing will also be assessed — so make sure you use **good English** with **specialist psychology vocabulary** where appropriate.

- Try to **structure** your answer in an **organised** way. Your answer needs to be **clear** and **coherent**. Before you start, it's worth jotting down a quick **plan** of what you want to write so that you don't just end up with a really jumbled answer full of **irrelevant information**.

DO WELL IN YOUR EXAMS

Index

Index

Index

Index

Index

social exchange theory 54
social learning theory 61, 68, 90, 95, 96, 122, 141, 145
social neuroscience 78, 79
social penetration theory 56
Social Readjustment Rating Scale (SRRS) 104, 105
social support 114, 115
socially sensitive research 49
soft determinism 44
Solyom et al 47
somatosensory cortex 10, 12
Spearman's Rho 30
Sperry 11
split brain surgery 11
split-half method 20
standardised research 21
statistical significance 27-29
stress
  individual differences 110, 111
  management 112-115
  measuring 104-107, 109
  physiology of 100-102
  role in illness 102, 103
  sources of 104-109
stress inoculation therapy 114
Strickland et al 144
structure of personality 2
Stunkard et al 97
sub-culture bias 42
summary of the exams 152
Sumter et al 146
superego 2, 3
  role in criminality 134
Sutherland 135
Sweeney 103
Sykes 125
sympathomedullary pathway 100

T

tables 24
taste aversion 90
Taylor et al 111
temporal validity 20
test-retest method 20
test statistic 27
testing theories 18
testosterone 50, 61-63, 119, 130
thematic analysis 22
theory of mind 76
theory of planned behaviour 150
theory of reasoned action 150
Tinbergen 120
token economies 88, 138
Thibaut and Kelley 54

Thompson 64
tolerance 140
'top-down' approach 128
Turner's syndrome 62
twin studies 47
two-tailed tests 28, 37
Type I error 28
Type II error 28

U

ultradian rhythms 16
unconditional positive regard 8
unconscious mind 2
universality 42
unrelated measures 29
unrelated *t*-test 34

V

validity 20, 21, 81, 82
  assessing 21
  concurrent 20
  ecological 20
  face 20
  improving 21
  temporal 20
Valzelli and Bernasconi 118
Van Goozen et al 119
Vaughn and Leff 84
ventromedial hypothalamus (VMH) 92, 97
verbal summaries 24
vicarious reinforcement 90, 95, 122, 124, 145
victim surveys 127
violation of expectation (VOE) research 74, 75
Virkkunen et al 118
virtual relationships 56, 57
visual cortex 10
Vogele et al 111
Vygotsky 72, 73

W

Wagenaar 143
Walster et al 53
Walters 117
Waxler-Morrison et al 114
Wegman et al 17
Weisner and Wilson-Mitchell 60
Wernicke's area 10
White 53
Whiting and Edwards 69

Wilcoxon test 32
Williams (1986) 68
Williams (2000) 102
Wilson and Daly 121
Winch 52
Wing and Jeffrey 99
Winn et al 92
withdrawal symptoms 140
Wood et al 73
worked exam questions 156-161
workplace stress 108, 109

Y

Yerkes 49
Yochelson and Samenow 132

Z

Zahavi 50
Zhang et al 141
Zimbardo 123, 136
zone of proximal development 72, 73